DATE DUE

MR 3 '95			
NO 9 '95			
MR 30 '99			
AP 3 0 '99			

Painful Inheritance

Life Course Studies

David L. Featherman
David I. Kertzer
  General Editors

Nancy W. Denney
Thomas J. Espenshade
Dennis P. Hogan
Jennie Keith
Maris A. Vinovskis
  Associate General Editors

Painful Inheritance

Health and the New Generation
of Fatherless Families

Ronald J. Angel
Jacqueline L. Angel

THE UNIVERSITY OF WISCONSIN PRESS

The University of Wisconsin Press
114 North Murray Street
Madison, Wisconsin 53715

3 Henrietta Street
London WC2E 8LU, England

Library of Congress Cataloging-in-Publication Data

Angel, Ronald.
Painful inheritance: health and the new generation of fatherless
families / Ronald J. Angel, Jacqueline L. Angel.
288 p.   cm. — (Life course studies)
Includes bibliographical references and index.
ISBN 0-299-13960-3   ISBN 0-299-13964-6 (pbk.)
1. Fatherless family—Health and hygiene—United States.
I. Angel, Jacqueline Lowe. II. Title. III. Series.
RA418.5.F36A54   1993
306.85′6—dc20   93-18788

To Tonie and Joe,
who despite growing up in fatherless families
became magnificent parents

Contents

Figures

Tables

Preface

Since the Second World War, the American family has changed dramatically, and although most children still grow up with both parents, for an ever-growing number of children, father no longer plays an active role in family life. Since at least the 1970s, the growth in the number of female-headed families has drawn increasing scholarly and public attention. Many social critics view the growth in the number of female-headed families as part of the general decay of the social structures that form the basis of our social order; others view it as the emergence of just another family form, neither better nor worse than any other. Regardless of one's views on the rise in the number of fatherless families, however, it is clear that for many female-headed families, poverty is an ever-present reality. The long-term consequences of this poverty for the physical and mental health of both women and children are, as yet, poorly understood.

Issues surrounding the decline of the two-parent family and the corresponding increase in the proportion of families that are headed by women are politically and emotionally charged for many reasons. One of the major reasons is that although the number of female-headed households is growing among all groups, the proportion of fatherless black families is over twice that of fatherless white families, and black female-headed households are far worse off economically than their white counterparts. The same is increasingly true for Hispanics. Discussions of the rise in the proportion of fatherless families, therefore, must immediately come to terms with the issues of race and Hispanic ethnicity. Yet many observers fear that focusing special attention on female-headed families and households, especially among blacks and Hispanics, runs the risk of labeling these families as abnormal and of blaming the victims for their situations. Despite its politically charged nature, the serious social and economic plight of a large fraction of female-headed families has been so well documented that we cannot avoid the conclusion that we are dealing with a new phenomenon that has unique causes and consequences.

In recent years, numerous studies of the economic plight of single mothers have appeared. These document the seriously deteriorating economic situation of poor female-headed families. Many fatherless families are dependent on welfare, and the cuts in health, housing, and nutrition programs have had serious consequences for their well-being. The problem is compounded by the perception of many middle-class Americans that welfare programs are not working. This perception has resulted in growing resistance to the taxation that is necessary for the support of single mothers and their children. The spread of antitax and antiwelfare sentiments at a time when the number of single-parent families is growing rapidly means that the well-being of a large fraction of our population is in jeopardy.

What, then, is the purpose of another book on single mothers and their children? Although the economic situation of female-headed households has been well documented, we know relatively little about the physical and mental health of either children or adult women in such families. We know even less about how race and Hispanic ethnicity interact with poverty to affect the health of these women and children. Large differentials in family income are unjust in and of themselves, but if living in poverty undermines the health of women and children in single-parent households, the existence of huge differences in family income that are based on the marital status and sex of the head of household are intolerable.

Because of the rapid decline of the two-parent family in our inner cities, from now on a majority of inner-city children will grow up without a father. Any negative consequences of father absence, therefore, will affect the health and well-being of large numbers of the most vulnerable members of our society. We will all pay the price of the neglect of these children, and it is imperative that we begin to understand how the physical and mental health of women and children is affected by poverty and single motherhood if we are to responsibly address their needs. The costs of neglect may be a painful inheritance of poverty and illness that is passed down from one generation to the next.

Our basic objective in this book is to document the impact of minority group status, gender, and poverty on the physical and mental health of children and adult women in fatherless families. Although each of these factors is associated with disadvantage, in combination, their impacts are magnified, placing poor, minority, fatherless families at very high risk of physical and mental illness. Of course, it is impossible to study health without simultaneously examining economic status. Family income and parental employment are major determinants of the health risks women and children face, as well as the type and quality of medical care they receive. Consequently, any examination of the health impact of single motherhood must identify the broader social forces that affect the economic situation of female-headed families. In the following chapters we examine the economic well-being and the physical and mental health of three generations of women and children in female-headed households.

Before proceeding, we should place our discussion of the health consequences of the decline of the two-parent family into a larger perspective and show how our study builds on a tradition of concern for the consequences of single motherhood for both women and children. Such a perspective will help the reader understand some of the major issues in the debate over the causes and consequences of single motherhood, especially of the role of race and Hispanic ethnicity in this debate. Let us begin by noting that although the plight of single mothers and their children reclaimed public and scholarly attention in recent years, the causes of the rise in the proportion of female-headed families and the consequences of fatherlessness for children have been the object of research and speculation for some time.

The issue first emerged as a major social issue in 1965 when Daniel Patrick Moynihan drew attention to the problems of the black family in his report, *The Negro Family: The Case for National Action* (Moynihan 1965). In that report, Moynihan marshaled a massive amount of statistical data to show that among poor blacks the family was ceasing to function as a viable entity and that the black community had adopted what he called a "matriarchal structure" that, he said, "because it was out of line with the rest of the American society, seriously retards progress for the group as a whole (29)." Even though Moynihan made it absolutely clear that discrimination and the economic and social disadvantages that blacks had suffered in American society since slavery were the major causes of the disruption of black family life, such an analysis was seriously out of step with the political climate of the day, and the report was violently attacked as racist (Rainwater and Yancey 1967). As a consequence, for the next ten years social scientists essentially avoided the issue of race and family structure.[1]

But, as it turned out, the problems of poor minority mother-only families were very real, and the problems of the poor and of female-headed households turned out to be far more serious than cultural adaptationist theorists claimed. The situation of our inner cities and of the poor continued to deteriorate, and by the 1980s the plight of single-parent families could no longer be ignored. Between 1960 and 1988 the proportion of families headed by single mothers more than doubled, such that by 1988 16 percent of non-Hispanic white children, 27 percent of Hispanic children, and 51 percent of black children were living in female-headed families (U.S. Bureau of the Census 1989c). If these trends continue into the future, approximately half of all children, and over 85 percent of black children, will spend some portion of their childhood before they reach the age of sixteen in fatherless families (Bumpass 1984).[2]

Most early characterizations of poor, black, and Hispanic families shared aspects of the culture of poverty explanation originally proposed by Oscar Lewis (1966). For Lewis and others, chronic poverty results in self-defeating behaviors and attitudes that make it almost impossible for its victims to escape. Although Lewis clearly stated that the objective situation in which the poor find themselves is the basic cause of the problem, identifying culture and the individual's own attitudes and behaviors as the immediate cause of their failure to move ahead in life was seen by many critics as blaming the victims themselves for their own plight. Such theories were widely condemned as little more than the value judgments of middle-class white observers who failed to appreciate the adaptive aspects of this supposed culture of poverty (Stack 1974).[3]

Not surprisingly, the response by many blacks and their supporters to the characterization of the black family as pathological was hostile, as any criticism of the black family, intact or otherwise, was seen as denigrating and racist (Rainwater and Yancey 1967). For defenders of the black family, ghetto life and its institutions represented a cultural adaptation unfamiliar to white Americans. Black institutions, they claimed, could only be understood in terms of black values. The fact that many of these institutions had been shaped in response to white racism lent a moral legitimacy to criticisms of research conducted by middle-class white researchers. The vicious attacks on Moynihan and Lewis clearly had their intended effect, and for at least ten years, few researchers dared to venture into the realm of race and the family. Few were willing to engage in any investigation that could be construed as involving value judgments about minority group culture, and, as a consequence, relatively little research on black or Hispanic single-parent families was conducted during the 1970s.

In the 1980s the political climate changed as Americans awakened to the extent of the physical and social decay of our inner cities. The explosion of crime and violence and the apparently endless supply of drugs that are part of the massive social disorganization of our poorest neighborhoods forced the problems of the inner city into the public limelight and back onto our social scientific research agenda. Only this time, unlike during the Johnson years, a different coalition led the assault on the problem of poverty and family dissolution. Rather than a "war on poverty," President Ronald Reagan presided over a conservative "war on welfare" that succeeded in cutting back, or slowing the growth of, many social welfare programs on which single mothers and their children rely (Katz 1986, Palmer and Sawhill 1984). Although Reagan made the reduction in the scale of the welfare state one of the central objectives of his administration, the decline in funding for welfare programs actually began in the mid-1970s during the Carter administration. Reagan was really no more than the standard-bearer for a new public mood and a changed political climate. His administration's early success in its assault on welfare was made possible by a growing middle-class resentment toward the tax burden that the public believes such programs represent.

During the 1980s both social scientists and social welfare professionals who were in direct contact with the inner city began to document the seriousness of the plight of many female-headed minority families. The taboo against the study of the minority families that had halted research for a full decade was abandoned in the face of evidence of serious social problems associated with fatherlessness in our inner-city ghettos and barrios. Numerous studies based on census data and large-scale social surveys clearly showed that female-headed households, especially among blacks and Hispanics, suffered serious economic hardship (Garfinkel and McLanahan 1986; McLanahan and Garfinkel 1989; Bane and Ellwood 1986, 1989; Tienda and Angel 1982). Ethnographic researchers drew poignant pictures of female-headed families coping with poverty and documented how chronic poverty affects norms concerning sexual behavior and marriage among young people (Stack 1974, Anderson 1989, Sullivan 1989).

By the 1980s many observers began to document the fact that this new poverty involves more than just a lack of income and often brings with it serious social pathologies. What was perhaps most useful about this research was that it began to document serious differences within the population living in poverty. The poor are a very heterogeneous group, and this new research began to provide clearer delineations between the vast majority in poverty who are poor only temporarily and the much smaller minority who are chronically poor. Although our welfare system is suited to help the former, it is poorly equipped to deal with the latter. The new research showed that each of the groups in poverty has its own set of problems that require specific solutions.

This research also made it abundantly clear that cuts in social programs for the poor have a serious impact on the welfare of single mothers and their children. In recent years declines in infant mortality have slowed, and if it were not for the fact that extremely low birth-weight infants can be saved by technical innovations, infant mortality rates would have increased (Grad 1988). Today the United States ranks twentieth among industrialized nations in infant mortality (ibid.), and among the poor many children are born underweight and suffer lifelong health consequences (Smythe 1988, Children's Defense Fund 1987). The number of children who are fully immunized against the childhood illnesses, including polio, diphtheria, pertussis, measles, tetanus, and mumps, that killed and crippled so many children early in the century has dropped as the result of cuts in funding for federal immunization programs (Children's Defense Fund 1987, Smythe 1988). Since the children of single mothers so often live in poverty and rely on federal support for their health care, these cuts have had a disproportionate impact on them.

Although the poor have always been with us, major structural changes in the U.S. labor market since World War II have created a new depth of poverty in America's inner cities. Some have used the term *hyper-ghettoization*[4] to emphasize the fact that although conditions in the inner city have never been good, today they are particularly serious. This new poverty has taken on disturbing features that make it qualitatively different from the poverty of earlier decades. Today, America's inner cities are beset by unprecedented levels of social disorganization as well as problems of drug abuse and violence.

Some observers have used the term *underclass* to characterize those who live in the poorest and most socially disorganized neighborhoods (Wilson 1987, Moore 1989, Auletta 1982). This term refers to more than just poverty; it is intended to distinguish poverty that results from low wages and temporary setbacks from that form of chronic poverty (with its accompanying social pathologies) that seriously damages its victim's capacity for self-sufficiency and that is passed on from one generation to the next (McLanahan and Garfinkel 1989). The underclass, then, consists of individuals who we might think of as having internalized poverty and who have little hope of escape.

In previous years these families might have been referred to as multiproblem families. They have always been with us, and perhaps the term *underclass* is just a new name for them. Yet the underclass seems to be a new phenomenon, representing a kind of damage associated with poverty that is uniquely modern. The term *underclass* and the concept it conveys are behavioral, but although they are based on individual responses to poverty, they are intended to characterize entire neighborhoods. The underclass is not defined by the presence of a few multiproblem families but rather by a lack of social organization and a near-total collapse of the community-level mechanisms of social control (Auletta 1982). William Julius Wilson notes that although many inner-city neighborhoods have always been poor, not all that many years ago life in them was very different from what it is today. As he says, "unlike the present period inner-city communities prior to 1960 exhibited the features of social organization—including a sense of community, positive neighborhood identification, and explicit norms and sanctions against aberrant behavior (Wilson 1987: 3)." Today, this sense of community and the norms and sanctions that it brings with it are missing from many inner-city neighborhoods.

Of course, as one would expect with such a politically changed term, many critics object to the use of the term *underclass* because they see it, and similar labels, as drawing attention away from social inequality as the culprit in producing poverty and social disorganization and focusing attention instead on the behavior of the victims of our system of social inequality. The concept, after all, has much in common with earlier notions of the culture of poverty, and many critics of the term also object to making distinctions among the poor on the basis of various characteristics since they see such distinctions as resulting in excessive stigmatization of certain groups. Michael Katz, a historian of American welfare policy who is clearly sensitive to the consequences of social labels asks,

Why is it helpful to lump people with such varied problems as drug addicts, women supported by AFDC [Aid to Families with Dependent Children], and former mental patients in one category? Will it point policy in useful directions or increase compassion for the victims of America's structure of inequality? Even if, as I believe, the answer is no, the concept of an "underclass" serves a useful rhetorical purpose for the war on welfare. By drawing a sharp line between the working class and the very poor, it fractures a potential source of political mobilization, justifies mean and punitive social policies, and keeps the working poor at low-paid jobs, any jobs, to avoid descent into the underclass. (Katz 1986: 277)

This criticism is justified when *underclass* is used to refer to those for whom poverty is only temporary. Clearly, being poor and being a member of a social class characterized by chronic poverty, crime, drug abuse, and other social pathologies are not the same. And, indeed, the very use of a special term suggests that there is something more serious about the poverty experienced by the underclass than that experienced by the working poor.

Christopher Jencks also questions the usefulness of rolling numerous problems into one package rather than treating them separately (e.g., Jencks 1991). As he notes, the standard indicators of underclass neighborhoods are high crime rates, high school dropout rates, few employed adults and youth, and a large proportion of fatherless families. Treating all of these problems as if they were part of the same package obscures the fact that for different groups some of these things are getting better at the same time that others are getting worse. Jencks notes that although the number of out-of-wedlock births and unemployment rates among black adolescents is a near-disaster, school achievement scores and graduation rates have been improving.

The term *underclass,* then, may produce more disagreement than consensus and perhaps it should be dropped, but even if it is exchanged for some other label or for no label at all, it is imperative that we do not lose sig'it of the reality to which it refers. Although it would be tragic to unnece sarily create invidious distinctions among members of the politically :akest members of our society, it is becoming clearer every day that the poverty that many of today's poorest inhabitants of our inner cities experience is of a qualitatively different sort than that experienced by the poor of earlier eras. The new chronic poverty involves much more social disorganization, and it leads to far more serious and long-lasting social and health problems than does short-term poverty.

Criticisms of the concept of underclass remind us that, as we noted above, the poor are a heterogeneous group. The population in poverty consists of at least three groups: (1) the working poor whose earnings are insufficient to lift them out of poverty; (2) the episodically poor whose poverty is the result of the loss of a job or some other temporary setback; and (3) an ever-growing number of chronically poor who are still a small minority but for whom poverty and social marginality are permanent and passed on from one generation to the next. Traditional income support programs like AFDC may address the problems of the first two groups by providing transitional support. The last group, however, needs a far more comprehensive set of services if the quality of their lives is to be improved. This heterogeneity among the poor must be kept continually in mind in any examination of the health consequences of fatherlessness.

Obviously, not all single mothers are members of the underclass, however it is defined, nor are most dependent on welfare. Single motherhood represents only one risk factor for chronic poverty, and, in and of itself, single motherhood probably does not have serious consequences for the well-being of a woman or her children. In combination with low education, few job opportunities, and a conflict-ridden environment, however, single motherhood may represent a major risk factor for long-term poverty and its damaging health consequences. Because of our gender-based system of occupational segregation, women have fewer job opportunities and earn less than men. Women with small children and few job skills are very unlikely to become self-supporting. Since many young single mothers face nearly insurmountable barriers to economic self-sufficiency, the health and well-being of an ever-growing fraction of children may be affected.

As we noted earlier, our objective in this book is to examine the health of three generations of women and children in fatherless families and to determine the institutional and individual factors that affect the health of single women and their children. We have organized the following chapters such that we begin with an overall assessment of the magnitude of the problems faced by fatherless families, proceed to an examination of the health-related social welfare programs that they rely on, and end with a detailed examination of research into the health consequences of single motherhood for children, their mothers, and grandmothers. Since each chapter is self-contained, a brief summary of each will allow the reader to choose those he or she is most interested in.

Chapter 1 introduces the concept of fatherlessness and presents a discussion of the consequences of different types of single motherhood. In this chapter we develop a theoretical model of the causes and consequences of single motherhood and spouse absence across the life course. Chapter 2 places the problem of poverty and the dramatic rise in the number of female-headed households in a historical perspective. In this chapter we document the serious economic vulnerability of fatherless families and compare the extent of welfare dependency among blacks, Hispanics, and non-Hispanic whites. In chapter 3 we compare the family support systems of the United States to those of the more developed social welfare states of Europe and describe the various programs that affect the health and economic well-being of fatherless families in the United States. In chapter 4 we examine important issues in the measurement of physical and mental health in community samples and discuss problems in establishing the validity of measures of both physical and mental health for children and adults.

In chapters 5 through 7 we summarize what is known about the impact of single motherhood, divorce, and father absence on the health of three generations of women and children. In chapter 5 we examine the consequences of divorce and single motherhood for the health of children. In chapter 6 we review the literature on the physical and mental health consequences of single parenthood for mothers and present some new findings based on recent data to explain how the burdens of single motherhood affect single mothers' physical and mental health. In chapter 7 we speculate on the health consequences of spouselessness for older women and discuss the growing phenomenon of the multigenerational household headed by grandmothers. Finally, in chapter 8 we discuss the possible future of health policy in the United States as it affects fatherless families and offer various policy options for meeting the physical and mental health care needs of single mothers and their children.

A Note on Our Data Sources

Although the problem of single motherhood has drawn increased attention, data on the health consequences of father absence are sparse and of mixed quality. Few longitudinal studies include detailed information on the marital history and the health status of women and their children. Although a large literature clearly documents the economic plight of fatherless families, few of these studies include good measures of either physical or mental health. And the rather immense medical and clinical literature on children's mental and physical health provides very little information on how family structure affects health levels. In this book, therefore, we rely on various data sources, none of them ideal, to provide as complete a portrait as possible of the health of women and children in female-headed families. Many of the conclusions that we draw are based on inferential and indirect evidence from studies of adolescent mothers and currently unmarried mothers. What we intend to do is paint a composite portrait that will provide useful evidence concerning how father and spouse absence affect the physical and mental health of women and children. We also hope to provide some useful suggestions for further research.

Acknowledgments

The research for this book would not have been possible without the support of numerous agencies and organizations. While working on the manuscript, Ronald Angel was supported by the National Institute of Mental Health, the Institute for Health, Health Care Policy, and Aging Research at Rutgers University, and the Population Research Center and the Hogg Foundation for Mental Health at the University of Texas at Austin. While at Rutgers University, Jacqueline Angel was supported through a postdoctoral traineeship in mental health services research from the National Institute of Mental Health. She was also supported by a postdoctoral traineeship in the demography of aging from the National Institute on Aging while at the Population Research Institute of the Pennsylvania State University. This book has also benefited from the helpful suggestions and criticisms of many colleagues and friends at Rutgers University, the Pennsylvania State University, and the University of Texas at Austin. We thank them all for their invaluable support.

Painful Inheritance

1

Single Motherhood and Health across the Life Course

We set the stage for our analysis of the health of women and children in fatherless families by reviewing scholarly explanations of the causes and consequences of single motherhood. To provide a focus for our discussion of the impact of single motherhood on health, we develop a conceptual framework in which we place the issue of female headship in a life course perspective and elaborate the health consequences of various routes to single motherhood. We use this conceptual model to develop basic hypotheses focusing on the physical and mental health consequences of fatherlessness for children and of spouse absence for younger and older adult women. Because in the United States, emotional and behavioral problems, as well as violence and neglect, have replaced acute illness as the major threats to the well-being of children, we begin here our examination of the degree of association between these problems and fatherlessness.

Let us start, however, by defining the object of our analysis, the fatherless family. We use *fatherless* interchangeably with such terms as *female-headed, mother-only,* and *single-parent* to refer to households and families in which no male is present. Obviously, fatherlessness can be temporary or long term, and the intensity and duration of an adult male's involvement with the family has important implications for the welfare of all concerned. A short period without a male breadwinner, for example, usually results in less severe deprivation than a more protracted period without his economic contribution. Our definition of fatherlessness, however, includes both short-term and long-term male absence. Our primary focus is on those families that, at any particular point in their life course, are headed and maintained by females. To identify the unique health vulnerabilities of the members of these families, throughout our discussion we compare the health and welfare of their members to that of the members of families headed by both a husband and a wife. The traditional two-parent family, then, serves as our point of reference for determining the health consequences of fatherlessness.

Recent media coverage of the problems of female-headed households has resulted in the popular notion that fatherlessness is a new phenomenon. This is hardly the case. The fatherless family was rather common in earlier centuries. Because of occupational hazards and other health risks, many men died in their prime and left widows and orphans to fend for themselves. These fatherless families were dependent for their welfare on the charity of others and, not infrequently, were condemned to life in the poorhouse (Axinn and Levin 1975, Katz 1986, Mencher 1967). Today, widowhood among women with small children is rare, and the vast majority of single mothers have never been married or are divorced. So although the female-headed family has always been with us, the phenomenon we are dealing with in this book is new, especially, as we will show, in terms of its magnitude.

Why, though, the concern for the health of single mothers and their children? After all, for a large fraction of these families fatherlessness is only a temporary phenomenon, and for the rest welfare and Medicaid are available if they are needy. Indeed, were the rise in single motherhood a short-term trend, or one that affected only a small fraction of women and children, or even one that did not result in serious economic hardship for a large number of families, we would have less cause for concern. However, there can be little doubt that single motherhood as a major social phenomenon is here to stay. On the basis of informed demographic projections, we can expect nearly half of all children alive today to spend some portion of their childhood in single-parent families (Bumpass 1984). Nor can there be much doubt that a disproportionate fraction of these families will live in poverty and be exposed to the health risks associated with a disorganized physical and social environment (U.S. Bureau of the Census 1989a). Despite recent attempts to extend Medicaid coverage to more needy families, many of them do not receive adequate medical care. The result may be seriously diminished health levels and an increased vulnerability to both acute and chronic disease.

The health consequences of fatherlessness, therefore, must be a central concern for American health policy, since the productive potential of future generations, as well as the health of a large number of young mothers, is at stake. We thus begin by asking how fatherless families fare and whether there are any significant effects of single motherhood on the health of children and of unassisted parenthood on the health of women. Health and illness, in a strictly clinical sense, are determined by such factors as genetic endowment, nutrition, and exposure to pathogens. From a larger perspective, health is shaped by social factors that increase or decrease one's exposure to health risks. Poverty, violence, and the lack of adequate medical care are the most serious threats to health in the United States today, and finding solutions to these problems requires far more than the skills of clinical medicine alone.

In the United States today, few Americans pay for medical care out of pocket. Rather, most medical care is paid for by employer-sponsored insurance plans or by combined federal/state programs such as Medicaid and Medicare. Yet, nearly thirty-seven million Americans are without basic health insurance (Woolhandler and Himmelstein 1989). Clearly, those economic and political forces that place private insurance out of reach of millions of Americans and that determine eligibility for state-sponsored insurance programs have a direct impact on the health of fatherless families. It is imperative, therefore, that we begin to understand the broader social, economic, and political context within which health and illness are produced and in which health care is provided.

Before we proceed to a closer examination of the health and welfare of fatherless families, we mention an important social change that has taken place during the last thirty years and that has profound implications for the distribution of illness among different age groups in the United States. Only a few decades ago poverty among the elderly was common, but as a result of increases in Social Security and especially as a result of the indexing of benefit levels to the rate of inflation, serious poverty is much less common among the elderly today (Myles 1984, Preston 1984). Unfortunately, since our economic pie is only finite and since expenditures for social welfare programs generally can grow only so fast, programs for the elderly have benefited at the expense of those designed to ensure the health and welfare of children.

Today, poverty is concentrated among families with children, a disproportionate number of which are female-headed. In the struggle for social resources, including those aimed at the preservation of health and the treatment of illness, poor children are at a distinct disadvantage. The shift in the burden of poverty from the elderly to the young has important implications for the health of future generations. As we demonstrate in subsequent chapters, the problem is compounded by the fact that although the poor include all racial and ethnic groups and all family types, a disproportionate number of the poor live in black and Hispanic female-headed households. Minority group children who grow up in single-parent families, then, are at particularly high risk for the negative health consequences of poverty.

Age, therefore, is a serious risk factor for poverty in the United States today as the very young, who are the most vulnerable among us, are at highest risk. Age is an important factor in the study of the health consequences of fatherlessness for another reason. As we will document, the age of the mother and the timing of her entry into single motherhood have important implications for her own health and welfare as well as for that of her child. In recent years, much attention has been devoted to the study of the consequences of adolescent motherhood for the social and economic welfare of young women and their children. This literature clearly shows that in conjunction with other factors, such as lower social class membership and minority group status, early pregnancy undermines a young woman's educational and economic opportunities and often has adverse effects on her child's health, primarily through an increased risk of premature birth and low birth weight. We can reasonably assume that the accumulated disadvantages of lower-class origins, minority group status, early pregnancy, poverty, and single motherhood result in a less than optimal child-rearing environment.

Much of the literature we review in later chapters also documents the serious psychological impact of divorce on children's health. The data clearly show that the conflict typical of a disintegrating marriage and the stresses brought about by a contentious divorce can seriously undermine a child's sense of security and result in serious emotional problems. As the result of divorce, many women and children suffer dramatic declines in income and are exposed to stresses they have not been used to. It is not surprising, therefore, that change of the magnitude that often accompanies divorce is stressful for adults and children alike. The situation of mothers who have never been married is rather different. The economic and social stresses that they and their children are exposed to are not the result of some dramatic change in marital status but are typically much more chronic and, often, more serious. The route by which a woman arrives at single motherhood as well as her age when she becomes a single mother, then, have important implications for the consequences for her own health and the health of her children.

Although knowledge of the economic, social, and health consequences of single motherhood is growing, much more research is needed before we begin to understand the joint effects of single motherhood, minority group status, and poverty on the physical and mental health of the mother herself and on the health of her children. To a large extent, our lack of knowledge concerning the impact of family structure on health results from a lack of appropriate data. We have good information on differences in morbidity and mortality between blacks and whites, the rich and the poor, and the well educated and the less educated, but we have very little information on the net impact of family structure on any aspect of health.

As we emphasize throughout this book, many, if not most, of the health disadvantages that children in mother-only families suffer are associated with poverty and reduced access to health services, especially those aimed at prevention and those designed to deal with mental and emotional problems. In subsequent chapters we summarize the medical and epidemiological literatures dealing with the effects of poverty on children's health and review several community studies of the impact of family and household structure on the health of women and children. Although we summarize the major clinical findings on the health of poor children, studies of treated samples are typically based on highly select and nonrepresentative samples. Rarely do they provide detailed information on a child's family situation. Our major sources of data, therefore, are community surveys in which we are able to identify fatherless families. Our ultimate objective in this book is to summarize what is known of the long-term consequences of single motherhood for women and children and to identify the mechanisms through which any negative health effects we might identify operate.

Since we have little reason to believe that single motherhood, in and of itself, has any significant impact on the health of women or children, in the following chapters we attempt to determine the extent to which any negative health consequences we may find are due to poverty and the stresses of unassisted parenthood. Our basic motivation for examining the health effects of single motherhood arises from the fact that households headed by women are often subjected to stresses from multiple sources, both economic and psychosocial. Female-headed households typically have much lower total incomes than two-parent households (Angel and Tienda 1982, Sweet and Bumpass 1987), but in addition, single mothers who have no other adult present to help with household tasks must manage by themselves all of the domestic responsibilities involved in maintaining a family. These women are often at risk of what we call "role overload" as the result of the excessive burdens of the combined responsibilities for the economic well-being of the household and the domestic demands of unassisted parenthood. "Role overload" refers to a situation in which being the sole breadwinner (or dependent on welfare), in combination with the demands of being both mother and father to her children, creates strains that undermine a woman's health and, potentially, that of her children. Clearly, although all single mothers have multiple demands placed on them, they do not all experience role overload in this negative sense.

new family type are complex, and many explanations have been offered. Some scholars see the decline of the two-parent family as an inevitable consequence of modernization and of women's liberation from economic dependence on men (Popenoe 1988, Farley 1988). From this point of view, the modern family has been stripped of the economic functions that it served in earlier ages when family stability was ensured by the members' mutual dependence on one another. Such modernization theorists hold that because it has ceased to serve a clear mediating role between the individual and the larger society, the family today is held together by little more than tenuous bonds of affection and sentiment that are easily broken by the individualistic orientation of modern life.

Another set of explanations for the emergence of fatherless families has been offered by critics of welfare programs who place the blame for the decline of the two-parent family squarely at the feet of the welfare state itself (Gilder 1981; Stockman 1986; Freeman 1982; Murray 1984). In the view of these critics, the availability of welfare encourages the dissolution of the family since it provides alternative sources of income for women and penalizes marriage because of work and marriage disincentives that make it rational for married couples with low earnings to separate.

Yet it is clear that father absence is not a single phenomenon and that the rise in the number of female-headed families is the result of a complex set of factors. The consequences of father absence depend on the social and political context in which it occurs. In an affluent and progressive country like Sweden, where nearly half of all births occur outside of marriage, father absence has no serious social or economic consequences (Popenoe 1988). In Sweden, out-of-wedlock births are not stigmatized, and the extensive family support system of the Swedish welfare state ensures fatherless families an adequate level of material well-being. In contrast, in the United States, which does not have a formal family support policy, the consequences of father absence depend on a woman's social class. Although marital disruption causes serious emotional and economic strain for all who go through it, for most middle-class women divorce and single motherhood usually do not result in destitution.

The consequences of single motherhood, however, are rather different for young minority group women, and among the inhabitants of our most seriously disorganized inner-city neighborhoods, an increase in adolescent pregnancy, in conjunction with an absence of marriageable males, has made marriage a rare event (Wilson 1987). Few young inner-city mothers ever marry their child's father, and for these women and their children single motherhood often means a life of chronic poverty and welfare dependency (Wilson 1987, Garfinkel and McLanahan 1986). The economic plight of these women and their children is truly serious, and the social disorganization in which they often live results in major threats to both their physical and their mental health. A combination of low income, out-of-wedlock pregnancy, and a lack of education provides new generations of poor single mothers few opportunities to escape poverty. These families, then, represent a society apart from the mainstream, one in which mothers and children are often chronically poor and dependent on welfare and one in which men play a peripheral role in family life.

As father absence becomes a permanent characteristic of many poor families, we might expect to see a rise in a "matriarchal" family pattern that includes some combination of grandmothers, mothers, and grandchildren but no economically active male. We use the term *matriarchy* to emphasize the emergence of a social system in which women must rely on one another and in which lineage is, in effect, through the female line.[1] Our use of *matriarchy* is, of course, ironic, since although women are the family decision makers, they have little economic or political power. As fatherlessness and spouse absence become more prevalent, they also characterize a larger fraction of the family life course. From this point on, many families will go through their entire childbearing and child-rearing years with no contact, or only casual contact, with adult males, and as a consequence, many older females will have spent a large portion of their lives single and will have fewer economic, perhaps even social, resources than women who spend their lives married.

In fact, in recent years we have witnessed a dramatic growth in the number of households headed by grandmothers and older women, especially among minority groups. For many of these women spouselessness is a life-long state, and grandmotherhood, which for many poor women occurs quite early in life, brings with it the responsibility for two younger generations, a daughter and the daughter's children. The fact that few adolescent mothers are in any position to support themselves means that they often have no place to turn but to their own mothers. As the result of an increase in adolescent pregnancy among minority groups, this family pattern is becoming more common in the inner city and is an important part of the emergence of the new matriarchy.

Perhaps some data would help to bring the point home. Figure 1.1 shows that in 1984 over 10 percent of black family households included a grandmother and that in over half of these households (53.6%) the grandmother herself was the head of household. As in other areas, Hispanics are intermediate between blacks and non-Hispanic whites in both the number of households containing a grandmother and in the number of such households in which the grandmother is the head. These data clearly indicate that female headship is more common among blacks and Hispanics throughout the life course than it is among non-Hispanic whites. The

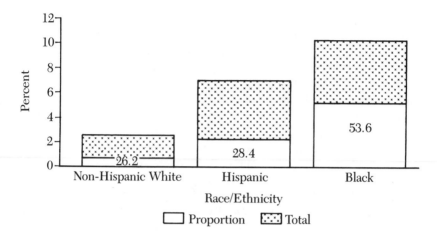

Figure 1.1. Percentage of Grandmother-Headed Households as a Proportion of Households Containing Grandmothers. *Source:* 1984 Survey of Income and Program Participation, Wave 1 (SIPP).

increase in the number of female-headed families among young black and Hispanic women will have repercussions in years to come in the number of families headed by grandmothers. If recent trends continue, and once again we have little reason to expect that they will not, a significant portion of black and Hispanic women will spend their childbearing years without husbands and will find themselves responsible for daughters and grandchildren later in life. As we will show in chapter 7, households headed by grandmothers, like households headed by younger single women, are heavily dependent on welfare.

Extended female-headed households (those consisting of the nuclear family and other relatives, including grandmothers) exist for several reasons, one of the most important of which is economic necessity. In the absence of employable (and therefore marriageable) males, single women must rely on one another and often form multigenerational households consisting of grandmothers, daughters, and grandchildren (Stack 1974; Shimkin, Shimkin, and Frate 1978; Staples 1986; Tienda and Angel 1982). The high rate of adolescent pregnancy is one of the driving forces behind the increase in this female-based family pattern (Bumpass and McLanahan 1989, Garfinkel and McLanahan 1986). A young mother with little to offer employers and few options in day care has little choice but to remain in her mother's home. Although AFDC allows women to maintain their own households, if only marginally, for very young mothers the responsibilities of running a house and caring for a child are often more than they can deal with, and many have nowhere else to turn but to their own mothers. In such situations the senior female is burdened with the domestic responsibility for two younger generations. Recent media coverage has dramatized this situation with stories about grandmothers who are the only responsible adults available to care for their grandchildren since the mothers are drug abusers, are in trouble with the law, or neglect their children (Gaines-Carter 1992, Gross 1989).

Among the very poor, then, necessity often leads women to rely on one another and leads young mothers to turn to their own mothers for support. This arrangement, although it might not be what either the daughter or her mother would prefer, allows the household to pool the economic and domestic resources of its members (Angel and Tienda 1982, Tienda and Angel 1982). Pooling resources is one way of dealing with shortages of both money and time (Angel and Tienda 1982). Someone to help with child care and with other household chores can be a great help. Multigenerational households may have positive effects in alleviating some of the psychological stress experienced by single mothers and, thereby, protect women and children against some of the negative health consequences of poverty (Angel and Worobey 1988a). Having another female around, especially one's own mother, to assume some domestic and child care responsibilities can make life a bit easier, even if the household's overall economic situation is not dramatically improved. Living with her mother may even make it possible for the young woman who has a child out of wedlock to resume her education or gain work experience.

Such a living situation, therefore, has clear potential benefits for young mothers. However, this benefit is bought at a price, and it is the senior female who must often pay it. The increased responsibilities accompanying caring for both children and grandchildren can significantly elevate the stresses grandmothers experience, especially since a large fraction of lower-class female-headed households are plagued by problems of poverty, drug abuse, and unemployment (Gaines-Carter 1992, Gross 1989, Bohlen 1989). We usually think of grandmotherhood as a privileged and enjoyable time of life. But if it involves a return to the responsibilities of motherhood, as when a woman must assume a large portion of the responsibilities for her grandchildren because her daughter is incapable of doing so, it can become burdensome (Burton and Bengtson 1985).

When parents are unable or unwilling to care for their children, grandmothers may be the only available care givers, but they are clearly no replacement for effective and caring parents. The strains of poverty and the seriously dysfunctional nature of many families that find themselves in this situation undermine the ability of the older woman to effectively raise her grandchildren. Why should she be able to do any better with her grandchildren than she was able to do with her children? How, for example, can she make sure they complete their education without the help of their parents? How can she counteract the powerful peer influences that her grandchildren will be exposed to outside her home? In most cases she cannot, and in years to come, more and more poor children will spend at least some portion of their childhoods living with their grandmothers instead of their parents.

Although we are painting a bleak picture by focusing on poor single-parent families, single mothers are a highly diverse group. Some are professional women with high educational levels and high income. Some are divorced middle-class women who have suffered serious economic losses as the result of divorce but who are able to maintain a middle-class life-style with a combination of earnings and child care payments from the absent father. Others are young never-married women who have not completed their education and who have little to offer employers. Each of these families is in a very different situation, and the combination of the age of the mother and the route by which she became a single mother has important implications for her welfare and that of her children.

Since these various types of single motherhood have such serious consequences for the health and economic welfare of both adults and children and since blacks, Hispanics, and non-Hispanic whites differ greatly in the type of single motherhood that typifies each group, we summarize the different routes by which a woman can become a single mother or grandmother in the conceptual model presented in figure 1.2. This model illustrates the complexity of the phenomenon of single motherhood. As we will show subsequently, there are large differences in the health of mothers and children in different types of female-headed families. We will also show that the sequencing and the timing of the completion of education and first birth have important implications for the welfare of both the mother and her children. The various sequences presented in figure 1.2, then, provide the conceptual framework for the rest of this book.

Figure 1.2 presents four ideal-typical family life courses consisting of four possible variations in the sequencing of the completion of education, first birth, and subsequent marriage and fertility for a woman and her daughters. These patterns are only illustrative; there are obviously many variations on these four sequences depending on the timing of the various life events and the remarriage and subsequent divorces and remarriages of any of the women involved. They serve to make our point, however, and the reader is free to add whatever variations he or she sees fit. These four hypothetical family life cycles are based on a woman's entire life course, which is divided into broad categories at the top of the figure. The model begins at the left side of the page with adolescence and ends on the right side of the page with grandmotherhood. Clearly, not all women become grandmoth-

Figure 1.2. Four Alternative Family Life Cycle Sequences

ers, in which case these sequences are truncated. Nonetheless, these four variants of the family life cycle portray the major transitions that a woman and her daughter experience during the senior female's lifetime.

These hypothetical sequences illustrate that the timing of marriage, education, and fertility for both the senior female and her daughter has important implications for the timing of the older woman's entry into grandmotherhood and the probability that she will end up in a multigenerational household. The first sequence, labeled A, is what we might consider the traditional life cycle. In this sequence, a woman completes her education, leaves her own parents' home, perhaps works as a single person, and then marries in her early twenties. She then becomes a mother herself. Her own daughter follows the same path, marries at approximately the same age and gives birth to grandchildren. Both grandparents enter their empty nest period in mature adulthood without the responsibilities of the daily care and support of children or grandchildren. The fact that the family remains intact throughout its reproductive life cycle allows the daughter to complete her education and to postpone fertility until she is economically ready to assume the responsibility of children. The grandparents are then relieved of both the economic and domestic responsibility for the immediate care of children or grandchildren. If the senior female in such a situation becomes widowed, she may move in with her children, but in such a situation, the younger generation is in charge.

The second sequence, labeled B, is similar to sequence A except that the parents divorce before the daughter leaves home. The household then becomes fatherless and in all likelihood suffers a serious drop in income. Such a breakup may or may not affect the daughter's ability to complete her education, to marry, and to reproduce in the way outlined in sequence A. If the daughter marries and eventually completes the traditional sequence, her mother enters late adulthood as a single grandmother but not burdened with responsibility for later generations. As we will show in chapter 5, the timing of the divorce is crucial in determining what impact it will have on the children.

Since as we noted earlier, a mother's marital disruption increases the probability that her daughter's own marriage will end in divorce or that she will have an illegitimate child, marital disruption may be transmitted from mother to children. In sequence B_2 the daughter follows her mother's pattern and divorces. If the daughter does not remarry, her mother may enter late middle or early adulthood as a single grandmother with a single daughter. As a result of divorce, then, a woman may find herself burdened with the responsibility for both her daughter and her daughter's child. Of course, there are several other possible sequences implicitly in variants B and B_2. Either the grandmother, her daughter, or both can remarry, divorce a second time, and so on, creating several variations. These models, however, serve to emphasize the point that the sequencing and the timing of the various family life events have important implications for the welfare of several generations.

The final sequence, labeled C, is of particular interest since it deviates so dramatically from the traditional sequence (A) and is almost a defining characteristic of the urban underclass. In this sequence a woman has a child out of wedlock very early in life. Her daughter follows the same pattern, and the older woman becomes a grandmother at a relatively early age. What is unique about this sequence is that it never includes men, except, perhaps, in a casual or peripheral way. Such families face a double jeopardy: they lack a male breadwinner throughout their family life course, and because of the extremely limited earning capacity of the women, they exist near or below poverty even when family members work.

Clearly, families that follow pattern C and are fatherless throughout all or at least most of their life cycle are at particularly high risk of welfare dependency. Although they may not be on welfare continuously, their precarious economic positions often mean that they move in and out of the welfare system. A certain number of adolescent mothers remain on welfare continuously, and given current trends in the economy and the educational profile of the urban poor, it is likely that this number will increase. The rise of this family pattern among the poorest segments of our society, then, creates a situation in which escape from chronic poverty is almost impossible either for individuals or for entire families. The adults and children in these families face the highest mental and physical health risks in our society.

These four patterns form the framework for our subsequent discussion. They are useful in identifying the sources of the potential health consequences of the duration, timing, and type of single motherhood for both women and children. Perhaps it would be useful before we proceed to state some general hypotheses concerning how we might expect fatherlessness and spouselessness to affect the health of the members of female-headed households. We will present three general sets of hypotheses focusing on the health effects of female hardship for children, young mothers, and older women.

1. We expect children who spend some substantial portion of their childhoods in poor female-headed households to experience more acute physical illness than children in two-parent families, largely as the result of greater stress and less adequate medical care. In addition, because a single mother may find it difficult to provide adequate supervision and direction to her child, we expect children in fatherless families to be at higher risk for behavioral and emotional problems. Finally, we expect the children of divorced parents to be negatively affected by the emotional turmoil leading up to the divorce and the disruption of the divorce itself. We expect pattern C in our conceptual model to have the most negative impact on children's health.

2. We expect to find that single mothers are at high risk for emotional problems because of the increased burdens associated with poverty and unassisted parenthood. We also expect any potential negative health effects for young mothers to be largely the result of divorce, low education, adolescent pregnancy, and poverty.

3. We expect single grandmothers who are economically responsible for one or more younger generations to be in poorer emotional health than married grandmothers or those whose children are economically indepen-

dent. Again, we expect any negative health effects experienced by older women to be the result of low education, family burden, and poverty.

In the chapters that follow we will review the existing literature to determine to what extent previous research can help us in testing these hypotheses. We will also present some of our own findings concerning these issues and make the best inferential case possible. Unfortunately, because the data to directly test the health consequences of our different life course patterns do not exist, our discussion will be based on inferences from descriptive and cross-sectional data. Information on the health effects of single grandmotherhood is particularly sparse, and our discussion of the potential health risks of single grandmotherhood focuses on the situation of older single women. One of our major objectives in this book is to provide the impetus for further research, and we hope that our discussion of the problems of single mothers and their children will stimulate interest in the collection of data appropriate to the examination of the long-term health consequences of single motherhood at different points in the life cycle.

Single Motherhood and the New Morbidity

As we noted earlier, the United States, along with the rest of the developed world, has achieved the longest life expectancy at birth in human history. Although infant mortality rates in the United States remain high in comparison to other developed nations, the morbidity and mortality experiences of even the poorest Americans reflect the shift in causes of death from acute to chronic illness. For the most part, children in the United States do not suffer from the infectious diseases that kill millions of young people in the Third World, and since the major chronic illnesses are largely a function of aging, even poor American children are fairly healthy. As a consequence, in the contemporary United States the major threats to children's health and well-being consist of external, socially influenced health risk factors, such as family violence and substance abuse. In addition, problems such as learning disabilities and emotional and behavioral disturbances have replaced infectious diseases as the major childhood illnesses. This package of emotional, behavioral, and developmental problems has been referred to as "the new morbidity" (Haggerty, Roghmann, and Pless 1975); it will be the major focus of chapter 5.

There can be little doubt that emotional problems are a serious threat to the welfare of children and adolescents. Although there is no way of knowing for sure, researchers estimate that somewhere between 10 and 30 percent of children experience at least one significant behavioral disorder at some time in their childhood (Haggerty 1983). In addition, approximately one out of every five adolescents has a clinically diagnosable psychiatric illness (Offer, Ostrov, and Howard 1983). The most frequently reported behavioral problems for children are those related to school, and while it is possible to view these as an inevitable part of growing up, problems that interfere with school and with normal socialization can limit the long-term opportunities for the children who experience them.

Because, as we will show, single women are subjected to stresses from several sources, they and their children are at increased risk of physical and mental distress. It is imperative, however, that we emphasize at the outset that we are not implying that single motherhood is inherently detrimental to the health of mothers or their children. Our position is that since in the United States, unlike Sweden and other European countries, single motherhood is often associated with serious economic and social stress, it may increase the risk of illness for its members, especially when combined with the economic and social disadvantages of minority group status.

Consequently, throughout the book we employ the epidemiological concept of *risk* to characterize the potential consequences of single motherhood for the health of children and adults. Being at risk for illness, or poverty, or whatever simply means that one has a higher chance than someone who is not at risk of developing the illness, of being poor, and so on. Risk, of course, is a matter of degree, and some people are at higher risk of poverty than others because they have low education and few jobs skills or are disadvantaged minority group members. The accumulation of risk factors greatly increases the chance of a negative outcome. Yet, although poor single-parent families are more likely than more affluent two-parent families to experience the negative health consequences of poverty, not all do. Many, if not most, single-parent families function quite well, and their members suffer no long-term ill effects. In this sense, single motherhood is by itself only one risk factor among others for ill health.

As with risk factors generally, the health consequences of single motherhood depend on its association with other risk factors. As we will show, if a single mother has other social and economic resources to call on, the health consequences of not having a husband may be negligible. In the absence of such resources, however, single mothers and their children may experience serious negative health consequences. In addition to risk, our discussion focuses on the concept of *health*. Although we will discuss the meaning of health in greater detail in chapter 4, the concept is so central to our entire discussion that before proceeding we must give a brief description of what we are referring to when we speak of health.

For almost everyone, the word *health* has a clear meaning. When we say that someone is healthy, we usually mean that he or she is not suffering from some obvious disease. In everyday use such a definition is clear enough, but for research purposes we need a far more precise definition of health. When we investigate the impact of father absence on either mental or physical health, what me mean by health and illness should be unambiguous. Unfortunately, as we will show in later chapters, in much research this is not the case, and when some people imagine they are measuring health, they are often measuring something else.

Health, to begin with, is a multifaceted phenomenon; in the broadest sense it consists of physical, mental, and social components. A healthy person is one who has no apparent physical or mental illness and who functions well at work or at school as well as with friends and family. Deficits in any one of these areas can flow over and affect others. When a person becomes physically ill, the illness often affects his or her psychological state and, ultimately, his or her social functioning. Social functioning is central to our definition of health, since the inability to interact with others is not only the result of ill health but a cause of poor mental and physical health as well. There is a large body of evidence that shows that the absence of adequate social support can lead to poor physical and mental health and even premature death (House, Landis, and Umberson 1988). As single mothers lack a confidant and often have no other adult to turn to for emotional and instrumental support, many are at risk of inadequate social support and its associated health risks.

The literature on the impact of father absence on health is rich in certain areas and sparse in others. For example, we know a great deal about the impact of divorce on children's mental and social functioning, but we know less about the mental health of children of never-married mothers and even less about the physical health of children in female-headed households. Nonetheless, there is enough evidence to indicate that father absence has different effects on various dimensions of health. In the contemporary United States few children, even those from the poorest families, suffer serious physical illness. Perhaps there may be some subtle effects of father absence on physical health that are difficult to measure in large samples, but on the basis of objective criteria we review in chapter 5, it appears that children in two-parent and single-parent households have fairly similar levels of physical health.

This is not the case for mental and social health. Children in single-parent and two-parent families differ significantly in emotional and social well-being. The literature clearly shows that marital disruption has serious negative effects on the psychological health of both mothers and children. The children of divorced parents are more depressed and have more problems in school and with social interactions than children in intact families. Some studies suggest that the negative consequences of family disruption can last into adulthood. Girls who grow up without a father, for example, often have difficulty in relationships with men when they become adults (Hetherington 1989). It appears, then, that physical health is much less affected by father absence than mental health.

Clearly, both physical and mental health are affected by income and social class. Those at the bottom of the income distribution are at higher risk of poor physical and mental health than those with higher incomes. Since in the United States health insurance is largely an employment benefit, a large number of the families of unemployed workers must rely on government-financed medical care. Such care may be of a lower quality than that received by families who can choose their own physicians or health plans. Since we suspect that the poverty many single-parent households experience lies at the core of any physical and emotional problems they experience, we will concentrate heavily on the economic plight of single mothers and pay close attention to those governmental programs that affect the health of women and children in female-headed households.

Health as a Political Issue

In the following chapters we demonstrate that the income and health programs of the American welfare state have been, and continue to be, crucial in ensuring the health of women and children in fatherless families. Proposals for changes in AFDC and other health-related federal and state programs must be informed by a clear understanding of the consequences for the health of future generations. We, like everyone else, have our preferred solutions for addressing the health care needs of single mothers and their children, but we also realize that even the sincerest attempts to improve the lives of the poor have unforeseen consequences.

Welfare policy in the United States is currently at a crossroads, and future directions in public policy concerning poverty generally and programs that affect health specifically will be shaped by political debates that are taking place during a period of economic retrenchment and renewed doubts concerning society's ability, or even its responsibility, to ensure the health and economic welfare of all those who are unable to care for themselves. The coalition between blacks, labor unions, and liberal Democrats that made the Great Society programs a possibility has collapsed. Today, the defenders of the welfare state have no coherent agenda, and because the political basis of the welfare state has never been as secure in the United States as in Europe, social welfare programs, especially those that affect single mothers and children, are under attack. Both liberals and conservatives are searching for new policy directions that will ensure the health and welfare of the poor, who are increasingly made up of mother-only households, while respecting basic American values of self-sufficiency.

At least two of the basic assumptions on which welfare policy in the United States is based have come into serious question in recent years. Americans have always assumed that there is adequate work available for all those who want it. The employment programs of the War on Poverty and current jobs training programs aimed at welfare recipients are based on the assumption that if only the unemployable were made more like the employable through training and job placement programs, they could become self-supporting, or at least reduce their dependence on the state. Unfortunately, it is becoming increasingly clear that basic changes in the national economy have resulted in the loss of employment opportunities in the inner cities. The loss of entry-level jobs in the inner city, for which there seems to be no immediate cure, combined with the serious skill deficits of many urban residents make large numbers of our poorest citizens fundamentally unemployable. Expectations that poverty can be eliminated through fostering self-sufficiency are, in our opinion as well as in the opinion of others, unrealistic.

The second assumption that informs welfare policy is that poverty, for the most part, results from temporary setbacks. Welfare is designed to provide help for short periods until a family gets back on its feet. Longer-term dependence on public transfers has historically been discouraged by stigmatizing those who receive it (Katz 1986, 1989). Despite the stigma, however, the number of families who must rely on welfare because they have no alternatives is growing. Although they may not rely on welfare on a continuous basis, many single-parent families never manage to completely escape poverty. For many single mothers and their children poverty is an ever-present possibility and long-term self-sufficiency an elusive goal.

The rise in the number of female-headed households and the limited earning capacities of many single mothers have added to the growth of a new class of people who have little chance for social mobility. The decline of stable working-class communities and the decay of the traditional two-parent family have resulted in a growing problem of chronic poverty that has contributed to serious social disorganization in our inner cities. The loss of stable communities and the increase in the amount of drug abuse and violent crime are among the greatest tragedies of contemporary poverty. Because of our gender-based system of social stratification and the chronic poverty experienced by so many fatherless families, many children will grow up in very poor households and will be exposed to the health risks of a disorganized and unsupportive social environment.

The Two Societies: Concluding Remarks

The dramatic increase in the number of female-headed households has resulted in what we might characterize as a two-tiered system of child rearing consisting of (1) two-parent households in which domestic and economic roles are shared by two adults, and (2) female-headed households in which the entire burden of economic and domestic life is borne by a single parent. This two-tiered system has potentially serious implications for the physical and emotional health of children as well as for the health of their mothers and grandmothers. As more women enter the labor force, the prices of housing and other durable goods are increasingly determined by dual-earner households, and the high cost of basic necessities, in conjunction with the generally lower earnings of women, results in a marked disparity in the income of two-parent and single-parent households.

We have argued here that the routes by which women become single mothers interact with their race and ethnicity to place young black single mothers at a far greater disadvantage than older middle-class divorced non-Hispanic white mothers. As a social problem, single motherhood is a multifaceted phenomenon. Many fatherless families experience no problems, while others essentially cease to function as families. In earlier days these families were labeled multiproblem families. Today, they are placed among the underclass. Whatever label we use, however, it is clear that our current welfare system does little to help these families escape poverty, nor does it preserve the dignity of the dependent poor.

We would expect the poverty in which many female-headed families live, in conjunction with the absence of another adult in the household, to increase health risks for children and to contribute to a household environment in which health care is provided less effectively than in dual-parent households (Cherlin 1982). Such a potential health care disadvantage might result from several sources. Perhaps most obviously, the generally lower earnings of women often increases the exposure of children in female-headed households to the health risks associated with poverty. In addition, because they less often have private medical insurance, female-headed households are disproportionately dependent on Medicaid for basic medical services (Davis and Schoen 1978; Cafferata, Berk, and Jones 1987). As a consequence, children in female-headed households may receive lower-quality medical care than children in two-parent households (Wolfe 1980).

In the following chapters we elaborate on these issues and examine the health consequences of father absence for women and children in great detail. Because our conception of health and illness is far broader than their narrower clinical definitions and because health and illness are defined, created, and responded to in specific social, economic, and political contexts, we pay a great deal of attention to federal and state programs that have even an indirect impact on health. A housing program that ensures that children live in a healthful environment in which they are not exposed to the dangers of lead-based paint, for example, has clear health benefits. By the end of this book, then, the reader will be aware of what is known of the physical and mental health consequences of single motherhood and fatherlessness and of how that impact differs for blacks, whites, and Hispanics. Our purpose is not to further any particular approach to meeting the health care needs of women and children. Rather, we wish to inform the discussion of the issue and make it clear that a great deal of work must be done before we truly understand their health care needs, let alone before we are able to prescribe effective cures.

2

The Magnitude of the Problem
Demographic and Economic Dimensions

In the United States today most of us take good health for granted. America, along with the other industrially developed nations of the world, has achieved the lowest mortality rates and the longest life expectancies in human history. These gains are the result of increases in material well-being as well as advances in medical care. It is a simple fact of life that as nations become richer, they become healthier. Middle-class Americans are about as healthy as they can be, and given the state of our knowledge concerning health and illness, they live about as long as human beings possibly can. Among the poor, especially among the minority poor of America's inner cities, however, life is different. Even as we approach the end of the twentieth century, major social class and racial differentials in the prevalence of various diseases persist. The poor are more likely than middle-class Americans to develop and die from the complications of such chronic diseases as cancer, diabetes, obesity, and hypertension, and in some of our central cities, infant mortality rates among blacks are nearly three times the national average (Children's Defense Fund 1990a, Grad 1988). In cities like Washington, Baltimore, Detroit, and Philadelphia, infant mortality rates approach those of the Third World, and the United States as a whole ranks twentieth among major industrialized nations (Children's Defense Fund 1991).

Although acute disease has largely been controlled, minority group children and the poor continue to experience a disproportionate amount of illness as the result of infectious agents and environmental toxins, such as lead (Children's Defense Fund 1990a). Most tragically, the recent epidemic of AIDS has struck savagely at both children and adults in poor and minority communities, and the number of cases of tuberculosis, which had become a minor health problem after the discovery of effective antibiotics, is again on the rise (Children's Defense Fund 1991). In addition to increasing the risk of disease, poverty and minority group status undermine the quality of health care adults and children receive. Black Americans wait longer for organ transplants and often seek medical care later in the course of diseases like cancer, decreasing the likelihood of long-term survival. Children, of course, are among the most helpless victims of these threats to health, and it is because of their extreme vulnerability that the situation of single-parent families demands our attention.

Although federally financed health care for the poor through Medicaid has greatly increased the use of medical care by the poor, the children of the poor are still less likely than the children of the middle class to be fully immunized or to receive dental and mental health care (Children's Defense Fund 1990a). Generally reduced access to preventive and high-quality curative health care widens the gap in health between middle-class and poor children and undermines their ability to compete in school and in the labor market. It is clear, therefore, that the remaining differentials in health levels in the United States are, for the most part, the result of the risk factors associated with poverty, and because blacks and Hispanics are the poorest groups in our society, they, along with women and children, bear a disproportionate share of the illness burden.

In a book dealing with the health of women and children in fatherless families, it is imperative that we document the extent and nature of the poverty experienced by families maintained solely by women before we proceed to a detailed examination of the health consequences of fatherlessness and a review of the governmental programs designed to address them. The health vulnerability of fatherless families is particularly severe since the combination of poverty, early childbearing, and low education that often accompanies single motherhood can undermine both the health status of children and the amount and quality of the medical care they receive. A mother's educational level is one of the most powerful predictors of the health of her child (e.g., Wilcox-Gok 1985). Because of the potentially serious health vulnerabilities of women and children in single-parent families, we take a close look at the demographic and economic characteristics of fatherless families and also document the extent of their dependency on governmental programs designed to maintain their health and welfare.

Single mothers as a group have extremely low earnings, and although over half are self-supporting, a disproportionate number are dependent on welfare for protracted periods. The evidence we review reveals large racial and ethnic differences in the income and the extent of welfare dependency of fatherless families. Although single mothers of all racial and ethnic groups are frequently poor, among blacks and Hispanics, long-term welfare dependency is rapidly increasing. In what follows we examine the growth in the number of fatherless families over the last forty years and compare the economic situation of black, Hispanic, and non-Hispanic fatherless families to that of non-Hispanic white single-parent households and to that of two-parent households.

The Growth in Fatherlessness

The dramatic post–World War II growth in the number of fatherless families has been a universal phenomenon that has affected all racial and ethnic groups. Among black Americans, however, the decline of the two-parent family has proceeded at a particularly rapid pace. Figure 2.1 shows just how rapid the increase in the number of female-headed families with children under 18 years of age has been. Between 1960 and 1989, the proportion of children living in families headed by women more than doubled, but since blacks started out so much higher than non-Hispanic whites, by 1989, more than half of all black children were living in fatherless families.

This rapid change in family structure means that the traditional family and the child-rearing practices we associate with it are, for a large fraction of our population, a thing of the past. If, as many believe, the type of adults we become depends on the type of families we grow up in, the future may be very different from the past. Not only will a large proportion of children in single-parent households be subjected to extended bouts of poverty and its attendant health risks but many will grow up without a male role model. For a large number of these children the men they will come to know will have only casual contact with the family and will contribute little to family welfare. Inevitably, these children's sex-role socialization and their notions of men's role in the family and in the society at large will be very different from that of children who grow up with an economically active father who serves as an authoritative role model. The social consequences of such a large number of children growing up without male role models is a huge unknown, and it may have subtle indirect effects on physical and mental health.

Whatever its ultimate health and social impact, however, it is clear that this growth in the number of single-parent families is an important factor in the increase in chronic poverty among black and Hispanic Americans.

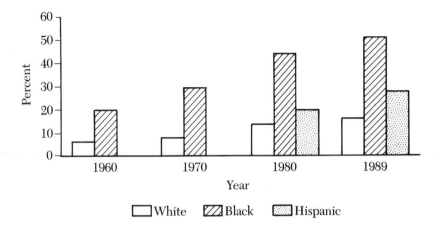

Figure 2.1. Children under 18 Years in Mother-Only Households by Race and Hispanic Origin. *Source:* U.S. Bureau of the Census (March 1989) CPS Series P-20, no. 445, table C, p. 3.

A high concentration of female-headed households is one of the defining characteristics that many investigators have employed to identify underclass neighborhoods (Auletta 1982, Moore 1989, Wilson 1987). Because of very high rates of long-term unemployment, such neighborhoods contain few marriageable males (Wilson 1987, Kasarda 1985), and because of the multiple disadvantages that young, poorly educated black and Hispanic mothers face in the urban labor market, few have much chance of supporting themselves or of earning much above poverty level incomes. These are hardly the optimal conditions for effective parenting and the development of the best physical and mental health.

In the popular media and even in scholarly journals, the discussions of the problems of chronic poverty and female-headed households have focused on blacks. Indeed, it is easy to get the impression from the popular media that the problems of the underclass are exclusive to blacks (Gross 1989). But the problems of poverty and family disruption are not just black problems. They are the problems of any group that has been on the losing end of the changes in the American economic system that occurred after World War II. In the contemporary United States the low-skill entry-level jobs that allowed generations of earlier European immigrants to escape poverty have disappeared. Few opportunities remain for even the most motivated inner-city youths who might be willing to start at the bottom and work their way up (Kasarda 1985).

Although the data do not cover as long a period for Hispanics since the

U.S. Census Bureau did not provide information separately for Hispanics before 1980, figure 2.1 shows that in the nine years after the 1980 census, the proportion of Hispanic children living with only their mothers increased rapidly. These trends have dramatic long-term implications. If the decline in the proportion of black families headed by both parents were to continue at anywhere near its current rate, and there is no reason to imagine that it will not, the vast majority of future cohorts of black children will spend at least some portion of their childhood in fatherless families (Bumpass 1984). Although rates of fatherlessness are lower among Hispanics than among blacks, these data suggest that the same forces that are causing the decline of the two-parent family among blacks are affecting Hispanics as well. As Hispanics follow blacks into the central cities, where job opportunities are limited, we can expect the number of female-headed families among Puerto Ricans and Mexican-Americans to grow rapidly (Moore 1989, Wilson 1987).

Figure 2.1 shows that the rate of father absence among Hispanics has followed the black pattern since 1980 and is currently intermediate between that of blacks and non-Hispanic whites. By the time of the 1980 census, over one-fourth of all Hispanic children under age eighteen were living in a female-headed household, and, as with blacks, there is little reason to believe that these trends will reverse themselves or even slow significantly in the future. The disruptive forces associated with minority group status, such as low education and unemployment, that have placed great strains on the black family are having a similar impact on the Hispanic family (Moore 1989). Among lower-class blacks and Hispanics, the two-parent family is beset by seriously disruptive forces that even the traditional familism of Hispanics appears unable to overcome.

It might be useful before we proceed for the reader to know that our previous research has shown that on most socioeconomic indicators, Hispanics are intermediate between blacks and non-Hispanic whites. Although Hispanics have never borne the burden of slavery, certain Hispanics share with blacks many of the labor force disadvantages that plague our inner cities, and consequently, on many social indicators they approximate blacks. Although they often lag behind blacks, as in the number of female-headed families, Hispanic families are clearly experiencing many of the same social forces that have led to the disruption of black urban family life. We should also note that our research clearly shows that Hispanics are a very diverse group and that not all can be considered disadvantaged minorities. Puerto Ricans are perhaps most similar to blacks in terms of socioeconomic disadvantage, while Cuban-Americans are in most regards other than culture indistinguishable from non-Hispanic white Americans.

The Demographic Causes of Single Motherhood

In a strictly demographic sense, the growth in the number of fatherless families is the result of two complementary trends: (1) an increase in the proportion of all births occurring outside of marriage, and (2) declining marital fertility (Cherlin 1981). These trends are really two sides of the same coin, since although the total number of illegitimate births has remained about the same since the 1960s, births to unwed mothers make up a larger fraction of all births as married couples are having fewer babies. What has changed dramatically in recent years is the greater tendency for unwed mothers to remain unmarried and to keep their babies. Even very young mothers are keeping their babies rather than giving them up for adoption as they did more frequently in the not so distant past. If AFDC has had any effect on the number of female-headed families, it may be because it allows mothers who might otherwise give their babies up for adoption to keep them and even to form their own households.

Figure 2.2 makes this point in a dramatic way. The left-hand panel shows that for all three racial and ethnic groups, only a minority of adolescent mothers have ever been married. In addition, figure 2.2 reveals some dramatic differences among blacks, Hispanics, and non-Hispanic whites. Virtually none of the young black mothers have ever been married and Hispanics again fall between blacks and non-Hispanic whites. Only 35 percent of young Hispanic mothers have ever married. The right-hand panel shows rather dramatic racial and ethnic differences in marital status even among older single mothers. Less than 50 percent of black single

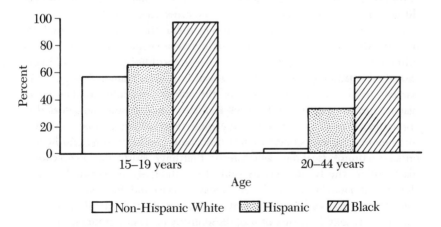

Figure 2.2. Proportion of Never-Married Mothers by Age, Race, and Hispanic Ethnicity. *Source:* U.S. Bureau of the Census (1989) CPS Series P-20, no. 433, table 9, pp. 46, 50, 54.

mothers aged twenty to forty-four have ever been married, and only 67 percent of single Hispanic older mothers have been married. Clearly, if these patterns continue into the future, an ever-larger fraction of all births will be to single mothers.

The marital status of the mother at the time of the child's birth has important implications for both the mother's economic welfare and her child's. Even though many divorced mothers receive little help from their ex-husbands, a substantial number receive at least some child support (U.S. Bureau of the Census 1986),[1] and although their income drops precipitously after divorce, many of these women have job skills that allow them to support a family. Unfortunately, as figure 2.2 shows, a large number of never-married mothers are adolescents with little education and few job skills. The number of adolescent mothers who eventually marry the child's father is decreasing, and since the fathers are often unemployable, these women are very unlikely to receive any aid from them.

As in other areas of life, the situation is more serious for black and Hispanic adolescent mothers, since a smaller fraction of these young mothers than of non-Hispanic white young women ever marry their child's father (Bumpass 1984). The mother's youth, her minority group status, and her interrupted schooling, then, offer bleak prospects for improving her lot through her own efforts and greatly increase her chances for long-term welfare dependency. Because of low educational levels and emotional immaturity, many of these mothers are incapable of providing an optimal home environment for their child's physical, cognitive, and psychosocial development.

Racial and ethnic groups differ in ways other than the number of children born out of wedlock. Their divorce rates differ, as do their rates of remarriage after divorce. Needless to say, remarriage has an important impact on the economic status of single mothers and their children. A woman who remarries within one or two years of her divorce in all likelihood ends up in a better economic situation than a woman who does not remarry at all, or one who does so only after a long interval. The fewer marriage options available to black and Hispanic women are revealed in remarriage rates as well as in first marriage rates. Divorced black and Hispanic mothers are less likely than non-Hispanic white divorced mothers to remarry (Bumpass 1984). Because of a serious shortage of employable black males, the remarriage as well as the marriage prospects for black women are poor (Wilson 1987). As Hispanics are exposed to the disruptive strains of poverty and the social disorganization of inner-city life, the number of marriageable males among these groups is also dropping, decreasing the chances of remarriage for a larger number of divorced Hispanic females (Moore 1989).

Out-of-wedlock births, the interruption of schooling, a lack of marriage-able males, and few employment opportunities, then, have serious social and economic consequences for adolescent mothers and their children. The long-term spells of welfare dependency and poverty that accompany father absence for many families in the inner city may seriously harm the physical and mental health of both mothers and their children (Carballo and Bane 1984, Children's Defense Fund 1990a). For blacks and Hispan-ics, the situation is exacerbated by the fact that the economic and social disadvantages of single motherhood are often magnified by minority group status. Black and Hispanic single mothers and their children are therefore at particularly elevated risk of physical and emotional illness.

The Economic Plight of Fatherless Families

The loss of a father has always been an economic disaster for families. In earlier centuries when widowhood was much more common than it is to-day, the death of a husband usually thrust a woman and her children into poverty and forced them to rely on charity or to enter the workhouse (Katz 1986, Mencher 1967). Even though widows were considered to be among the deserving poor, because of generally low levels of material wel-fare, their lot was a hard one. Unlike widows, though, unwed mothers have never been considered among the deserving poor, and their lot has been even harder. Although today the economic welfare of female-headed families is better by far than it was at any previous period in our history, single mothers and their children are still at the bottom of the economic heap.

Official governmental poverty figures paint a bleak picture for female-headed households. Figure 2.3, although it covers only thirteen years, il-lustrates our point that fatherless families with children under the age of eighteen have always fared much worse than two-parent families. This time series shows a constant level of poverty among female-headed fami-lies since 1975. In all years more than 50 percent of black and Hispanic female-headed households and nearly 40 percent of non-Hispanic white female-headed households were poor. The feminization of poverty, then, is not the result of a new tendency, for female-headed families always have been poor. Rather, it is the result of the fact that a larger fraction of all families fall into this category. Today, single mothers and their children comprise the largest segment of the population in poverty (Wilson and Neckerman 1986).

Yet as bleak as these statistics are, they actually understate the magni-tude of the problem. For a significant fraction of female-headed house-holds, serious poverty and welfare dependency last for long periods, and

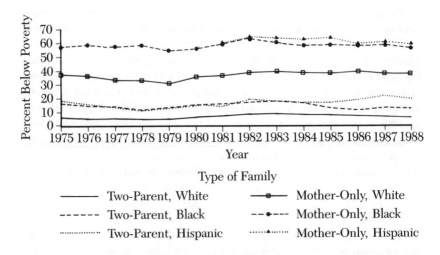

Figure 2.3. Poverty Status of Families with Children under 18 by Race and Hispanic Ethnicity: 1975–1988. *Source:* U.S. Bureau of the Census (1989) CPS Series P-60, no. 166, table 20, pp. 62–65.

even when it is not continual, many families never really manage to escape poverty and are on and off the welfare roles frequently. What is particularly troubling is that although the fraction of families that are chronically dependent on welfare is rather small, it appears to be growing (Garfinkel and McLanahan 1986). It is also important to remember that the definition of poverty is arbitrary. Even for many female-headed families who are not poor by official criteria, the true economic freedom that results from an adequate income is elusive. An income that places one above the federal government's official poverty line can still be quite low. In 1987, for example, a single woman with two children would have to have had an income below $9,056 to be counted as officially poor.

Obviously, an income of $3,000, $4,000, or even $5,000 more than this amount would leave a three-person family very little discretionary income. As we elaborate in greater detail in the next and in the final chapters, those individuals whose earnings are too high to allow them to qualify for Medicaid but who work at jobs that do not provide adequate family health insurance are the least well served by our current public/private health financing system. Many single mothers are exactly in this situation. Statistics that show that only a small fraction of poor families are continuously on welfare do not tell the whole story. For many of these families the escape from poverty is often brief, and for all intents and purposes they remain poor. In fact, for many, rising into the ranks of the working poor can mean a drop in real welfare because of the loss of benefits, including Medicaid. Clearly, this is a system that is not optimally designed to ensure the physical and mental health of single mothers and their children.

Yet many fatherless families do manage to escape poverty. Several studies based on longitudinal data have demonstrated that most families, including those headed by women, eventually find their way out of poverty (Duncan 1984, Garfinkel and McLanahan 1986). For single mothers the route out of poverty is often through marriage or remarriage. Using the Michigan Panel Study on Income Dynamics (PSID), in which a group of approximately five thousand families was followed for a ten-year period, Heather Ross and Isabel Sawhill (1975) found that in the early 1970s single motherhood was only a short transitional period for most women which usually ended in remarriage within three to five years. However, since that study was published, the transitional period during which single mothers remain unmarried has increased (Garfinkel and McLanahan 1986, Duncan 1984, Hill 1983). Within a relatively few years, then, single motherhood has for many women become permanent. It is probably not an overstatement to say that among the urban poor reproduction has essentially been separated from the institution of marriage, and as a consequence, poverty is often an inevitability.[2]

Although welfare provides a real safety net for single mothers and their children, it cannot, and perhaps should not be expected to, provide them a middle-class life-style. Figure 2.4 shows that in all three racial and eth-

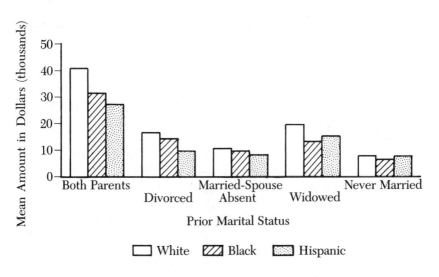

Figure 2.4. Family Income of Two-Parent and Mother-Only Households with Children under 18 by Race and Ethnicity: 1988. *Source:* U.S. Bureau of the Census (1989) CPS Series P-20, no. 433, table 9, pp. 46, 50, 54.

nic groups fatherless families have much lower incomes than two-parent families. Once again, we can see that families in which the mother has never been married are the worst off regardless of race or ethnicity. In 1988, never-married white mothers report incomes of $7,829; black mothers, $6,596; and Hispanic mothers, $7,540. These figures, however, understate the real income of fatherless families, since they do not include the value of in-kind transfer programs. Nonetheless, even with these additional transfers, never-married mothers and their children are not well off.

Table 2.1 presents more detailed evidence concerning the extent of welfare dependency among female-headed households. Almost half of black and Hispanic female-headed households receive AFDC. Female-headed households are also dependent on noncash transfers such as food stamps, Women, Infants, and Children (WIC), and the school lunch program. Black and Hispanic female-headed households are particularly dependent on these noncash programs. Clearly, if it were not for AFDC and the various health and nutrition programs that make up our welfare safety net, these women and their children would suffer serious deprivation and malnutrition.

One particularly troublesome aspect of single mothers' reliance on wel-

Table 2.1. Public Transfers Received by Two-Parent and Mother-Only Households with Children under 18 Years of Age (Weighted Data)

	Non-Hispanic White		Black		Hispanic	
	Two-Parent	Mother-Only	Two-Parent	Mother-Only	Two-Parent	Mother-Only
AFDC	1.4	24.3	7.1	44.6	7.5	43.8
Amount ($)	369	354	279	356	460	397
SSI	0.5	3.3	4.8	4.7	3.3	5.4
Amount ($)	345	269	322	309	279	386
Food Stamps	4.6	34.7	15.2	60.3	20.3	63.8
Amount ($)	187	158	197	188	169	159
WIC	1.5	3.5	2.8	5.4	4.5	4.7
School Lunch	61.5	72.2	77.3	87.6	74.4	89.5
N (unwgt)	(8984)	(1349)	(878)	(936)	(743)	(258)

Source: 1984 Survey of Income and Program Participation (SIPP) Wave I.

fare is the fact that it is not responsive to changes in the larger economy. As figure 2.3 shows, the proportion of female-headed families living in poverty remains fairly constant through good times and bad. For two-parent families poverty often results from downturns in the economy, and with two adults such families are often able to compensate for the loss of the earnings of the primary breadwinner, at least to some extent. When a plant closes or when jobs are scarce and the husband in a two-parent family loses his job, his wife can often take up at least part of the slack by continuing to work or by going to work if she is unemployed.

The possibility of a team approach to family income, then, gives a two-parent household greater potential economic adaptability. The poverty of mother-only families, however, is less often the result of aggregate economic fluctuations. Rather, it is usually the result of chronic unemployability and the inability of poorly educated single women to command anything near a living wage, especially if they must pay for child care. Because they lack a spouse who can go to work and contribute to total household income, single-parent families lack the economic flexibility of two-parent families. For these reasons their poverty is more enduring and less responsive to improvements in the economy. The real welfare of single mothers and their children has been influenced by another trend. As the result of inflation, the real value of AFDC and food stamps declined by over 30 percent during the 1970s and 1980s (Children's Defense Fund 1990a). Since these are the basic programs on which single mothers and their children rely and since substantial increases in welfare are unlikely in our stagnant economy, the overall situation of fatherless families may erode seriously in the coming years, and the physical and mental health of their members may well be affected.

The Inheritance of Poverty: Consequences for Health

One particularly troublesome aspect of this new chronic poverty is the possibility that it is transmitted from one generation to the next. If the daughters of women who have children out of wedlock are more likely to have illegitimate births themselves, the poverty that female-headed households experience could be transmitted from mother to child. The possibility that this inheritance of poverty also results in the inheritance of low levels of health is particularly disturbing. If this is the case, the children born to poor single mothers are handicapped before they even begin life. Unfortunately, since as we document in great detail in chapter 5, poverty, low birth weight, and diminished health tend to occur together, the possibility that diminished vitality and impaired life chances are transmitted from one generation to the next is very real indeed.

Although there are few studies that follow single mothers into adult-hood, the few that do paint a disturbing picture. They suggest that single motherhood and a life in poverty may, in fact, be passed on from mother to daughter. The mechanisms of this transmission are complex and involve interrupted schooling and early pregnancy for both the mother and her children (McLanahan 1985a; Furstenberg, Brooks-Gunn, and Morgan 1987). Variant III in figure 1.2 illustrates how poverty might be passed on from mother to daughter. Because this possibility has such clear impor-tance for health, we briefly summarize the major findings concerning the impact of single motherhood on a woman's own life chances and on the long-term welfare of children.

In the United States education is a prerequisite for a good job as well as one of the most important predictors of good health. There is a large body of evidence that the type of family that one grows up in has an important impact on one's educational attainment and, consequently, on one's occu-pational attainment in adulthood.[3] Children who grow up in female-headed households complete fewer years of education than children who grow up in two-parent families (Duncan, Featherman, and Duncan 1972; Featherman and Hauser 1976a, 1976b). In a study that traced children from childhood into adolescence, Sara McLanahan (1985a) found that the children of single mothers are less likely to complete high school than chil-dren who grow up with both parents.[4]

These educational deficits experienced by the children of single moth-ers can result from many sources. The age of the mother is clearly an im-portant factor in determining the extent to which she values education and encourages her children to complete it. Many single mothers never complete high school and are less likely than college-educated middle-class parents to encourage their children to do well in school. In addition, the stresses of poverty and unassisted parenthood may undermine a mother's ability to discipline her children and to make sure they actually attend school and do their homework. A poor single-parent household may simply be too noisy and disorganized to allow children to complete their homework. Of course, if a child spends little time at home, the possi-bility for doing homework is undermined. Low education of the parent is also associated with less knowledge about disease and fewer visits to the doctor by children (Colle and Grossman 1978, Wilcox-Gok 1985).

For whatever reasons, many children of single mothers experience both academic and psychosocial problems during their school years. In a longi-tudinal study of the impact of a mother's age when she gives birth on the adjustment and behavior of schoolchildren, Kristin Moore (1986) found that early childbearing has serious long-term negative social and health consequences. In 1976, Moore initially studied a group of children who were between the ages of seven and eleven and then recontacted them four years later in 1981 when they were between eleven and sixteen. The children of young mothers were more likely to have run away, to have gotten into trouble, to have engaged in antisocial behavior, and to have done poorly in school than the children of older mothers. The educational deficits that result from this constellation of problems mean that as adults these children will be less competitive in the job market than children of older mothers or children who grow up with both parents. It is also likely that they will suffer more adult adjustment problems and have poorer mental health.

Adolescents who do poorly in school, of course, are likely to engage in other behaviors that have long-term negative implications for their economic and psychological well-being. In a study of the consequences of early childbearing, McLanahan (1988) found that girls who live in a single-parent household during adolescence are more likely than girls who grow up in two-parent households to become single parents. In addition, she found that growing up in a family that receives welfare increases the probability that a child will receive welfare as an adult. These findings suggest that welfare-dependent single-parent households do not provide young women with the skills necessary to escape poverty. These data again indicate that poverty and its associated health risks may be passed on from mother to children.

Other evidence indicates that in addition to low educational attainment, the children of single mothers experience many other problems later in life. In a study of the long-term consequences of single motherhood for a woman and her children, researchers found that although many young single mothers are eventually able to complete their education, to marry, and to find work, most of them suffer some long-term negative consequences (Furstenberg, Brooks-Gunn, and Morgan 1987). For example, the women who had their first birth at a young age had very unstable marital histories and earned less as adults than women who had their children later. In addition, their children experienced more behavioral problems and were more likely to drop out of school and to face restricted employment opportunities than the children of older mothers.

The evidence is fairly convincing, therefore, that early pregnancy and low educational attainment are the primary mechanisms through which poverty is transmitted from mother to children. The data are consistent in showing that a mother who has her children early is less able to provide them the opportunities that might help them get ahead in life (Hayes 1987; Moore and Burt 1982; Chilman 1983; Garfinkel and McLanahan 1986; Morgan and Rindfuss 1985). Women who have children early in life have a higher probability of economic hardship and divorce than women who begin their families in their twenties. Since they are little more than children themselves, many of these young mothers can provide neither the material nor the social and emotional resources their children need to develop optimally, and their children, in turn, will lack those skills when they become parents. With more young mothers keeping their children and facing a job market with fewer opportunities for the poorly educated, this situation will become increasingly serious in years to come. Again, this situation means that the physical and mental health of future generations of children in single-parent families may be compromised.

Another potentially serious consequence of early pregnancy and low education is the fact that women who have their first child at an early age have more children than women who have their first child later (Bumpass, Rindfuss, and Janosik 1978). Thus, the fewer economic and emotional resources that these single mothers have must often be spread among a larger number of children. Several researchers have shown that the number of siblings a child has influences the total amount of education he or she attains and, ultimately, affects his or her earnings potential (Featherman and Hauser 1976*a*, 1976*b*). Large families are simply able to do less for each child, and when there is little to begin with, children are inevitably handicapped. Larger families are also less able to ensure the physical and mental well-being of children. Children with many siblings tend to go to the doctor less often than children with fewer siblings (Colle and Grossman 1978; Horwitz, Morgenstern, and Berkman 1985; Tessler 1980; Wolfe 1980).

Conclusion: The Inheritance of Poor Health

There is ample evidence that single motherhood places both mothers and their children at elevated risk of poor physical and mental health, largely through its association with other health risk factors, such as early pregnancy poverty, and low education. We investigate below whether this elevated risk results in actual diminished health levels. The evidence we have presented here clearly demonstrates the low income of single-parent families. Many of these families would obviously have to do without adequate nutrition and medical care were they not provided by the state. What is particularly disturbing is the suggestion that poverty and its accompanying health risks are passed on from one generation to the next. Such a situation could lead to an accumulation of health disadvantages over generations, resulting in marked differentials in levels of vitality and productivity between the poor and those better off. Perhaps inherited poor health is another tragic legacy of the growth in the underclass.

The data also illustrate dramatic differences in income levels among white, black, and Hispanic fatherless families. As we noted, although all single-parent families are at elevated risk of poverty, black and Hispanic households are at particularly high risk. The legacy of diminished health, therefore, may be even more serious for those who have the fewest resources with which to cope. In subsequent chapters we will investigate how these differences in income and welfare dependency among black, non-Hispanic white, and Hispanic fatherless families affect the health and medical care use of women and children.

Of course, we should conclude this chapter by noting that not all women who become pregnant as teenagers are doomed to a life of poverty, nor do they inevitably condemn their children to a life of poverty and poor health. Some teenage parents are able to finish their education and succeed admirably as adults. A teenage mother's later success or failure depends on her personality and drive as well as on the sources of economic and social support at her disposal (Furstenberg, Brooks-Gunn, and Morgan 1987). A middle-class white teenage mother who is taken in by her family and who is therefore able to complete her adolescence as if the pregnancy has not occurred obviously has a better chance of later success than a poor central-city adolescent whose family cannot or will not help her. Of course, as we will show, race and Hispanic ethnicity influence the availability of such social support.

Teenage pregnancy, then, is only a risk factor for poverty, albeit a serious one; in and of itself, it need not spell disaster. B___ n combination with other disadvantages, such as a disrupt___ ___ poverty, or rejection by one's parents, ado___ ___nd of any possibility for social mobility an___ ___ical and mental health. Even with the gr___ ___omes for single young mothers, it is clear ___ ___oor backgrounds face particularly serious ___ ___tion and providing for their children. Bec___ ___many fatherless families, they must rely ___ ___s that contribute to the maintenance of l___ ___ealth and welfare of single mothers and th___ ___quacy of programs such as AFDC, food s___ ___basic nutrition and health care. Because ___ ___ in the maintenance of the physical and mental he___ ___mbers of fatherless families, in the next chapter we examine welfare and health policy for the poor in the United States and summarize the basic income and health programs that ensure their welfare.

3

Family and Health Policy in the United States and Europe

Although we usually do not think of health as a commodity, those goods and services, such as adequate nutrition, safe housing, and timely medical care, that ensure one's physical and mental well-being must be purchased, either by the individual or by someone else. The economic, political, and social factors that increase or decrease a family's access to these goods and services, therefore, directly influence the health of its members. Because access to basic nutrition, housing, and health care is so central to maintaining health and avoiding illness and because single mothers and their children are disproportionately dependent on the state for these goods and services, we must examine the package of state and federal social welfare programs that guarantee the basics of good health to fatherless families. To provide a comparative perspective on the situation of fatherless families in the United States and to illustrate some possible alternatives for their care, we compare family policy in this country to that of other developed nations. We review the major health-related governmental programs that are central components of the American welfare state and summarize the changes that health-related state and federal programs have undergone in recent years. And we review what is known about the effectiveness of these programs in maintaining the health of women and children in fatherless families.

The Welfare State in Europe and America

The United States differs substantially from other developed nations in the role that the state plays in the preservation of the health and welfare of its citizens. Most developed nations provide their citizens with universal health care coverage, and most provide some form of financial support to all families with young children, regardless of income. In fact, in some advanced social welfare states like Sweden, family support programs are so generous that they make it possible for a woman to raise her children alone without suffering the serious economic hardship that often accompanies single motherhood in the United States. These differences in the extent of health-related welfare coverage have measurable impacts on health. The United States exceeds most developed nations in levels of infant mortality (United Nations Children's Fund 1989), and many children in single-parent households lack adequate immunization against the acute diseases of childhood and suffer significant physical and mental illness (Angel and Worobey 1988a; Hetherington 1989; Kellam, Ensminger, and Turner 1977; Zill and Schoenborn 1990). Why, one wonders, is the United States so different in its approach to ensuring the health and welfare of both adults and children? Many explanations have been offered, and we will discuss some of these later, but first let us provide some specifics concerning differences between the United States and other developed nations in state-sponsored programs designed to ensure the health and welfare of adults and children.

Although programs such as workers compensation, accident insurance, and retirement income were introduced in Germany and other European countries as early as the 1880s, it was only after World War II that the social welfare state became a universal feature of modern capitalist society in Europe and America.[1] The expansion of state control and coordination that the war required, in conjunction with the greatly increased scale of postwar economies and the emergence of poverty as a major social problem, made large-scale planning an accepted part of the state's role. Today, we take for granted programs such as Old Age Security and Disability Insurance, Medicare, Medicaid, Unemployment Insurance, and Aid to Families with Dependent Children that were nonexistent only a few decades ago. These programs have become such an integral part of modern society that even the most conservative observer would hesitate to advocate their total elimination.

Despite the universal nature of the post-World War II growth in the state's role in ensuring the health and welfare of citizens, the extent and nature of coverage differs greatly. In the United States the welfare state is

Table 3.1. Universal Entitlement Family Support Programs for Selected Industrialized Countries

	Income Maintenance				Child Support[a]	Early Childhood Care or Education	Food Stamps	Health Services	Parental Leave
	Family Allowance	Child Allowance	Refundable Tax Credits	Housing Allowance					
Great Britain	+	+	+	+	•	•	•	+	+
Norway	+	+	+	+	+	+	•	+	+
France	+	+	•	+	+	+	•	+	+
West Germany	+	+	+	+	+	+	•	+	+
Sweden	+	+	•	+	+	+	•	+	+
Australia	+	+[b]	•	•	•	•	•	+	•
Canada	+	+[c]	+	•	•	•[d]	•	+	+
United States	•	•	+	•	•[e]	•[f]	•[g]	•[g]	•

Source: Kamerman (1984); Kamerman and Kahn (1978, 1988).

Note: + Indicates the presence of some type of support for single-parent families.

• Indicates that benefit is not an entitlement to families with dependent children.

[a] Guaranteed government collection of child support payment from absent parent.
[b] Includes only a Class A Widow's Pension.
[c] Dependent child tax credit available only in the province of Ontario, Canada.
[d] Currently considering expansion of compulsory early childhood education and care for young children.
[e] Wisconsin has experimental program to enforce child support provisions for single-parent families.
[f] Child care tax credit benefit is available.
[g] A means-tested program exists.

Whether or not a single mother feels excessively burdened depends on how she views her various roles and also on the other economic and social resources that she has at her disposal. A well-educated professional single mother with an adequate income is obviously better able to deal with the economic strains of single parenthood than a poorly educated single mother with a marginal job. The very poorest single minority mothers, who are frequently trapped in the inner city where they are exposed not only to poverty and heavy role demands but also to the health risks associated with a seriously disorganized social environment, may experience serious role overload and its consequent ill effects.

In a society in which race and ethnicity continue to limit opportunities for social mobility, the problems of single motherhood are inevitably bound up with those of race and Hispanic ethnicity. As we will demonstrate, the disruptive effects of poverty and unemployment fall most heavily on blacks and Hispanics, for whom post-World War II changes in the urban job market have had the most serious effects on family life (Tienda 1989; Kasarda 1989; Wilson 1987; Garfinkel and McLanahan 1986). Although the number of fatherless families among Hispanics is still lower than among blacks, the structural factors that have placed extreme strains on the black family are affecting Hispanics as well. As they move to the central city, where job opportunities for both males and females are limited, the number of female-headed Hispanic families will continue to grow (Moore 1989, Tienda 1989, Tienda and Angel 1982).

This growth in the number of poor minority single-parent families has serious implications for the racial and ethnic distribution of wealth in the future, as well as for the differential prevalence of illness. As the population ages, fertility differentials between blacks, Hispanics, and non-Hispanic whites may result in the emergence of an age-graded racial and ethnic system of social stratification in which a predominantly white and politically powerful gerontocracy consumes a disproportionate share of our aggregate resources, while a poor and predominantly black and Hispanic lower class, consisting largely of women and children, receives less. In such a political and social environment, health programs targeted to the elderly may benefit at the expense of those targeted to children and the poor.

A New Family Form: Fatherlessness Institutionalized

As we have already noted, it is becoming increasingly clear that the growth in the number of fatherless families is not a passing phenomenon. Rather, what we are witnessing is the rise of a new family form, one in which men play a peripheral role. The reasons for the emergence of this rather underdeveloped by world standards. For example, sixty-seven countries, including all industrialized nations except the United States, provide some form of family allowance or child benefit to families with children (Kamerman 1984, Kamerman and Kahn 1978). Typically, these benefits are paid for each child in a family regardless of the family's income, and payments usually continue until the child completes his or her mandatory education.[2] Such benefits are clearly an important source of income for single-parent families.

Table 3.1 summarizes the major family support programs for selected industrialized nations. As we can see, the most progressive welfare states, like Sweden, provide the entire range of family support and health care. In Sweden a single working mother with two young children receives a child support benefit for each child (collected, if possible, from the noncustodial father), a housing allowance, and generously subsidized child care (Kahn and Kammerman 1983). In Norway, which also has a generous family support system, a single mother receives a child allowance, tax allowances and child care tax credits, a child care cash benefit, an education benefit, a housing allowance, and much more (Kammerman and Kahn 1988). The average child allowance for a single mother with two children in Norway in 1985 was approximately $217 (U.S. equivalent) a month, which in combination with other social insurance benefits provides an adequate standard of living. Finland also provides generous support to families, including single-parent families. In 1988, the package of Finnish family supports included, among other things, a universal child allowance, an income-tested housing allowance, maternity leave, and a home care or child-rearing allowance. As a consequence, a single mother with two children receives about 60 percent of the income of a comparable two-parent family (ibid.).

In France, which has a pronatalist family policy, families with young children are eligible for a package of family support programs that makes it possible for primary care givers to remain at home (ibid., 87). These include a family allowance (provided to families with at least two children), a family allowance supplement, a young child allowance, a prenatal allowance, fully paid maternity leave covering sixteen weeks from the time of birth, parental leave, a housing allowance, and a free preschool education (Questiaux and Fournier 1978). Such welfare benefits are not contingent on a family's income, and everyone with children is entitled to receive benefits.

For numerous reasons that we shall discuss below, the welfare state in the United States is less developed than it is in Europe (Wilensky 1975). A greater emphasis on individual responsibility for one's own welfare, a deep distrust of centralized government, and the more peripheral political role of labor have resulted in a much more fragmented and less inclusive system. The United States, for example, is one of only two developed economies without a national health insurance scheme; the other is South Africa. Nor do we have anything approaching the family income support programs of most Western European nations (Kamerman 1984, Kamerman and Kahn 1978). Nonetheless, even in the United States the welfare state plays a central role in maintaining the health and welfare of the poor. AFDC, Medicaid, and other means-tested programs have greatly improved the lot of single mothers and their children (Schwarz 1988). In the absence of the various programs that provide income, food, and medical care to those who could not otherwise afford them, both children and adults would suffer far greater deprivation than they do and the health levels of the poor would be far worse than they are.

Reductions in funding for these programs seriously endanger the health and welfare of the women and children who rely on them (Physician Task Force on Hunger in America 1985, Children's Defense Fund 1990). Figure 3.1 shows that although infant mortality rates dropped throughout the 1970s and early 1980s, the decline stopped in the mid-1980s (Grad 1988). Cuts in health care and nutrition programs for pregnant mothers have particularly serious implications for black infants, whose mortality rate was twice that of white infants in 1986. The infant mortality rate for blacks in 1986 was as high as that for whites in 1970. Blacks, apparently, are exposed to a health care environment that is at least sixteen years behind the times.

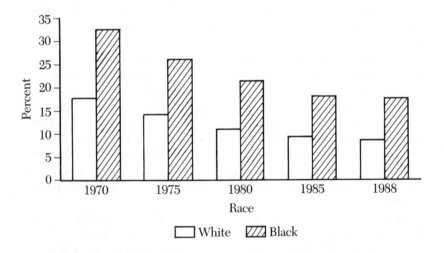

Figure 3.1. Infant Mortality Rates by Race: 1970–1988. *Source:* CDF (1991): 144.

Birth is dangerous for the mother as well as for the infant. In 1986, nearly four times as many black women died in childbirth as white women (U.S. Bureau of the Census 1989*b*). The infant mortality rate is a sensitive indicator of a population's overall health level, and the extremely elevated rate for blacks, which in some cities such as Washington, D.C., is still over twenty deaths per one thousand births, indicates serious problems in the area of maternal and infant health care. Clearly, then, the children of the poor are extremely vulnerable to reductions in basic support programs, and the racial disparities in health that persist in the United States represent one of the most serious failures of our social welfare and health care systems.

Although reductions in funding for welfare programs began during the Carter administration, President Reagan made the reduction of social spending the cornerstone of his domestic policy (Palmer and Sawhill 1984, Block et al. 1987). During the early Reagan years, major steps were taken to dismantle programs for children and the poor. The objectives of the Reagan welfare reforms were threefold: (1) to limit the number of eligible welfare recipients; (2) to reduce total expenditures for welfare programs; and (3) to shift control of spending for specific welfare objectives from the federal government to the states by providing funding in the form of block grants (Colby 1989, Palmer and Sawhill 1984). Ultimately, the Reagan administration intended to reduce the role of the federal government in welfare and to return control of specific programs to the states. By the later years of the Reagan administration, however, the political climate had changed, and more moderate welfare policies were enacted in the Family Support Act of 1988 (Cottingham and Ellwood 1989). These set the stage for welfare reform into at least the beginning of the 1990s.

Health-Related Governmental Programs in America

What follows is a brief description of the major federal and state programs that affect the health of both women and children in female-headed households. Although programs such as AFDC, food stamps, and housing assistance are not health programs in the strictest sense, they provide the income, nutrition, and housing support that ensures the health of children. We begin with a discussion of those programs that affect children. As we are also interested in the health of adult women, we also review those programs, such as Social Security and Medicare, that provide income and health care to older single women. For each program or group of programs, we summarize its basic purpose, outline the eligibility criteria, and explain how it has been affected by legislative and funding changes since the early 1980s.[3] We also review evidence of the effectiveness of maternal and child health programs.

Aid to Families with Dependent Children

The most important—and clearly the most controversial—program for the support of children in poor single-parent families is AFDC. This program began formally in 1935 with the passage of the Social Security Act, of which it was a minor part. Originally, the program was labeled Aid to Dependent Children (ADC) and was intended to provide minimal support for the relatively small number of fatherless children that existed at the time. However, the AFDC rolls grew steadily during the 1950s and 1960s, and during the decades of the 1970s and 1980s, the number of families on AFDC increased dramatically as the number of poor single-parent households increased.

AFDC is the major source of income for poor female-headed families. It is a means-tested cash assistance program that provides income to eligible families with dependent children. In most states families with one parent and those with a disabled parent are eligible, but in some states two-parent families with an unemployed father also qualify. The program is funded jointly by the federal and state governments. States administer the program under federal guidelines, although each state is free to establish its own income eligibility requirements and benefit levels.

States vary widely in the number of persons receiving assistance and the amount of benefits received. The disparity in AFDC payments is one of the program's most troublesome features. For example, the average monthly payment in Alabama was $118 in 1989. In that same year the average payment was $539 in New York and $517 in Wisconsin (Children's Defense Fund 1990a). Of course, the cost of living differs among states, but even when differences in the cost of living are taken into account, huge disparities persist. This is illustrated when payment amounts are compared to the 1988 federal poverty threshold for a family of three. In Alabama the average AFDC payment amounted to approximately 15 percent of the poverty level, while in New York it represented nearly 69 percent and in California, 88 percent. After adjusting for inflation, the average AFDC grant for a family of four has fallen by 38 percent since 1970 (ibid.). This drop is the result of the fact that AFDC payments, unlike Social Security payments, are not indexed to the inflation rate. In recent years, only in California and Maine have AFDC payments kept pace with inflation. Many critics who blame AFDC for the rise in the number of female-headed families ignore the fact that the real value of benefits has dropped significantly at the same time that the number of fatherless families has increased.

In 1981 Congress enacted major reforms in AFDC that were proposed by the Reagan administration. These changes resulted in greater restrictions on eligibility for AFDC and reductions in the amount of benefits (Palmer and Sawhill 1984). Some of the specific changes required states to set the maximum gross income a family can receive from all sources including AFDC at 150 percent of the poverty level for each state. In addition, they required that a stepparent's income be counted toward eligibility, and among other restrictions, a limit was placed on child care expense deductions. Although some of these reductions were reversed in 1984, most of the work disincentives and inequities built into AFDC remain.

In addition to these changes in the amount of income a woman can earn and still qualify for AFDC, other changes in the determination of eligibility were introduced. States now have the option of counting other transfers, such as food stamps and housing subsidies, as income. Further, states were given the option of requiring that AFDC recipients participate in "workfare" programs as a condition for receiving benefits. As early as 1967 a work incentive requirement was made part of AFDC, and President Jimmy Carter proposed a program to provide full-time public service employment to AFDC recipients (Gueron 1987). President Reagan's proposal, in contrast, did not offer to provide jobs but merely required that recipients work in return for receiving benefits. None of these workfare programs have been implemented except in demonstration projects.

These new eligibility restrictions resulted in a significant reduction in the number of women and children eligible for AFDC and in a reduction in the average size of benefits received. Throughout the 1960s and 1970s welfare reform proposals focused on increasing the work incentives in AFDC, primarily by allowing recipients to keep some fraction of their payments even when they had earnings. These proposals were aimed at ensuring that the marginal tax rate associated with earnings made work worthwhile. So at the same time that the Reagan reforms reduced AFDC rolls, they increased the work disincentives in the program. Had the pre-Reagan eligibility criteria not been altered, in 1985 between 400,000 and 500,000 additional families would have been eligible to receive AFDC than was the case under the new restrictions. In addition, for those who remained eligible to receive benefits, monthly payments were cut on average by $150 to $200 dollars a month (Palmer and Sawhill 1984).

Medicaid

Medicaid is the major federally sponsored program for providing medical care to the poor. Eligibility for Medicaid is closely tied to AFDC, since recipients of AFDC are automatically entitled to Medicaid coverage. In some states, families with incomes about the level at which they would qualify for AFDC are eligible to receive benefits if they meet other criteria, such as having an unemployed head. Since April 1990, states are required to provide coverage under Medicaid to all pregnant women and children under six in families with family incomes below 133 percent of poverty level. By 1987, over 23 million Americans received Medicaid benefits, yet this program covers less than half of all households with incomes below poverty level (U.S. Bureau of the Census 1989b). Medicaid is jointly financed by the state and federal governments, and each pays about half the cost. The state administers the program under federal guidelines, although, as with other programs, each state sets its own rules for eligibility, benefit coverage, and payment levels.

Early Reagan welfare reforms slowed the rise in the cost of Medicaid indirectly by limiting the number of eligible AFDC recipients. As a result of the direct link between AFDC and Medicaid, cutbacks in the number of AFDC-eligible participants also reduced the number of individuals eligible for Medicaid (Kimmich 1985). In addition, since most poor families move in and out of poverty, their eligibility for AFDC changes over short periods and, consequently, so does their eligibility for Medicaid.[4] Families with incomes near poverty level are particularly disadvantaged, and as a consequence, in 1986 nearly 20 percent of children under 13 had no health insurance (Smythe 1988).

Despite some cutbacks early in the decade, changes in the law during the latter half of the 1980s extended coverage to hundreds of thousands of low-income pregnant women whose incomes were too high to qualify for AFDC. Medicaid now covers all children under six years of age in families whose incomes fall below 133 percent of poverty level (Children's Defense Fund 1991). Currently, Medicaid coverage is mandated for all pregnant women and infants in families with incomes below the poverty level, with states having the option of extending eligibility to families with incomes as high as 185 percent of poverty level (Children's Defense Fund 1987).

One of the major obstacles to the receipt of medical care that poor families face is the fact that because of rather low payment levels and cumbersome reimbursement procedures, many physicians will not take Medicaid patients. A number of states have increased reimbursement for obstetrical services to encourage physician acceptance of Medicaid patients (Fossett et al. 1990). Further changes will eventually extend coverage to all needy children. Beginning in 1991, states are required to cover all medically needy children older than six years of age in stages until by the year 2002 all children under eighteen in poor families will be covered (Children's Defense Fund 1991, Rosenbaum and Johnson 1986).

Another change that has improved the availability of health care for women and infants was the increase in the number of managed care arrangements, such as health maintenance organizations (HMOs), that offer maternity-related services to Medicaid-eligible families under federal sponsorship. The number of HMO Medicaid beneficiaries enrolled increased from 282,000 in 1981 to two million by 1986 (Rosenbaum et al. 1988). Despite this, many states have not extended coverage to all potentially eligible families, and many of those that have impose other restrictive eligibility criteria. These usually require that the family have only one parent or that the head of household be unemployed. One of the major injustices in our health insurance system arises from the fact that many poor families in which both father and mother work are uninsured because they do not meet these restrictive eligibility requirements.

Early Periodic Screening, Diagnosis, and Treatment

One of the most important health-related components of AFDC is a special preventive health care benefit for poor children. The Early Periodic Screening, Diagnosis, and Treatment (EPSDT) program, a 1967 amendment to Title XIX of the Social Security Act, offers medical screening as well as diagnosis and treatment to Medicaid-eligible children and adolescents. This program has been shown to be extremely cost-effective, largely because it is medically effective. One study, for example, found that Michigan's EPSDT program substantially reduced the medical care costs associated with Medicaid. The mean annual Medicaid costs for persons eligible for the 1979 Michigan EPSDT program were significantly lower ($312.09) than for non-EPSDT participants ($358.62). Although lifetime savings were not estimated, the analyses revealed that even after controlling for the costs of the program itself, the net reduction in medical costs due to EPSDT was almost $4 million, representing a 7 percent decrease in medical costs for the year (Keller 1983). The study also showed that the EPSDT program had a positive impact on the health of children by reducing the number of referrals for serious health problems.

South Carolina provides an example of the successful implementation of the EPSDT program. Through the use of an extensive outreach effort, that state has increased screening rates and access to medical care for needy mothers and children. In addition, home visits for all Medicaid-eligible newborns in South Carolina, including those families that initially declined EPSDT services, have been expanded and their quality improved (Liu 1990). Given the clear lifelong payoff to such interventions early on, this program might well serve as a model for other states.

Women, Infants, and Children

Adequate nutrition is clearly a crucial requirement for good health, especially in childhood when development is proceeding so rapidly. The WIC

program provides vouchers for the purchase of prescribed foods for pregnant and nursing women and for children under five years of age (Physician Task Force on Hunger 1985). The program also provides health care
screening to high-risk pregnant women, infants, and children under age
five whose family incomes fall below 185 percent of poverty level. The
U.S. Department of Agriculture (USDA) funds the program, and states
distribute the vouchers through local health centers and clinics.

The WIC program is targeted specifically to poor neighborhoods. Communities are designated as needy and therefore entitled to participation
on the basis of several economic and health indicators such as the unemployment rate and the infant mortality rate. In 1987, roughly four million
mothers and infants were served by the WIC program (U.S. Bureau of the
Census 1989*b*). Because of its demonstrated effectiveness and the clear
necessity for the program, its budget was spared the cuts that other programs experienced during the early 1980s. In fact, spending for WIC has
increased almost 90 percent since 1981 (ibid.). As is the case for EPSDT,
not only is the program medically effective but its cost-effectiveness has
been clearly demonstrated. For every dollar spent on WIC, $3 are saved
in medical care costs for children in the first year of life (Children's Defense Fund 1990*a*). Unfortunately, although there is ample evidence that
money spent on prenatal care and on nutrition early in life has clear long-
term health and economic benefits, only eight states and the District of
Columbia supplement federal funding for WIC (ibid.).

The Maternal and Child Health Block Grant

The Maternal and Child Health Block Grant was created as part of the
Omnibus Budget Reduction Act of 1981 (Office of Technology Assessment
1987). This bill consolidated several categorical health services programs
for women and children. As with other Reagan era reforms, the purpose
was to give states greater control over setting priorities and funding levels. States use block grant funds to make payments to clinics, hospitals,
and other health care facilities so that they can provide health care to poor
women and children. Since it is administered with no clear eligibility criteria, coverage varies from state to state. States are not required to furnish
data on the sorts of services they provide or on the characteristics of the
populations they serve, so we know little about the extent of coverage or
the effectiveness of the program (Blank and Brock 1987).

Future Possibilities

Although they are not universal programs and do not cover everyone in the
country, we would like to review two demonstration projects aimed at improving birth outcomes for the children of single women. We suspect that
future innovations in providing care to single mothers and their children

will develop out of such experimental programs. The first demonstration project, Healthy Start, is a state-funded program in Massachusetts begun in 1985. The objective of this program is to facilitate access to postpartum care for mothers whose incomes are between 100 and 185 percent of poverty level. The program seeks to reduce complications following delivery and to provide infants with adequate pediatric care. Early evidence suggests that it has been a huge success. Women who have participated in the program were far more likely than those who have not to receive postpartum care (Kogan, Leary, and Schaetzel 1990).

As we have shown, teenage pregnancy is one of the major social and health problems we must deal with as a nation. Early pregnancy is detrimental not only to the health of the child but also to the social well-being of the mother. For this reason, programs aimed at the reduction of teenage pregnancy promise high potential health payoffs. The second demonstration project represents an apparently successful attempt to deal with the potential negative effects of teenage pregnancy. Project Redirection, which has been implemented in Boston, Massachusetts, New York City, Phoenix, Arizona, and Riverside, California, is designed to help enhance the self-sufficiency and parental competence of pregnant teens and teen mothers. The program achieves these goals by means of a range of services, including extensive employment training and counseling in education, parenting, health, and life management.

The intervention is based on a three-prong approach: each participant is provided (1) a community "mentor" to serve as her role model, (2) a personalized work schedule designed by staff members, and (3) opportunities to participate in peer counseling groups to discuss mutual problems. An evaluation of the success of the program after five years provides strong evidence for its effectiveness. A random sample of program participants had better work histories and higher earnings and were less reliant on welfare than a matched sample of nonparticipants (Polit 1989).

Besides having beneficial effects on the mother, the program also benefited children. The children of participants scored better on a battery of cognitive, social, and emotional developmental assessment tests than the children of nonparticipants. Given the serious long-term consequences of teenage motherhood for both the mother and the child, such innovative programs appear to be well justified. After all, an ounce of prevention is worth a pound of cure. And as we have noted before, there is incontrovertible evidence that money spent on prenatal and infant care has more of a payoff than money spent at any later time in the life course.

Food Stamps

The family nutrition program, more commonly known today as the food stamp program, issues food vouchers to eligible low-income families and individuals. These vouchers can be used to purchase specific food items at retail stores. Like AFDC, the food stamp program is federally financed and administered by the states. The USDA shares half of the costs for administration of the program with individual state departments of welfare or social services. Roughly 83 percent of AFDC households received food stamps in 1987 (Children's Defense fund 1990*a*). As with AFDC, however, there is great variation in coverage by state; in our nation's capital, for example, less than half of AFDC households receive food stamps.

The price that individuals are charged for the stamps depends on their family size and the family's income after taxes. Beginning in 1977, free food stamps were made available to low-income households, and by 1987, the program served seven million households and roughly nineteen million people. Federal expenditures for the program totaled nearly $11 billion in 1987. As the result of Reagan reforms, new income ceilings were introduced to reduce the number of those eligible for food stamps. Individuals with pretax incomes above 130 percent of poverty level or after-tax incomes above 100 percent no longer qualify.

As with AFDC, there are large disparities among states in the amount spent on food stamps. In 1989, the combined value of AFDC and food stamps provided an Alabama family of three with the equivalent of 45 percent of the 1988 federal poverty threshold. In contrast, in California the combination of AFDC and food stamps provided the same family of three with the cash equivalent of 102 percent of the poverty threshold.

National School Lunch Program

The federal government also sponsors nutritional programs for poor children. The national school lunch program (NSLP) was initiated in 1946 in response to evidence of widespread malnutrition among draftees during World War II (Physician Task Force on Hunger in America 1985). Congress mandated free or reduced-price lunches for needy children by providing cash reimbursements and government surplus food items to local schools. In 1966, the program was expanded to include the school breakfast program (BP), which serves breakfast to children from low-income families. Today, these programs are important guarantees of nutritional adequacy for children in fatherless families.

Both the breakfast and lunch programs are federally funded and state administered. Children in families whose incomes fall below 185 percent of poverty level are eligible to receive school lunch and breakfast free or at a reduced cost. Over 80 percent of schools offer either breakfast or lunch, or both. In 1987, 24 million children participated in the lunch program, and 3.6 million children participated in the breakfast program.

Housing Assistance

The U.S. Department of Housing and Urban Development (HUD) and Farmers Home Administration (FHA) share the financial responsibility for funding the housing assistance program. The goal of these agencies is to improve the quality of housing for low-income families. Housing assistance includes both subsidies for rent in the private market and the construction of subsidized housing units by local municipalities. In 1987, an estimated 4.2 million households received some form of housing assistance, for example, low-rent public housing and rural housing loans. Approximately 40 percent of those who receive rental assistance are nonelderly families, for example, female-headed households (Colby 1989).

Housing assistance for the poor has declined sharply in recent years. The number of newly assisted households declined from approximately 300,000 in the period between 1976 and 1980 to about 100,000 in the period between 1981 and 1984 (Palmer and Sawhill 1984). Consequently, by the end of 1985, there were roughly one million fewer households receiving assistance than would have been the case had the pre-Reagan policies remained in place. In addition to reducing the number of households eligible for assistance, the amount that tenants are required to pay was increased from 25 to 30 percent of their total income. The lack of adequate housing is one of the major problems faced by the poor in general and by female-headed households in particular.

Summary of Program Benefits for Children

These programs, then, form the safety net that ensures the health and material welfare of children. The health-related services that these programs provide are particularly important in guaranteeing the health of poor infants and children, especially those born to teenage mothers. The evidence is clear that medical care early in pregnancy increases the probability of a positive birth outcome and optimal development later in life. In addition, proper nutrition, immunizations, and adequate medical care reduce the risk of serious illness for young children. Unfortunately, even with this increased availability of financing for preventive and treatment-focused health care, the poor face other barriers to adequate health care. Recent analyses of data from the American Medical Association reveal that the number of obstetricians and gynecologists is far lower in inner-city neighborhoods than in more affluent neighborhoods, and physicians in more affluent neighborhoods treat relatively few Medicaid patients. For this reason, expanded Medicaid eligibility will not necessarily improve the availability of medical care for low-income pregnant women. Because we are also interested in the health and welfare of older women, before proceeding, we must review three of the major health-related federal support programs for elderly and disabled adults. These programs have been the major reason for the decrease in poverty among the elderly.

Social Security

Old Age, Survivors, and Disability Insurance (OASDI), or Social Security, as it popularly known, is a national insurance plan that provides retirement income to older citizens. The program is financed by a payroll tax on employees and employers during a person's working lifetime. The size of the payment one receives in retirement is based on the amount of ones contribution during his or her working years. Unlike means-tested programs, OASDI payments are adjusted annually for inflation.

Many single older women do not qualify for OASDI because they have not been employed for the requisite period. A minimum of forty quarters or ten years of work experience is required to receive benefits. However, women whose husbands die qualify for benefits in the form of survivorship insurance, and women who suffer major losses in functional capacity qualify for disability insurance. Thirty-eight million Americans received Social Security benefits in 1986. Average payments were $489 for retirement, $488 for disability, and $444 for widows.

In 1981, the Reagan administration proposed major reforms in Social Security to address the urgent problem of a rapidly depleting trust fund. The proposal was unanimously turned down by Congress, but a modified version was accepted in March 1983. This plan resulted in a sizable increase in trust fund revenues through higher payroll tax rates and taxation of half of Social Security benefits for beneficiaries with total incomes above certain levels (Palmer and Sawhill 1984). In addition, the age at which a person can retire and still receive full benefits will increase from sixty-five to sixty-seven beginning in the next century. Although these changes still result in some loss of income to middle-class recipients in years to come, low-income beneficiaries who also receive Supplemented Security Income (SSI) will be better off because of the increases in SSI mentioned below.

Supplemental Security Income

SSI is a federally funded and administered means-tested program that provides cash assistance to poor aged, blind, or disabled persons. This program is important in the context of our discussion of the female-headed household since it provides assistance to low-income elderly women who live with their daughters and grandchildren. The increase in the number of multigenerational female-only households makes this a potentially important source of income for such households.

To be eligible for this program, an individual must be at least sixty-five years of age, blind, or disabled and have little other income or personal assets. For older women who qualify for Social Security but who receive low monthly payments, this program serves as a supplement to OASDI and other in-kind benefits. For those women who do not qualify for Social Security, SSI is a purely means-tested benefit similar to AFDC. In 1987, there were 4.4 million SSI recipients (U.S. Bureau of the Census 1989*b*). SSI was one of the few welfare programs that not only survived but benefited from the Reagan reforms. Rather than reducing benefits, Congress in 1983 increased monthly benefits to offset reductions in cost-of-living increments. In addition, benefits are adjusted for inflation annually.

Although AFDC and SSI are the major sources of income for the majority of impoverished single mothers and older women, both groups depend heavily on other types of assistance. These provide basic necessities, such as food, medical care, and shelter. Since they have an important impact on the health and welfare of female-headed households, we will briefly describe some of the major noncash programs.

Medicare

Medicare, a federally funded and administered health insurance plan for the elderly, is the largest health insurance plan in the United States. Over 32 million elderly Americans were enrolled in this program in 1987. Nearly all elderly women sixty-five and older are covered, regardless of work history. Medicare complements Social Security benefits by partly reimbursing payments for hospital and physician services. This program helps the elderly with low incomes in two very important ways: first, it protects the aged from any large short-term medical care expenses, and second, it allows those who might not seek medical care because of its cost to receive it (Davis 1985).

Medicare includes both hospital (HI-Part A) and supplemental medical (SMI-Part B) insurance. The hospital insurance portion of Medicare (Part A) is funded through a joint employer-employee payroll tax and covers inpatient service costs and certain follow-up care. The medical insurance program (Part B) is financed through a combination of general federal revenues and participants premiums that are used to reimburse enrolled members for utilization of doctor's services. The program costs the federal government over $80 billion, which comprises two-thirds of total federal expenditures for health care.

The rising cost of medical care for the elderly has created serious problems for this program. The rapid growth of Medicare costs forced Congress to introduce major reforms in the way reimbursements are paid. The major change was in the payment system of medical services to hospitals in which rates for hospital services were determined in advance. Under the previous system, hospitals had been reimbursed for what they actually spent. As yet, the impact of this new payment system on the costs of medical care services is unknown. Proposals for freezing the price of physician care have had little success, but debates still continue about the measures that should be taken to restrain payments for such services. As yet, the elderly have no protection against catastrophic illness or coverage for long-term care.

These programs form the core of the health-related social welfare system of the United States. As we noted at the outset, the unique aspect of this set of programs that distinguishes them from those of the other developed nations is that except for Social Security and Medicare, they are targeted to the poor. Because it is impossible to understand our system of means-tested social welfare without understanding how culture and ideology have influenced its development and how they limit alternatives for reform, we end this chapter with a discussion of the basic philosophy that informs welfare and health care policy in the United States. Although we discuss these issues in greater detail in chapter 8, we must briefly discuss how the changing economic context of the debate over health care for fatherless families has affected public programs. We must also point out the important historical role that race has placed in the development of U.S. welfare policy.

Citizenship Right versus Charity

To understand why the United States has taken such a radically different course from Europe in dealing with the income and health needs of families and children, it is useful to begin with values and ideology. Welfare policy in the United States has always maintained a sharp distinction between entitlement programs for the middle class, which are treated as earned citizenship rights, and means-tested welfare programs like AFDC, which are clearly labeled and stigmatized unearned transfers of money from the middle class to the poor. Aversion to the dole has historically been so strong in the United States that the passage of the Social Security Act of 1935 was possible only because the Roosevelt administration was careful to make sure that Social Security was seen as a self-supporting annuity or insurance scheme from which individuals were to draw on the basis of what they had contributed (Derthick 1979, Orloff 1988).

The political constituencies that benefit from and support entitlement and means-tested programs differ greatly in economic and political power. Middle-class elderly white Americans have been much more cohesive and effective in furthering their interests than have minorities and the poor.

For example, OASDI guarantees the retirement income of the middle-class white elderly and has expanded much more rapidly than programs for the poor. Table 3.2 compares the increase in federal spending for OASDI and AFDC from 1950 to 1988. Although both programs have grown extensively, spending for Social Security has far outstripped spending for the poor. The political and fiscal crises of the welfare state, then, are likely to affect the poor to a greater extent than the middle class. Attempts by the Reagan administration to reduce the cost of Social Security in 1981 resulted in only small savings and quickly came up against massive and effective opposition by the elderly and their representatives. AFDC,

Table 3.2. Expenditures for Selected Transfer
Programs, 1965–1988 (in Billions of Dollars)

Year	OASDHI[a]	AFDC[b]
1965	18.1	1.7
1966	20.8	1.9
1967	25.5	2.3
1968	30.2	2.8
1969	32.9	3.5
1970	38.5	4.8
1971	44.5	6.2
1972	49.6	6.9
1973	60.4	7.2
1974	70.1	7.9
1975	81.4	9.2
1976	92.9	10.1
1977	104.9	10.6
1978	116.2	10.7
1979	131.8	11.9
1980	154.2	12.4
1981	182.0	13.0
1982	204.5	13.3
1983	221.7	14.2
1984	235.7	14.8
1985	253.4	15.4
1986	269.3	16.3
1987	282.9	16.7
1988[c]	300.5	17.1

Note: Data from U.S. Department of Commerce,
Bureau of Economic Analysis.
[a]Old Age Survivors, Disability, and Health Insurance Benefits.
[b]Aid to Families with Dependent Children.
[c]Based on average for first three quarters of 1988.

however, was cut drastically and the number of eligible individuals reduced significantly.

It is in this context of differential political power and the resistance of the middle class to greater tax burdens that the situation of female-headed families must be understood. As the number of poor female-headed families grows, resistance to programs for their support is likely to increase, creating a serious dilemma for public policy and potentially affecting the welfare of millions of children. In the United States the later development and less complete nature of the welfare state has resulted in a situation in which society's responsibility for the support of families with unemployed or unemployable parents continues to be a matter of debate. The relative success of an attempt to slow the growth of welfare programs attests to Americans' conflicting attitudes toward welfare for the poor. Although Americans have come to view Social Security for the elderly as a citizenship right, our attitudes concerning the support of the poor remain much more ambiguous.

Because of higher death rates, wars, and occupational hazards, during most of our early history many women became widows fairly early in life. Although Americans have always felt that the able-bodied poor have no right to be supported at the public's expense, widows with children have been treated much more compassionately. Even the most conservative critics of welfare concede the particularly difficult situation of widowed mothers. Since their plight is not of their own making, they have always been considered among the deserving poor, especially if their husbands were killed in war (Katz 1986, Mencher 1967).[5] However, much more hostility has been directed toward women who become pregnant out of wedlock. Charity, many have felt, merely encourages these women to have children and to become dependent on the community.

Throughout the eighteenth and nineteenth centuries, poverty in the United States was largely the inevitable consequence of limited material wealth and, for the most part, was viewed as the result of the individual's own moral failure (Mencher 1967, Axinn and Levin 1975). Such simplistic views concerning the individual's responsibility for his or her own poverty were shattered by the massive economic dislocations of the Great Depression that put large numbers of middle-class individuals out of work. Such massive unemployment made it clear that local economies were part of a larger global economy and that large-scale structural factors were responsible for creating poverty. The scale of poverty that the depression created sensitized the nation to the more enduring problem and forced the state to directly address the problem of poverty in the postwar period (Weir, Orloff, and Skocpol 1988; Mencher 1967; Axinn and Levin 1975). If in preindustrial Europe and in America poverty was an unavoidable consequence of a relatively low overall standard of living, in the contemporary United States that is much more difficult to accept in light of our enormous material wealth.

Although the poor today would be considered well-off by nineteenth-century standards, the gap between the incomes of the most privileged individuals and the least privileged is extreme. This fact complicates attempts to eliminate poverty, since although the elimination of absolute poverty is an obtainable objective, the elimination of relative poverty requires equalizing the incomes of the rich and the poor rather than simply providing a minimum subsistence level income to those at the bottom.[6] There is very little support for a massive redistribution of income in the United States. Such an equalization of income would clearly conflict with many Americans' belief that an individual's income should reflect his or her own efforts. In this country welfare is limited to dealing with absolute poverty and ensuring that no one lacks the basic necessities for survival. Although there are some glaring shortcomings, for the most part programs like AFDC, Medicaid, and food stamps have succeeded in ensuring a minimal level of welfare for the poor (Schwarz 1988). Dealing with the consequences of relative poverty will prove much more difficult.

Economic and Political Factors Affecting the Future of Health-Related Welfare Programs in the United States

Despite the fact that it is by now well established in all developed nations, many of the basic goals and assumptions on which the welfare state is based have come under increasing attack in recent years, especially in the United States.[7] The recession of the 1970s and the relatively stagnant economy that followed it, combined with the tremendous increase in expenditures for federally supported employment, housing, and health programs, have created a backlash from middle-class voters that has resulted in a general erosion of many programs for the poor (Weir, Orloff, and Skocpol 1988; Palmer and Sawhill 1984; Kimmich 1985; Block et al. 1987). Although no major welfare programs have been eliminated, slowed funding for health and welfare programs at a time when the population in need is growing and when inflation has reduced the value of benefits has, in effect, shrunk the relative size of the piece of the economic pie that goes to the poor. The growing opposition to welfare and the backlash by the middle class to taxation is occurring at a time when poverty and the potential threat to health it represents is on the rise (U.S. Bureau of the Census 1989a). Despite twenty years of effort since President Johnson's War on

Poverty, homelessness and substantial hunger continue to plague the nation, and the risks to health they entail are clearly substantial (Physician Task Force on Hunger in America 1985).

Because blacks in general and black fatherless families in particular are at high risk of poverty, black single mothers and their children are at seriously elevated risk of poor physical and mental health. The impact of race, therefore, must be a central focus of our discussion of the health of mothers and their children. In the United States the race problem has had a major impact on the development of health-related welfare and social security policy generally (Wolters 1975; Derthick 1979; Skocpol 1988; Orfield 1988). Domestic employees and agricultural workers were excluded from coverage under the Social Security Act of 1935, thereby denying old age insurance to the vast majority of blacks, who were employed primarily in these occupations.

Although race has been only one of many factors that have influenced the development of American health and welfare policy, in our highly race-stratified society it has inevitably had an important impact. Federal policy has been very responsive to local constituencies, some of whom have been concerned with maintaining established racial disparities in income and political power. The historical insistence by southern states on local control of welfare was largely a response to the fear that a uniform national payment schedule would help free blacks from their traditional economic dependency on local whites (Skocpol 1988, Quadagno 1988). The health care of many black fatherless families has been undermined by the coupling of Medicaid and AFDC because states have historically been granted the right to determine eligibility criteria for the latter. Some states have kept qualification levels for AFDC so low that many needy families are excluded from the program and, consequently, denied coverage by Medicaid. This is one of the reasons for the recent reforms in Medicaid that have uncoupled participation in this program from qualification for AFDC.[8] Even with these recent reforms, however, many black and Hispanic fatherless families receive less medical care than they need.

In addition to race, other aspects of American culture have influenced the development of social policy toward the poor. Because of the widespread fear that a formal income support system for families would make reliance on public funds legitimate, the United States is almost alone among industrial democracies in never having had a universal family support system (Rodgers 1982; Kammerman 1984; Weir, Orloff, and Skocpol 1988). In the United States income support for families with children is part of a means-tested welfare program that stigmatizes the receipt of benefits. Unfortunately, because medical care for the poor has been tied to welfare, it too has been stigmatized, and many individuals are, no doubt, discouraged from seeking the help they need.

The assumption on which welfare policy in the United States has been based since the eighteenth century, that there is sufficient work for all who want it, is by this point in the twentieth century obviously untrue. The concentration of poor, often female-headed, minority families in the inner city and the flight of manufacturing and service jobs to the suburbs have created a situation in which a low-skilled work force has few legitimate sources of income other than government transfers. During the 1970s, this led the poor and their advocates to attempt to redefine welfare as a citizenship right (West 1981, Burke and Burke 1974). As part of this effort welfare rights organizations encouraged poor families to apply for welfare, and by now most eligible families receive at least some support (Ellwood 1988). Whether the medical care they receive as part of this package is adequate or not is, as yet, a question we cannot answer unambiguously.

Although the extent of coverage of the welfare state differs from one nation to another, the universal expectations that the state bears ultimate responsibility for the welfare of individuals has structured the postwar social and economic policies of all Western societies (Flora and Heidenheimer 1981; Kammerman and Kahn 1977; Furniss and Tilton 1977; Esping-Andersen 1985; Gronbjerg 1977; Derthick, 1979). In both Europe and America, macroeconomic policies aimed at full employment, as well as the social welfare guarantees that most people now view as a citizenship right, are part of the increasing intrusion of the state into the economy and into organized social life more broadly.

In both Europe and America, the evolution of the welfare state and government's response to poverty have been structured by conflicting political forces (Wilensky 1975, 1976, 1981; Weir, Orloff, and Skocpol 1988; Derthick 1979). Conflicts among capital, labor, and the middle class, which in the United States have been confounded by serious racial antagonisms, have resulted in different political coalitions in various countries at various times. In Europe the welfare state was brought about largely through the efforts of labor-based Socialist parties that, in coalition with centrist parties, generated broad-based demands for direct state intervention aimed at full employment and the maintenance of health (Esping-Andersen 1985, Furniss and Tilton 1977, Flora and Heidenheimer 1981).[9] The welfare state in Europe, then, is largely the product of reformist attempts to ensure citizenship rights and economic security while retaining the basic institutions of capitalist democracy. In the United States, which has never had a labor party, this reformist political agenda has been furthered by the Democratic party, which has espoused policies aimed at guaranteeing broad social welfare through tax and spending programs and limited state regulation of the economy.

The philosophy of the welfare state has historically met with much more resistance in the United States than in Europe, where labor parties have exercised much more political power. This has had important implications for the financing of health care for the poor. Even in the face of strong opposition, however, the growing problems of poverty and inadequate health care coverage in the United States make the continuation and probably the expansion of the welfare state inevitable. The rapid increase in the cost of programs such as Medicare and Medicaid has forced the federal government to attempt to contain the costs of providing medical care through bureaucratic means. These attempts inevitably lead to a greater intrusion by the federal government into the private sector. What remains to be seen is just how rapidly the welfare state, including its health care component, will grow in the United States in years to come and how the programs that ensure the health and welfare of fatherless families will evolve.

That evolution, of course, depends both on the rate of growth in economic productivity and on political forces. As health and welfare programs grow, they tend to alter the political environment in which they operate. The major opposition to the welfare state in both Europe and the United States arises primarily from the size and expense of the programs that guarantee everything from medical care to a retirement wage for the middle class and income support for the poor. Postwar experience with such programs, including Medicare and Medicaid, has shown that they have a tendency to expand indefinitely (Burtless 1986, Myles 1984). Such programs, in fact, appear to generate their own demand, and this process has no apparent limit.

In addition to the sheer size of the expenditures for health and welfare programs, the rate of increase causes alarm in the public mind. The rapid increase in expenditures during the 1960s and 1970s accounted partially for the Reagan administration's mandate to reduce spending during the early 1980s. Table 3.3 reveals that by 1986 expenditures for social welfare programs in the United States accounted for 18.4 percent of total gross national product and 48 percent of total federal and state government outlays. As large as this fraction of the budget is, however, it was down from over 57 percent in 1975, indicating that attempts to restrain the growth of the welfare state have had some impact. A major objective of those who support public funding for health and welfare programs, then, has been to defuse the hostility that the tax burden creates among the middle classes, who must bear the major tax burden (Wilensky 1975, 1981). Health and welfare programs, of course, are affected by public perceptions. In spite of

Table 3.3. Social Welfare Expenditures under Public Programs as Percent of GNP and Total Government Outlays, 1969–1986

Year	Total Amount[a]	Total GNP[b]	Percent of Total Government Outlays
1960	52.3	10.3	38.4
1970	145.9	14.7	48.2
1975	290.1	19.0	57.3
1980	492.5	18.5	56.5
1985	730.4	18.5	51.2
1986	770.5	18.4	47.9

Note: Data from U.S. Social Security Administration, *Social Security Bulletin* (November 1988).
[a]In billions of dollars.
[b]Gross national product.

the obvious success of the welfare state in guaranteeing income and health care to the poor and the middle class, programs like AFDC are often portrayed as failures (Schwarz 1988). This may be a result of unrealistic expectations. Despite the enormous scale of income maintenance programs, no nation has been able to eliminate poverty or the major social problems, such as drug abuse and crime, that follow in its wake. Health and welfare programs for the poor, therefore, are influenced by public perceptions that are often based on erroneous or incomplete information.

Hostility to the welfare state has another source. Since expenditures for public welfare absorb such a large fraction of our aggregate income, the expense of the welfare state creates a perceived problem of investment. Many critics believe that the relatively high marginal tax rates that are necessary to support health and welfare programs discourage investment in productivity-enhancing enterprises by decreasing the real return on such investment (e.g., Gilder 1981). Simply put, this means that it hardly pays for a person or a firm to risk money by investing in new production processes if any gain is taxed away. The arguments over the apparent conflicts between public expenditure and private investment are heated and complex, and we cannot review them in detail here. We will only say that some analysts of a leftist pesuasion argue that the conflict concerning the way in which our national income is spent has resulted in a fiscal and political crisis of the state that must certainly affect the future of health and welfare programs for the poor (Castells 1980, O'Connor 1973).

It is impossible to deny that the gap between government revenues and outlays for social welfare programs has clearly contributed to the massive budget deficits that we have witnessed in recent years. The enormous size of the federal budget deficit, which has grown dramatically since the 1970s, has captured the public's attention and is clearly a matter of concern. Since it would be political suicide for any politician to suggest that Americans are undertaxed, suggestions from both liberals and conservatives for reducing the budget deficit involve budget cuts. These suggestions differ only in what should be cut, but given the relative strength of the constituencies that support each part of the federal budget, health and welfare programs that benefit fatherless families are clearly at risk.

Of course, as many analysts have observed, there is no inherent limit to what a society can spend on social welfare or on health care.[10] Nor are high marginal tax rates necessarily a deterrent to savings and investment. Japan has a far more progressive tax structure than the United States, and this has certainly not undermined investment there (Kuttner 1984). Many European nations have much higher tax rates than the United States, and as we have noted, all provide some degree of income support and publicly financed health care to their citizens. Decisions concerning how a nation's domestic product is invested or consumed are really political choices that reflect the power of the various constituencies that are affected by the way in which the aggregate economic pie is divided. In a real sense, then, there is no real economic crisis of the welfare state, only a political one. Expenditures that enhance the health and education of the work force clearly enhance productivity. Unfortunately, whatever the truth of the matter, the perception of an inherent conflict between welfare expenditures and investment, especially in combination with the sort of revenue system that we have in the United States which relies on highly visible personal income and property taxes, results in widespread hostility to social welfare programs.[11]

Conclusion

We have illustrated the extent to which the health risks faced by women and children in fatherless families are influenced by economic and political factors. Poverty, especially in combination with low education and early fertility, places single mothers and their children in an extremely vulnerable economic position and undermines their political power at the same time that it increases the health risks they are exposed to. This vulnerability can be passed on from mothers to children, resulting in the intergenerational accumulation of risks to health. Because of post-World War II changes in the economy and the increase in the number of fatherless families, the health and welfare of a substantial fraction of America's children will be affected by future developments in the programs that ensure their health and welfare. The centrality of politics and economics to the health of both adult women and children in fatherless families must be kept in mind as we proceed to more detailed investigations of the physical and mental health and medical care use of single mothers and their children. The health disadvantages that we document, especially for black and Hispanic fatherless families, are largely a result of their economic disadvantage and political powerlessness.

In chapter 8, we investigate potential options for ensuring health care to single mothers and their children. In chapters 2 and 3, we have intended only to document their extreme economic and political vulnerability and to identify the sources of the health risks they face. We end by reiterating the central lesson of this chapter. The economic cost and the growing resistance of the middle class to taxation illustrate the fundamental dilemma in providing the basics of good health to fatherless families facing our nation. At the same time that basic social welfare programs have succeeded in ensuring income and health care to a large fraction of both the middle and lower classes, the ever-increasing cost of these programs fuels strong political opposition. This opposition has been remarkably effective in slowing the growth of health-related programs for the poor. The future of the welfare state generally and of the programs that provide health care to the poor specifically will be determined by the success or failure of attempts to limit the cost of programs such as AFDC and Medicaid. As we document in chapter 8, many of these attempts may have beneficial effects on the health of poor single mothers and their children, but there are many risks involved as well. Since it is simply impossible to fund all the programs various constituencies favor, it is necessary to clearly identify those programs that are most central to the maintenance of the health of single mothers and their children.

4

Measuring Health
Physical, Emotional, and Social Aspects

Now that we have documented the serious economic and political vulnerability of fatherless families and summarized the federal and state programs that ensure the health of their members, we are ready to examine our basic dependent variable in some detail. Health, like wealth, is something that is taken for granted while one has it, but when one becomes seriously ill, the attempt to get well dominates one's life. Health is clearly one of the central components of overall well-being; in its absence, little else matters. Yet health is difficult to define and to measure. Does health, for example, consist merely of the absence of disease? Or does it consist of some positive quality above and beyond the absence of identifiable pathology? The answer to these questions depends on one's purpose, and in this chapter we develop a fairly broad definition of health. Although for many practical purposes the layperson's understanding of what health means is adequate (healthy people, for example, tend not to die), for research purposes the study of health involves a number of complex issues that even nonspecialists must understand if they are to critically assess the findings of research on the health of children and adults in community samples. Before we can proceed to an examination of the impact of family structure on the health of women and children in fatherless families, then, we must discuss exactly what health and illness are, how they are measured, and how they are influenced by culture, society, and family structure.

Neither health nor illness are unambiguous entities. Rather, they are global states that have physical, emotional, and even social components. Increasingly, both physicians and policymakers are concerned with more than the simple absence of organic disease in assessing health. With the passage of acute disease as a major threat to health, subtler aspects of health, including emotional and behavioral adjustment, have become matters of public as well as professional medical concern. Both laypersons and specialists increasingly recognize that deficits in any one area of health, whether physical, emotional, or social, can affect the others and seriously diminish the quality of one's life (Ware 1986). We will examine all of these dimensions of health, but we begin here by developing a model of the impact of social class, minority group status, and single motherhood on health.

The issues we deal with are both conceptual and methodological. As in most operational science, the measures we use to represent theoretical variables are imprecise to varying degrees. The fundamental intellectual and technical task facing the health researcher is to develop the best measures and techniques possible but also to clearly understand the limitations of commonly used measurement techniques. After all, in the social sciences generally, even the best manifest measures are only imperfect representations of the latent construct they are meant to tap. Before we proceed to details of measurement, however, let us briefly mention a few issues related to sampling, since the sample one employs in any study defines the population to which one can generalize the findings.

The fundamental requirement of any sample that is intended to be used to make generalizations to some larger population is, of course, representativeness. To determine whether the absence of a spouse affects the health of women or the absence of a father harms the health of children, it is necessary to measure health in large samples so that one can compare the health of individuals in single-parent families to the health of those in two-parent families. Unfortunately, much existing research on fatherless families is compromised by inadequate samples. For example, many studies document serious problems among children whose parents have divorced but fail to compare these children's problems to those of children in intact families. In the absence of a comparison group of children in two-parent families, it is impossible to determine whether the problems that children in divorced families experience are atypical (e.g., Wallerstein and Blakeslee 1989). After all, adolescence is a trying time of life, and even children in two-parent families occasionally have problems.

In addition to relying on inadequate samples, much of the existing research on differential health levels in community samples is compromised by serious flaws in the methodology used to measure health. In what follows we discuss the major problems in the measurement of health and illness in some detail. Since few researchers can afford to administer physical examinations to large samples of people, most research that is based on community samples employs more indirect methods for establishing differential health levels. As we demonstrate later in this chapter, the most commonly used techniques for determining health levels in surveys are affected by unknown amounts of random and nonrandom error. Random error compromises the reliability of the method used to assess health, while nonrandom error affects validity and can seriously bias results, especially in the analysis of the impact of race, Hispanic ethnicity, and poverty on health. Individuals from different cultural and socioeconomic groups often answer the same question concerning health in very different ways.

We realize, of course, that these issues will strike some readers as excessively technical or specialized, but they really are not. We understand that those interested specifically in the health consequences of single motherhood want straightforward answers to questions concerning the impact of the marital status of the mother on her health and the health of her children. Unfortunately, it is not that easy, and the problems we deal with here go well beyond mere technical detail. They arise, in fact, from our basic conceptualization of what diminished health means for women and children. Because so much public policy depends on how researchers measure health and because so much is at stake in the study of the health of the poor, unsophisticated or facile treatments of health are simply irresponsible. The critical and concerned observer does not have the luxury of treating basic issues concerning the meaning and measurement of health and illness as technical nuisances to be relegated to some easily ignored Appendix. We suspect, however, that because the issues we raise in this chapter are of such practical importance and because they are also intellectually interesting, most readers will find what we have to say fascinating and highly informative.

The Operationalization of Health Constructs

Health consists of at least three major dimensions, physical, mental, and social, and although it is possible to clearly distinguish among them conceptually, the operationalization of these constructs often loses much of the clarity.[1] Health can be defined either narrowly, as, for example, the absence of specific symptoms or conditions, or more broadly, in terms of an individual's overall perception of his or her general health or well-being. Once again, although distinct dimensions of health make sense to the researcher, they are experienced globally by the individual. Since they are so central to our understanding of the impact of single parenthood on the health of women and children, let us briefly review the most basic types of physical and mental health status measures used in community studies and then discuss those factors that potentially affect their validity.

1. *General Health Measures.* Perhaps the most direct way of assessing an individual's health is to ask the person to rate his or her health in terms of categories such as "excellent," "very good," "good," "fair," or "poor." Such global assessments are the most commonly used health measures because they are easy to administer and can be incorporated into general surveys that cover a variety of topics. The use of global assessments to compare health levels makes a great deal of sense, since how one feels is a very good reflection of one's overall health, and self-assessments of this sort have been shown to be associated with numerous outcomes including medical care use, psychological status, and even the probability of death (Angel and Guarnaccia 1989, Idler and Angel 1990a). Clearly, these measures tap some very important dimensions of one's overall health. We will employ such global assessments of health throughout the remainder of the book.

Perhaps the greatest weakness of such general assessments, however, is that they confuse physical and mental status and tell us nothing about the specific aspects of one's physical health that give rise to the global assessment. They are, consequently, quite ambiguous. The reader might ask himself or herself how he or she would answer this question. What sort of comparison does one make to determine whether one's health is excellent as opposed to very good or even fair? Compared to individuals in their twenties, the overall health of even a vital eighty-year-old is quite poor. Ambiguous questions of this sort require that the individual interpret what is being asked, choose his or her own criteria for determining the answer, and answer truthfully. Obviously, there is no guarantee that this subjective process will be the same for two different people, especially if they are from very different cultural groups. One individual may rate his health as excellent when his clinical condition is no different from that of someone else who rates her health as only good. Two major differences between health measures, therefore, are their degree of objectivity and their specificity. Questions concerning general health are clearly much more ambiguous than questions about specific symptoms.

2. *Physical Symptoms.* Another commonly used method for assessing physical health in community samples is to ask individuals whether or not they have experienced any of a list of specific symptoms during some period (e.g., Aday, Chiu, and Andersen 1980). Symptoms are essentially of two sorts: those that are strictly physical (toothache, bleeding gums, diarrhea, or pains and swelling in the joints), and those that are termed *psychophysiological* to emphasize the fact that they can have psychological as

well as physical causes. Psychophysiological symptoms often consist of ambiguous sensations like "sudden feelings of weakness or faintness" or "feeling tired for weeks at a time for no special reason." Unfortunately, for research purposes even fairly specific symptoms like heart palpitations and dizziness can have psychological origins, so it is impossible to develop symptom scales that measure only physical health or only mental health; such scales invariably measure aspects of both simultaneously.

Clearly, symptoms differ greatly in their severity and in what they mean for one's long-term health status. Everyone at some time or another suffers from a stuffy or runny nose. Children are particularly prone to a great number of such minor symptoms, and unless they occur with abnormal frequency, they are really not worth worrying about. Other symptoms, like chest pains or the unexplained loss of ten or more pounds, can have serious implications for one's long-term health. Symptom scales often combine symptoms of differing severity, so that a similar score can reflect very different health statuses depending on the specific symptoms experienced and their underlying cause.

In addition to questions concerning symptoms that one has experienced recently and that refer to one's current state of health, many surveys ask an individual if he or she has ever had any of a list of chronic conditions such as heart or liver disease or kidney problems (National Center for Health Statistics 1985). Or it is possible to let the individual report any illness that he or she has had during some period which has required staying in bed or changing his or her daily routine. These reports are similar to the medical history that a physician takes during a physical examination. Individuals who are less vital and who are prone to a larger number of illnesses report more specific conditions, especially if they have been told at some time by a doctor that they have the condition, than individuals with more vitality. In the following chapters we compare children and adults in female-headed and two-parent families in terms of both symptoms and conditions.

3. *Functional Capacity.* One very common and useful way of assessing health, or at least the manifestations of health, is to ask a person about his or her ability to perform certain tasks such as dressing oneself or going out alone (Katz et al. 1963). Such measures are particularly useful in assessing the health of older individuals since in the later years of life some people suffer serious functional declines. Questions about physical functioning usually ask the individual if he or she has any difficulty with such common activities of daily living as bathing, dressing, getting into or out of bed, eating, and going to the toilet (Branch and Jette 1982). Clearly, someone who needs help with such basic activities is not in optimal health. We will

employ such measures when we examine the health of older females (chap. 7).

Measures of functional capacity are particularly useful because they are specific and highly relevant to one's ability to perform necessary self-care tasks. It might even be the case that until an illness interferes with one's ability to perform such activities, it is not really perceived as serious by the individual. Although they provide information on specific functional deficits, however, such measures tell us nothing about the specific health condition responsible for the functional incapacity. The inability to get in or out of a chair or to climb a flight of stairs can be the result of several medical problems, and deciding why an individual is limited requires more specific information (Ware 1986).

4. *Symptoms of Mental Illness.* We can see that the measurement of physical health in community samples is somewhat imprecise. Measurement of mental illness, for which there is no well-understood organic cause or unambiguous set of symptoms, becomes even more difficult. Mental health is difficult to measure largely because it is difficult to define. It refers to internal psychological states that are not readily observable, and although mental illnesses have observable manifestations, such as delusions or the inability to function because of depression, in the absence of overt behavioral evidence we must rely on the self-reports of individuals themselves to make diagnoses. The basic problem in assessing mental health, then, is that it is entirely subjective, and individuals employ their own internal standards when answering questions about their feelings. The researcher has no guarantee whatsoever that different individuals interpret questions about their feelings similarly or that the tools they use tap the same underlying dimensions of mental status in different individuals.

Researchers have approached the problems in measuring mental health from two different perspectives. As with physical health, mental health can be operationalized as either global feeling states or as specific diseases. In many studies individuals are asked if they have experienced any of a number of psychological symptoms such as "I felt lonely," "I felt fearful," "my sleep was restless," or "I had crying spells" during some period. Such scales measure nonspecific depressive affect. These symptom scales are popular because they are relatively easy to administer, and they tap an individual's overall affective state. As with general physical symptom scales, however, such global affect scales tell us nothing about the specific psychiatric illnesses that an individual might be suffering from, or even that they are ill in any clinically meaningful sense.

In recent years a great deal of progress has been made in determining the prevalence of specific psychiatric illnesses as they are defined in the American Psychiatric Association's Diagnostic and Statistical Manual (American Psychiatric Association 1987). These new attempts to study specific mental disorders in the community entail the development of complex questionnaires that are based on clearly defined diagnostic criteria involving not only a set of specific symptoms but also clearly specified severity criteria and the requirement that the symptoms not be the result of drug or alcohol abuse (Robins et al. 1984). Since these instruments are, for the most part, administered by lay interviewers, the rules for classifying symptoms as normal or abnormal are determined by computer in accordance with prespecified algorithms. The usefulness of such scales is limited by the fact that since they are long and detailed, they cannot easily be incorporated into general surveys that gather information on other topics. In the following chapters we will rely on the more global measures of depressive affect to assess the mental health of women and children in female-headed families.

5. *Social health.* Social health is a complicated concept but one that is clearly related to mental and physical health. There is ample evidence that those who have adequate social support (which we might interpret as social health) enjoy better physical and mental health (House, Landis, and Umberson 1988). Individuals who lack a spouse or other confidant are more prone to depression than those with a spouse or intimate friend (Brown and Harris 1978). Social isolation increases the risk of complications from medical procedures (Nuckolls, Cassel, and Kaplan 1972). Some studies report that individuals who are more socially active live longer than those who are less active (Berkman and Syme 1979). Social involvement, then, is clearly an important cause as well as a consequence of physical and mental health. Those who are in good health are able to interact with others, and this interaction enhances physical and mental health. Those in poor health find it more difficult to maintain the social ties that help maintain physical and mental well-being.

Social functioning is particularly important in the assessment of the health of children. Behavioral and academic problems can be seen as failures in social functioning. The child's main developmental task is to become a competent and functioning adult. Problems in school or with authority figures undermine this process and have lifelong implications, and for children, behavioral problems are often the reason for contact with the mental health care system. As we demonstrate in chapter 5, since in the contemporary United States few children suffer from serious physical illnesses, the negative consequences of divorce and father absence are manifested less as physical health problems and more as behavioral and adjustment problems. Children act out their feelings by striking out against other children and against authority figures. They can also suffer from rather serious emotional disturbances that interfere with their socialization.

Culture, Social Class, and the Meaning of Health Indicators

One of the most serious problems one encounters in evaluating research on racial and ethnic group differences in health and health care use is that in much of it, the impact of culture and social class on an individual's responses to questions concerning global health states, symptoms, and past illnesses is ignored. Yet the anthropological, sociological, and psychological literatures make it abundantly clear that subjective assessments of health are not unmediated reflections of something we might consider "true health" but rather represent mental and linguistic constructions that are influenced by an individual's culture and social class (Angel and Guarnaccia 1989; Angel and Thoits 1987; Guarnaccia, Angel, and Worobey 1989; Kleinman 1977; Kleinman and Kleinman 1985; Kleinman, Good, and Guarnaccia 1986; Malgady, Rogler, and Costantino 1987).[2] Unfortunately, if groups with different social characteristics (e.g., blacks, Hispanics, or poor females) respond to questions concerning health differently than other groups, researchers who use such information to compare health levels can quite easily attribute substantive differences in health to what are actually differences in the way individuals from these different groups respond.

A dramatic example of how ethnicity can affect the results of supposedly objective and scientifically validated measurement instruments occurred during the 1930s and 1940s when many Spanish-speaking Hispanic children were labeled retarded by conventional IQ tests when, in fact, they simply did not score well on intelligence tests administered in English (Raftery 1988). Much of the current debate over IQ differences between blacks and whites focuses on whether or not tests that are based on the intellectual and social experiences of one group can appropriately be used to test the intelligence of another group that has been exposed to a very different set of experiences.

The problem is particularly serious in the study of health, since the vast majority of studies that deal with health differences between blacks and whites, between the middle class and the poor, and between children in divorced and intact families are based on subjective reports by survey respondents or their proxies. This information is highly personal, and only rarely can it be verified against objective external information. In the study of health, as in the rest of science, one always must ask whether the measurement device that one uses taps the same underlying phenomenon in different groups or whether its measurement function is significantly affected by characteristics of the groups studied. This may seem obvious, but it is surprising just how frequently the problem is ignored in published research. Since both physicians and survey researchers rely on an individual's reports of symptoms and feelings to make assessments, it is necessary to understand how such subjective information is influenced by social class and cultural factors if we are to begin to understand just how accurate it is and how much confidence we can have in group comparisons based on self-reported data.

Objective versus Subjective Health

Illness, as at it is experienced subjectively, is a different phenomenon from one's clinically ascertainable disease state. As a matter of fact, people often feel ill when there is nothing diagnosably wrong with them. It is common in medical sociology, therefore, to distinguish between "disease" and "illness." Disease refers to the organic or functional pathology that is the result of some disease process. Cancer and heart disease have clearly objective aspects that can be diagnosed through laboratory tests and the use of diagnostic instruments. Illness refers to the subjective experience of disease. Unlike disease as a clinical entity, illness cannot be objectively measured because it is a subjective experience that only the individual has access to.

Although the disease process is basically the same for everyone regardless of the social group they belong to, the subjective experience of illness is influenced by a person's culture, social environment, and psychological makeup (Angel and Guarnaccia 1989, Angel and Thoits 1987, Mechanic and Angel 1987). But what is even more important for our purposes, the subjective experience of illness involves the entire person, since in lived experience people do not clearly distinguish their mental, physical, or even social selves (Angel and Angel in press, Angel and Idler 1992). The distinction between mental and physical illness is more for the convenience of researchers than a reflection of how people experience their internal worlds.

When one is ill one experiences the phenomenon both as mood changes and as physical discomfort. This fact makes the assessment of a person's health difficult, and it is necessary to collect as much information as possible concerning all aspects of a person's health before making a judgment that he or she is well or ill. A doctor collects information from numerous sources, including laboratory tests, a medical history, and a physical examination, before arriving at a diagnosis. Researchers, however, often have only one source of information and must base their judgments on average differences between groups.

Making inferences about specific illnesses that people may have from reports of their symptoms and feelings is clearly dangerous. One cannot, for example, infer that an individual has heart disease solely on the basis of a report of chest pains. A definitive diagnosis requires much more detailed information, much of it more objective than the individual's report of symptoms. We do not mean to imply, of course, that subjective reports are always a distorted or inaccurate reflection of an individual's actual health status. Feelings clearly reflect underlying global health status, and for the individual the subjective experience is, for all intents and purposes, the reality. The way an individual feels determines how he or she functions socially and whether or not he or she seeks medical care. We merely wish to point out that subjective experience is a complex product of one's cultural, social, and psychological status as well as of one's actual physical status.

The situation is confounded further by the fact that health information is often collected from someone other than the individual of interest. Clearly, the accuracy of such information depends on just how well the proxy, which is what we call the individual who provides the information, knows the subject. Although a wife may be able to accurately report her husband's educational level, she may not be able to provide accurate information on the symptoms he has experienced or on his subjective health status. However, a mother is probably quite aware of her child's symptoms and feelings.

Proxy respondents are very common in the social sciences. In community studies we usually rely only on a mother's report of her child's health. Such information is very useful, but when interpreting it we must keep in mind that responses to questions concerning a child's health may be inaccurate, and as we will demonstrate later, they can be significantly affected by the mother's own psychological state. Consequently, a mother's response to questions about the health of her child only partially reflects the child's clinical status. Because of these limitations in measurement, when we attempt to assess the health levels of individuals in the community, it is imperative to keep in mind that what we are measuring is not health in a narrow clinical sense but more global aspects of social and personal functioning. Because the health of children is one of our major concerns in this work and because they are particularly vulnerable to the strains of poverty, it is important to more thoroughly develop our conceptualization of how culture, social class, and single parenthood affect children's health and a mother's decisions concerning appropriate medical care.

A Mother's Assessment of Her Child's Health

Most of what we might consider health care is not provided by professionals; for the most part, basic health care is either self-administered or provided by someone else at home. Indeed, for most of human history, as in
many parts of the world today, home remedies have been the only medicine
available. Even when more formal care is available, the decision to use it is
initially made at home, often by a parent or at the prodding of a spouse.
Most routine health care, therefore, is provided in what we might term the
informal medical marketplace, in which the initial evaluation of symptoms
is made in consultation with one's spouse or other household members
(Alpert, Kosa, and Haggerty 1967; Angel and Thoits 1987; Chrisman and
Kleinman 1983; Kellam, Ensminger, and Turner 1977; Litman 1974; Pratt
1976). Anthropologists refer to the process by which illness is recognized
and responded to initially as "lay consultation and referral" (e.g., Chrisman
and Kleinman 1983). As part of this process an individual may solicit the
opinions of those in his or her immediate social environment before seeking
the advice of professionals. As we are all aware, one need not even solicit
this advice; it is quite often volunteered.

Figure 4.1 summarizes our conceptualization of the informal health
care environment in which a child's health is determined and interpreted
by his or her mother (Angel and Worobey 1988a). Of course, this same

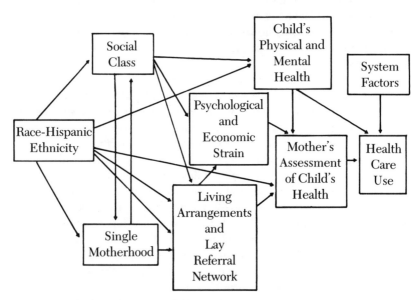

Figure 4.1. The Cultural and Social Context of Health Assessments

conceptualization can be applied to adults' assessments of their own health, in which case the focus is on the interpretation of one's own symptoms rather than those of one's child. Since race and Hispanic ethnicity affect all other aspects of the model, we conceive of them as contextual variables as well as attributes. Race and ethnicity are complex variables because they tap aspects of both culture and social class. These variables, therefore, affect all subsequent components of the model.

In this conceptual model we treat social class, measured by such variables as income and education, and single motherhood as exogenous and simultaneously determined. As we have shown, lower-class membership increases the likelihood of single motherhood, and single motherhood certainly increases the risk of poverty. In addition to affecting a woman's material resources, however, single motherhood affects her social resources, largely through its impact on her living arrangements, which determine the size and composition of her immediate lay referral network. These factors influence the amount of economic and psychological strain that the woman and her children experience. Poverty, the burdens of unassisted parenthood, and life in a deteriorated physical environment can greatly increase the health risks that both adults and children are exposed to. An extended family, or helpful and supportive relatives or friends, can help reduce some of these risks. Together, these factors influence what we might consider the child's actual, or clinically ascertainable, physical and mental health. Since, as we demonstrated in chapter 2, lower-class minority group mothers are frequently single, both their material resources and their social resources are often limited (Angel and Tienda 1982, Tienda and Angel 1982, Ross and Sawhill 1975). We would expect these disadvantages to adversely affect a child's actual health status.

In addition to influencing actual physical health, culture and social class also influence a mother's assessment of the severity of symptoms and constrain her decisions concerning the appropriate response to these symptoms (Angel and Worobey 1988*a*). One social process that we theorize influences a mother's evaluation of her child's symptoms is reference group comparison. Those in our immediate social environment, including other family members, neighbors, and even members of our racial or ethnic group, comprise a reference group against which we evaluate our own symptoms or those of our children (Angel and Thoits 1987). Among lower-class children, runny noses and ear infections are fairly common, so these symptoms may not strike a mother as particularly troublesome. She may consequently decide not to seek medical care, especially if she lacks the material resources to do so.

The point we wish to make is that a woman's perception of and her response to her child's symptoms, as well as to her own symptoms, is structured by a complex interaction of cultural as well as material factors. In earlier work we developed a theory of the existence of linguistic and cognitive "schema" through which perceptions of symptoms are filtered and which influence their interpretation as either serious or not (ibid.). By "schema," we mean culturally based structured ideas concerning which symptoms are physical and which are mental; which are serious and which are not; which go together and which are distinct; and which should be attended to and by whom. The existence of such schema is supported by an increasing body of evidence that demonstrates that people's evaluations of the etiology, severity, and appropriate course of action regarding specific symptoms and disease categories change as they migrate from traditional cultures to scientifically oriented developed societies (Angel and Guarnaccia 1989, Angel and Thoits 1987). Such change can occur as the result of actual migration or as the result of the modernization of a traditional society.

Culture and even social class, to the extent that it constitutes a subculture, provide the individual with a limited set of interpretive options for assessing the severity of symptoms and for making decisions concerning the appropriate course of action. We should anticipate a potential criticism here. Some people may feel uncomfortable even discussing culture as a factor that influences a mother's response to symptoms when material resources and limited access to medical care constrain her decisions concerning medical care for herself and for her child. We certainly do not intend to reduce economics to culture, nor do we wish to focus on individual behaviors to the exclusion of system-level factors as the determinants of health care use, and our model takes the availability of health care specifically into account in the determination of actual health care use. An entire set of economic and system factors, including the availability of child care for other children, the availability of transportation, the distance to the doctor, the availability of public or private insurance, and much else, influence a woman's ability to take her child to the doctor. Even with an appreciation of the importance of economic and structural factors, however, we simply cannot ignore the fact that a large body of research makes it abundantly clear that symptoms are interpreted differently by individuals in different cultural and social groups.

The impact of social class, then, takes place within specific cultural contexts that influence the impact of structural, economic, and psychosocial variables on evaluations of health and the actions one takes in response to symptoms (Angel and Thoits 1987, Zborowski 1952). Let us return for a moment to one key component of our model, the size and composition of a mother's lay referral network. The lay network is important in any discussion of health care in fatherless families specifically because making decisions concerning the severity of symptoms experienced by others, even when one knows them as well as a mother knows her child, requires judgments based on secondary information. The ambiguity inherent in assessing the severity and long-term implications of symptoms for children increases the psychological importance of confirmatory opinions. When a mother in an intact family discovers that her child has some particular symptom, she may solicit the opinion of her spouse as to whether he feels that the symptoms are serious enough to warrant taking the child to the doctor or at least taking special action, like keeping the child home from school. Even if a parent is fairly confident that a symptom is not serious, it is a normal human characteristic to desire the affirmation of others in such evaluations, especially since the salience of symptoms experienced by their children is likely to be quite high for parents. In the presence of ambiguous symptoms and persistent complaints from a child, a parent must decide between forcing the child into his or her normal routine or allowing the child to assume the sick role.

To summarize, there are several ways in which single motherhood can affect children's health or a mother's perception of it and thereby influence her response to her child's symptoms. Most obviously, the stresses and deprivations associated with living in poverty can actually impair the health of children in lower-class female-headed households. Low birth-weight infants born to young mothers experience a greater number of illnesses than other infants both at birth and later in life (Field 1981). Another possibility is that children in female-headed households manifest the stresses they experience somatically as well as emotionally and complain of more common childhood symptoms. Or finally, a single mother may, as the result of her own stress, view her child's health as poorer than it actually is. Since children's health is such a central consideration in the rise of the fatherless family, we should discuss the sources of information on a child's physical health and mental health.

Sources of Information on Children's Health

Information on a child's health comes from a variety of sources, including the child himself or herself, the child's parents, teachers, psychiatrists, psychologists, and pediatricians. Each of these individuals has a different perspective concerning the child's physical, cognitive, and social development, and the validity of the answers to questions concerning the child's health can vary depending on the person providing the information. Ideally, one would like information on the child's physical health and his or her behavior and emotional state from several of these sources, since the type of information each provides is different and, it is hoped, complementary.

To assess a child's physical health, for example, physicians rely on detailed examinations and the results of fairly precise laboratory tests. Such assessments are perhaps the most objective information available for assessing a child's physical health status. However, detailed physical examinations are far too expensive for most community studies, and information is usually provided by a parent or some other adult. Such information is obviously less objective than that provided by the physician. However, a parent is aware of aspects of the child's behavior and functioning that the physician may not find out about during a brief examination, and such information is useful for detecting large differences in the physical health status and social functioning of children in different sorts of families.

If judgments about the presence or absence of physical illness in community samples are difficult to make, judgments concerning mental illness are even harder, since mental illness is a more diffuse and imprecise concept than physical illness, and information concerning the child's behavior and emotional status is less objective than information concerning the presence or absence of physical symptoms. A diagnosis of mental illness in a child involves making inferences about internal emotional states from indirect evidence and behavior. If a child does not complain of depression because he or she lacks the vocabulary to do so, we must infer the state from his or her behavior. Of course, we do the same thing for adults, but adults play a much greater role in the diagnosis of their own conditions than do children, and they usually seek help for emotional problems on their own. When children are taken to a mental health professional it is usually at the instigation of someone else, such as a parent, a teacher, or the juvenile court.

Parents and mental health professionals provide very different sorts of information concerning a child's mental health since each uses a different set of criteria to assess the child's behavior. Typically, psychiatrists and psychologists attempt to identify constellations of behaviors and feelings that fit into formal diagnostic categories. Such diagnoses, ideally, dictate a course of therapy. Mothers are sensitive to disruptive or atypical behaviors or changes in their child's mood. They are less concerned with labels and attend more to the child's global functioning and emotional state. Teachers focus on yet another set of behaviors, those having to do with the child's academic performance and social interactions at school.

Each of these sources provides a different type of information concerning the child's functioning, and each is appropriate for a specific purpose. The treatment of clinical pathology requires a thorough clinical evaluation before therapy can begin, but detailed clinical assessments are obviously too expensive for community studies in which it is necessary to collect information on a large number of children to identify risk factors for mental and behavioral problems. Nonetheless, because they are the only sources of data available for studying children with serious mental illness, samples of patients in therapy or counseling are often used in the study of the mental health of children.

Much of the existing work on the mental health of children is based on small convenience or clinical samples, and the findings from these studies can be generalized to the larger population of children only with caution. Children who are brought to a mental health clinic or to a counselor may be very atypical and unlike other children in the community who have similar mental or behavioral problems. These children are a subset of all children with problems, and something about their family situation or their behavior singles them out for treatment. They may simply have more serious problems than other children. Children with mild forms of mental illness or mood disorders may never receive treatment from a professional, while disruptive or violent children may be very likely to be referred for counseling.

Obviously, the generalizability of findings concerning childhood physical and mental health problems is increased if they are based on representative community samples. Since in any cross section of the population of children at large only a few will have any particular health problem, very large samples are necessary to ensure enough cases. Of course, the collection of information from large samples requires the use of fairly inexpensive data collection techniques. Most studies rely on fairly general questions about symptoms and behavioral problems. Although such studies do not allow us to determine the prevalence of specific psychiatric diagnoses among children, they tell us something of the overall mental health and social functioning of children and allow us to identify those factors that increase or decrease a child's general well-being. For general purposes such as ours, which is to determine if father absence has a noticeable impact on the overall well-being of children, such data are useful.

The most commonly employed technique for identifying mental or behavioral problems in community studies is a behavior problem checklist.[3] A mother or some other adult usually reports whether or not the child manifests problem behaviors such as temper tantrums, destructiveness, problems in school, and mood changes. The information from problem checklists must be interpreted cautiously, however, since even normal children occasionally have problems in school, are moody, or defy authority. One must make a judgment as to when such behaviors are frequent or severe enough to be considered abnormal. Data from the National Health Interview Survey (NHIS) show that the majority of parents report that their children occasionally engage in problem behaviors.[4] Only a third of parents, however, report that their children frequently engage in disruptive behavior or have serious behavioral problems. It is clear, therefore, that we must be careful in how we use such data. If we employ overly liberal criteria, many children appear to have problems. If we use very conservative criteria, many children with significant emotional and behavioral problems may be missed.

How Accurately Can Various Dimensions of Health Be Measured?

Now that we have reviewed the basic conceptual and methodological issues involved in the definition and measurement of health, a concrete example of the ambiguity inherent in the measurement of health is in order. Of course, what we term "ambiguity" represents more than a mere nuisance or what we often term "measurement errors." Rather, it reflects the actual complexity of intrapersonal experience, and observed variation in responses to questions concerning health status tells us something about the complex cognitive processes involved in answering questions about health. The analyses we present here clearly illustrate how culture and language structure self-assessments and reports of overall health status.

As we noted earlier, information provided by questions concerning one's global health status are valid for the most part. Individuals who rate their health as poor have higher subsequent mortality rates than those who rate their health as better (Idler and Angel 1990a). Despite such broad validity, however, there is a great deal of variation, or what we might consider error, in self-assessments of health. Unfortunately, this error is often as large or larger than the average differences in health status between groups that are often detected. There is ample evidence that individuals with the same clinically assessed physical health respond to questions concerning specific symptoms, pain, and general health differently depending on other cultural and psychological factors (Angel and Idler 1992, Idler and Angel 1990b, Mechanic and Angel 1987). In this section we present some striking findings concerning just how much slippage there is in subjective measures of health.

Our data are from a large survey of Hispanic-Americans in the United States conducted between 1982 and 1984.[5] As part of this study each individual received a detailed physical examination, after which the physician rated the individual's health level as excellent, very good, good, fair, or poor. The individual rated his or her own health in terms of the same five categories. Table 4.1 presents a comparison of the responses of the survey participants to those of the physicians. The respondent's self-assessments are listed along the left margin and the physician's assessments along the top. The columns, therefore, refer to each category of the physician's assessment and add to 100 percent. The numbers in each column show how

Table 4.1. Self-Assessed and Physician's Assessments of Health for Mexican-Americans

Self-Assessment	Physician's Assessment of English Interview			
	Excellent	Very Good	Good	Fair/ Poor
Excellent	21%	16%	9%	10%
Very Good	27%	21%	13%	6%
Good	34%	38%	35%	27%
Fair/Poor	18%	25%	43%	57%
	100%	100%	100%	100%

Self-Assessment	Physician's Assessment of Spanish Interview			
	Excellent	Very Good	Good	Fair/ Poor
Excellent	7%	6%	4%	2%
Very Good	8%	7%	4%	4%
Good	35%	33%	28%	32%
Fair/Poor	51%	55%	65%	62%
	100%	100%	100%	100%

Source: Hispanic Health and Nutrition Examination Survey (HHANES), National Center for Health Statistics (1985).
Note: Because of rounding, proportions do not necessarily total to 100%.

individuals who physicians judged to be in similar health evaluated themselves. Since there were relatively few people who rated their health as poor, we combined this category with fair.

Because we know from our previous research that Mexican-Americans who have become acculturated into American society and who are fluent in English are very different in their responses to health questionnaires than Mexican-Americans who are less acculturated and who are not fluent in English, we separated the sample into those who answered the questions in English and those who answered them in Spanish (Angel and Thoits 1987, Angel 1984, Angel and Guarnaccia 1989). The top panel of table 4.1 refers to those who took the interview in English and shows that only 21 percent of those individuals whom the physicians judged to be in excellent health rated themselves as in excellent health, whereas 18 percent judged themselves to be in fair or poor health.

Clearly, there is a good deal of disagreement between the respondents and the doctors. Although these data are from Mexican-Americans only, there is no reason to believe that this basic relationship would not hold for other groups as well. To illustrate that culture (here level of acculturation as measured by language) plays an important role in the answers people give to such questions, we compare the second panel, based on respondents who took the interview in Spanish, to the first panel, based on those who took it in English. The disagreement between respondents and physicians is much greater among the respondents who answered the question in Spanish than among those who answered in English, suggesting that less acculturated individuals respond to questions concerning their general health differently than more acculturated individuals. These findings corroborate the anthropological data that we reviewed earlier that responses to questions concerning physical health reflect more than just clinical status.

Now we proceed to an illustration of how emotional status can influence reports of physical health. In this case we illustrate how a mother's assessment of her child's health is influenced by her own emotional status. As part of the same study from which table 4.1 was derived, we were able to identify pairs of mothers and children who were both in the study.[6] As part of the mother's examination she was given a checklist of common psychological symptoms, the Center for Epidemologic Studies Depression Scale (CES-D) (Robins et al. 1984). These items are commonly used to assess an individual's level of depressive affect or overall emotional state at any particular time. Like the adults in the study, the children received a full physical examination, after which the doctor rated their health as excellent, very good, good, fair, or poor. The mother then assessed her child's overall health using the same five categories.

Figure 4.2 shows the level of distress for mothers who reported different health levels for their children. Since a mother's distress level could be the result of real illness in her child, these depressive affect scores are statistically adjusted using the physician's examination to make the children comparable in terms of actual physical health.[7] This adjustment has the same effect as comparing the depression scores of women whose children have the same objective health status. This figure shows that even after this statistical adjustment for the physician's assessment is made, those mothers who reported the poorest health for their children also have the highest depressive affect scores. Since these associations are adjusted to take the child's objective health status into account, they provide fairly strong proof that a mother's mood status directly affects her assessment of her child's health. Mothers' reports, then, must be interpreted as revealing as much about the mother as the child.

For single mothers, the increased strain associated with maintaining a household and raising children alone might easily affect her perceptions of her child's health. Mechanic (1964) found that mothers who were under stress reported that their children had more illness than did mothers who

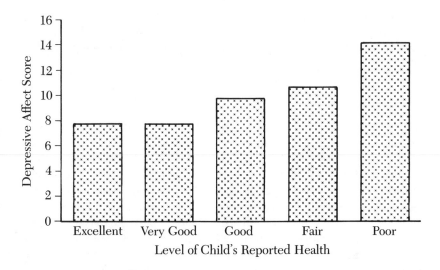

Figure 4.2. Average Mother's CES-D Score by Categories of Child's Reported Health. *Source:* 1984–1986 Hispanic Health and Nutrition Examination Survey (HHANES).

were not under stress. Although our data do not allow us to examine the possibility, it may be that stress not only increases a mother's report of the number of symptoms her child experiences but may also affect her assessment of the severity of such symptoms. These findings, then, illustrate that the family's emotional climate affects the health of all of its members. Although we do not have depression measures for the children in these households, the data we review in the next chapter lead us to suspect that a mother's depression affects her child's health as well. The data we review consistently show that a stressful home environment affects both adults and children. Father absence increases the financial and emotional strains a mother experiences and, thereby, undermines the well-being of the entire family.

These simple illustrations of the discrepancy between a physician's and an individual's assessment of his or her overall health and the reports of poorer children's health by emotionally distressed mothers make a much more general point. Although the sorts of measures that are typically used in community studies to assess health are useful and, in fact, the only sorts of measures that are practical enough and economical enough for comparing the health of large groups, they must be interpreted cautiously. When we compare the physical health levels of children or adults in poor female-headed households who are exposed to high levels of emotional stress to the physical health levels of individuals in less-stressed two-parent households using self-reported or proxy-reported measures, the differences in physical health that we find may be more a reflection of the differences in the emotional strain these families are under than of their actual physical health.

Concluding Remarks

The literature we have reviewed and the data we have analyzed above should make it clear that health and illness are extremely complex concepts that include interdependent physical, emotional, and social dimensions. It should also be clear that this complexity is compounded at the level of measurement and that it is impossible, in principle, to separate the physical, emotional, and social dimensions of health and illness using self-reported data. As refined as our measurement techniques become, they are incapable of unambiguously distinguishing between these various dimensions of health because of the simple fact that the physical, emotional, and social aspects of self are not experienced subjectively as distinct domains by individuals in lived experience.

In this chapter we have provided data showing that doctors and patients or research subjects often disagree rather dramatically in their assessments of the patient's overall health. We have also shown that depression affects a mother's assessment of her child's health. Although the data we have presented focus on children's health, our previous research clearly shows that emotionally distressed adults rate their own health as poorer than adults who are not distressed. Our results, however, reveal only the tip of the iceberg. There are many other factors that might influence the meaning and accuracy of the sorts of information that researchers must rely on to make group comparisons. The literature is filled with contradictory and inconsistent findings concerning the impact of attributes and characteristics such as race, Hispanic ethnicity, and marital status on health. Many of these contradictory findings are probably the result of inadequate measurement and a lack of clarity in what one means by health or illness. It is simply impossible to meaningfully draw conclusions about the health levels of different groups without a clear understanding of these difficulties. In the following chapters we will summarize what is known of the health of women and children in fatherless families, but the reader must always keep in mind that the objects of our inquiry, health and illness, are elusive concepts.

5

Growing Up without Father
Health Consequences for Children

In this chapter we assess the physical and mental health consequences of father absence for black, Hispanic, and non-Hispanic white children. As we showed in chapter 3, fatherless children in these three groups have a great deal in common, but they are also quite different. Although female-headed families are generally poorer than two-parent families, the combination of single motherhood and minority group status can make matters far worse. Unfortunately, the data to unambiguously determine how the combination of minority group status and father absence affects children's physical and mental health do not exist. Consequently, to begin to understand the health consequences of father absence for the health of children from different racial and ethnic groups, we summarize a great deal of data from various sources. Each of the data sources we employ suffers from certain shortcomings. Some are based on small clinical samples; others are studies of adolescent mothers who make up a large fraction of the population of single mothers but who are not necessarily typical of all single mothers; yet others lack appropriate control groups, without which we cannot with any certainty attribute the behavioral and health problems observed to father absence. Despite the shortcomings of any particular study, though, together they allow us to make a fairly comprehensive assessment of the more serious health risks faced by children in father-absent families.

Our objective here, then, is to develop a synthetic overview of the consequences of father absence for children's physical and mental health. The studies we review include (1) pediatric and community studies of the social factors affecting the physical, emotional, and social health of children; (2) epidemiological studies of the prevalence of health conditions among children in different living arrangements; and (3) more recent community studies of the prevalence of specific mental illnesses among children and adolescents. These studies address various aspects of the impact of minority group status, poverty, divorce, and single motherhood on children's health. We make no attempt to be exhaustive in our literature review. The published literature on the health of children includes thousands of articles and books, most of which provide little information on the health consequences of family structure. Instead, we focus on those studies that provide at least some indirect evidence of the impact of father absence on the physical and mental health of children.

As we pointed out in chapter 4, it is often difficult to differentiate between physical and mental illness in community studies. Nonetheless, in this chapter, we do so to draw some tentative conclusions concerning the consequences of father absence for each of these important dimensions of health. As we will demonstrate, father absence has a far more obvious impact on children's emotional health than on their physical health. Of course, the mental health consequences of divorce and single motherhood have received far more attention than have the physical health consequences of father absence, and the failure of many studies to find clear physical health consequences of father absence may be the result of insensitive measures. Relatively few studies of the impact of divorce or single motherhood include rigorous assessments of physical health. Although we will make some inferences concerning the physical health consequences of father absence based on findings from clinical studies of the health of poor children and the children of adolescent mothers, most of the information on the physical health consequences of father absence for children that we present is based on parents' general impressions of their children's health as well as their reports of medical conditions, symptoms, and acute illnesses. Such subjective information is clearly useful, but it lacks the objectivity of physicians' examinations and, as we demonstrated, its accuracy or meaning may be seriously affected by the parent's own mental state.

The situation is rather different when it comes to our understanding of the impact of father absence on the mental health of children. The literature on the emotional and behavioral problems experienced by the children of adolescent and single mothers is extensive. Much of it focuses specifically on the emotional and behavioral consequences of divorce, and most of it clearly shows that adolescent motherhood and the turmoil surrounding divorce have serious negative consequences for a child's social and emotional development. Because of the greater availability of information on the behavioral and emotional consequences of single motherhood for children, as well as the more obvious negative consequences of divorce and single motherhood for children's mental health, we devote a great deal of this chapter to a discussion of these outcomes. We also investigate how father absence affects a child's use of health services and present some recent evidence concerning the co-occurrence of mental and physical illness among children in father-absent and two-parent households. Before we proceed to the specific findings, though, we should devote some time to a discussion of the factors in a child's immediate world that affect his or her health.

Biological and Social Factors in Children's Health

A child's physical health is determined by genetic, family, social, and environmental factors. At the most basic biological level, a child's genetic endowment determines his or her overall level of vitality and affects the sorts of illness that he or she is prone to. Biology is not destiny, however, and this genetic endowment interacts with the child's physical and social environment to influence his or her overall health level and the specific illnesses he or she experiences in childhood (Starfield 1990, Willis and Walker 1989). A physically and emotionally resilient child has a better chance of thriving in a situation in which a less vital child might suffer serious illness.

A child's mental health is also affected by his or her immediate family and social environment. The evidence clearly shows that the emotional climate of the family can either enhance or diminish a child's emotional health (Garmezy and Rutter 1983, Litman 1974, Rutter 1985). A harmonious and well-functioning family can protect a child from the negative effects of poverty, whereas a dysfunctional and strife-ridden family can seriously harm even a middle-class child's emotional health. Children are particularly sensitive to family discord, and as we document in greater detail below, parental conflict often results in serious behavioral and emotional problems (Wallerstein and Blakeslee 1989; Wallerstein and Kelly 1975, 1980; Hetherington 1988a, 1989; Rutter 1985). Beyond the family and local social network, larger social and environmental factors affect a child's health. Exposure to environmental pollutants and living in a neighborhood beset by drugs and violence can clearly harm both a child's physical and mental health. One of the greatest tragedies we face today is that the physical decay and social disorganization of many of our contemporary urban neighborhoods place poor children at very high risk of emotional and physical illness (Hewlett 1991, Sidel 1986, Schorr 1988).

The determination of the sorts of health risks children in poor father-absent families face in the community is a difficult task. As we noted above, the amount of published information on the health of children is vast, but relatively little of it relates specific health problems to specific family structures. To understand how father absence interacts with other factors, such as poverty and the process of family disruption, to affect children's health in the real world, we draw heavily from a few community studies based on fairly large samples. To identify those factors that affect children's health for different racial and ethnic groups, we must have sufficient variation in household type and family income levels as well as sufficient numbers of blacks, Hispanics, and non-Hispanic whites. Most clinical studies of children's health do not include sufficient racial and ethnic variation for this purpose, nor do they provide information on the child's family structure. In addition, clinical samples can be very atypical of the general population in terms of health-related socioeconomic characteristics. Children who are brought to psychiatrists or other mental health professionals can be quite different from other children in the community with similar emotional or behavioral problems, most of whom receive no specialty mental health care at all.

As we showed in chapter 4, assessing either the physical or mental health of children in community studies is difficult, and many contradictory and inconclusive findings concering children's mental health in the literature are no doubt the result of methodological weaknesses in the way studies are carried out. In subsequent sections we will summarize and critique many studies based on different methodologies. Extensive criticism of each would result in a laborious and excessively technical presentation, and we refer the reader who is interested in a detailed discussion of the methodology of the assessment of children's health to the appropriate sections in chapter 4. In this and the following chapters our methodological critiques of specific studies will be general, and we will focus more on the substantive results.

Poverty and Illness in Infancy, Childhood, and Adolescence

For most Americans childhood is a healthy time of life. There is, of course, significant mortality associated with birth, especially for the poor and minorities, but in the United States today most children are born healthy, and since we have controlled the most serious diseases of childhood, few children die of acute causes (Rosenwaike and Bradshaw 1989). Yet, although overall serious morbidity and mortality rates for children are generally low in the United States, significant differences persist in the health of the children of the poor and of the middle class. The children of the poor are at higher risk of death during the first year of life and are more often damaged by the effects of lead poisoning and other environmental pollutants, including noise and stress, than middle-class children (Children's Defense Fund 1991, Starfield 1990). Although acute illness is a common occurrence in childhood (Garrison and McQuiston 1989), most of the common childhood illnesses occur more frequently among the poor than among the more affluent. We highlight here some of the major differences between the poor and the more affluent in patterns of morbidity, mortality, and health care use by children.

One of the most indisputable findings in the literature is that early prenatal care reduces the risk of low birth weight and, consequently, of poor infant health outcomes (Casper and Hogan 1991, General Accounting Office 1992). Yet, in 1988, nearly a quarter of pregnant women did not receive care during the first trimester of pregnancy. Of these, some did not receive care until the last trimester, and a certain fraction received no care at all (Children's Defense Fund 1991). Those most likely to do without adequate prenatal care are disproportionately black, Native American, Hispanic, or poor (Guendelman and Schwalbe 1986; Horwitz, Morganstern, and Berkman 1985; Kelleher and Hohmann n.d.; Moss and Carver 1992). Among these disadvantaged groups, even those who receive care often receive less care than is medically recommended (Children's Defense Fund 1991). One recent study reported an association between single motherhood, race, Hispanic ethnicity, and the quality of prenatal care for women (Hansell 1991). Unmarried mothers were less likely than married mothers to be regularly tested for medical problems that complicate pregnancy. In addition, single mothers were not given adequate medical advice regarding salt restricton and the use of diuretics. Hispanic mothers were tested for high blood pressure less often than non-Hispanic white mothers.

One of the most important predictors of successful birth outcome is adequate nutrition for the mother during pregnancy. Mothers who are malnourished during pregnancy are at higher risk of difficult pregnancies and of giving birth to low birth-weight infants (Children's Defense Fund 1991). One indication of adequate maternal nutrition is sufficient weight gain during pregnancy. In 1980, approximately one-third of all pregnant women did not gain as much weight as is medically recommended, and a disproportionate number of these women were poor and unmarried. One indication of the seriousness of this situation among minorities is the fact that 16 percent of black and Hispanic children experience growth retardation traceable to their mother's poor nutritional status. After birth, many poor children continue to be poorly nourished.It has been estimated that as many as 21 percent of all poor children under two years of age suffer from anemia (Children's Defense Fund 1991, Physician Task Force on Hunger in America 1985).

Low birth-weight is one of the most serious short-term as well as long-term threats to children's health. The consequences are tragic, particularly since they are relatively easily avoided given current medical knowledge. Seriously underweight infants often suffer neonatal complications, such as respiratory distress syndrome, hypoglycemia, jaundice, and other metabolic and neurological disorders (Granger 1982). These conditions can have long-term effects on development and health. Both poverty and adolescent motherhood are associated with low birth weight (Broman 1981). One quarter of the infants born to mothers aged fifteen or younger are premature, and, as a consequence, their mortality rates are twice as high as those of infants born to women aged twenty to thirty (Granger 1982, Menken 1972). Even among infants who are heavier, the APGAR scores (a measure of the child's vital status at birth) of the babies of teenage mothers tend to be lower than those of infants born to older mothers (Jones and Placek 1981). Since poverty and early pregnancy tend to occur together, the pregnancies of poor minority teenagers are, by definition, high-risk.

Several studies indicate that adolescent motherhood adversely affects children's later development as well. Field (1981) found that the children of adolescent mothers lag behind the children of older mothers in psychosocial development. When their infants were four months of age, for example, adolescent mothers rated their babies as less responsive and motorically less developed than did older mothers. The infants born to adolescent mothers were less responsive to the mother's attempts to keep them from fussing or crying than were the children of older mothers. Again, since minority group mothers are at elevated risk of both poverty and early pregnancy, their children are at high risk of these adverse outcomes. This risk is clearly demonstrated by a study that found that the children of black adolescent mothers from seriously economically and socially disadvantaged backgrounds were delayed in motor development when compared to the children of mothers in their twenties (Broman 1981). These motor delays were observed again a year later, when the infants of the black adolescent mothers had difficulty walking without support and displayed irregular gaits or posture. The children of many poor adolescent mothers, therefore, begin life with very serious developmental as well as social disadvantages.

One of the major predictors of educational and occupational success later in the life course is the rate of intellectual development in childhood.

The children of poor young mothers are often handicapped in this area as well, since low birth weight frequently results in markedly reduced intellectual functioning (Starfield 1990). The tragedy of the situation is compounded by the fact that even when the damage done by complications at birth might be overcome, poverty reduces the likelihood that a child will receive the help necessary to do so. The data show that there are fewer long-term consequences associated with prematurity for the children of more affluent parents than for the children of the poor (ibid.). Evidently, the enriched social and intellectual environments of the children of middle-class parents allow them to overcome initial intellectual handicaps. The children of poor single mothers begin life facing a true double jeopardy then. They are at elevated risk of low birth weight and its negative health consequences, and their mothers frequently do not have the personal, social, or economic resources to provide them with the remedial help that might compensate for a disadvantaged beginning to life.

Many other risks threaten the health of poor children, including those born to single mothers. The children of the poor are less likely than middle-class children to be fully immunized against diseases such as measles and rubella (Children's Defense Fund 1991). Recent data from Los Angeles County show that between 1985–1987 and 1987–1989 Hispanic preschoolers were at highest risk of measles during both periods (Ewert et al. 1991). Of course, for some diseases there are no effective vaccines. As the AIDS epidemic worsens, it disproportionately victimizes the children of the minority poor. Black and Hispanic children make up approximately one quarter of the population under fifteen but account for over three quarters of pediatric AIDS cases (Children's Defense Fund 1991). Many of these children are born to single mothers. In addition to being inadequately immunized, the children of the poor are more likely to suffer from hearing and vision disorders than children from more affluent families (Children's Defense Fund 1991, Dutton 1985, Starfield 1990). Therefore, the data clearly indicate not only that poor children are more likley than middle-class children to become ill but when they do, they are frequently sicker and suffer more long-term effects (Children's Defense Fund 1987, McCormick 1986).

In the United States lead poisoning remains one of the major environmental threats to children's health. Because they more often live in old, inner-city housing that was constructed before modern building codes were adopted, the children of the poor are frequently exposed to lead from lead-based paint and lead plumbing. Exposure from these and other sources can result in damage to the central nervous system and lead to such neurological problems as hearing loss and poor motor coordination. High lead levels in the blood can also result in impaired blood flow and growth deficits. But it is not just old housing that places poor children at risk. Congested urban environments are often seriously polluted by automobile exhaust that until recently contained high levels of lead. The magnitude of the problem of lead poisoning is best illustrated by estimates that one in six American children is at risk of lead poisoning and nearly half a million pregnant women are exposed to levels of lead that can potentially harm their unborn children (Children's Defense Fund 1991). Once again, since the children of single mothers are overrepresented among the poor, they are at significantly elevated risk of negative health consequences.

These data clearly document the elevated health risks faced by children born to single mothers. In an equitable medical care system, this elevated need should result in an equivalently elevated use of medical care. Yet this is not the case. To be sure, since the introduction of Medicaid, health care use by the poor in general has increased dramatically, but several studies reveal persistent social class and racial differences in visits to the doctor by children. Black and Hispanic children, the children of poorly educated parents, and children from poor families are taken to the doctor less often than more affluent white children with highly educated parents (Colle and Grossman 1978; Tessler 1980; Wilcox-Gok 1985; Wolfe 1980; Worobey, Angel, and Worobey 1988). Since single mothers are disproportionately members of minority groups, poor, and poorly educated, their children are less likely than children in two-parent families to receive the health care they need. The problem of poverty is compounded by family size, since poor families tend to be larger than more affluent families, and children from small families are more likely to be taken to the doctor than those from larger families (Colle and Grossman 1978; Horwitz, Morgenstern, and Berkman 1985; Tessler 1980; Wolfe 1980).

Families with low incomes often lack health insurance and a regular source of medical care, factors that are associated with lower physician use (Cafferata and Kasper 1985, Wolfe 1980). Although many single-parent families qualify for Medicaid, a significant number do not participate in the program, and many are clearly burdened by medical expenses. In one study, for example, investigators found that single-parent families spend almost two-thirds more for health care than two-parent families. These families clearly have less adequate health insurance, and it is likely that even with this added expense, many do without needed medical care.

Low-income families have less access to private practitioners than families with higher incomes and, consequently, more often rely on outpatient clinics, emergency rooms, or health centers for routine care (see Horwitz, Morganstern, and Berkman 1985 for a critical review). At such locations a child is likely to see a new physician who is unfamiliar with his or her case at each visit. Such discontinuous care may be of lower quality than that

received by children in two-parent families (Wolfe
poor fatherless families, therefore, face numerous
health care, and the evidence suggests that there
need for preventive and curative medical care a
less families (Cafferata and Kasper 1985; Caffera
Horwitz, Morgenstern, and Berkman 1985; Worob...,
bey 1988).

Emotional and Behavioral Problems in Childhood

Although childhood is a relatively privileged time of life in terms of physical health, it can be a traumatic time in terms of emotional development. Children and adolescents are engaged in the difficult task of becoming adults at a time of life when they lack the well-defined social statuses and power that those who successfully navigate this part of the life course will later acquire. The uncertainties of youth when combined with the insecurities of poverty or the trauma of a dysfunctional family can result in serious emotional turmoil and impaired social development. Although children are emotionally resilient, those whose emotional and social development is undermined can suffer serious lifelong consequences.

For many years prior to the development of pediatric psychiatry and our current methods for assessing childhood psychopathology, the emotional and behavioral upheavals of childhood and adolescence were considered unfortunate, but nonetheless normal, aspects of development. Moodiness, difficulties in school and the family, and behaviors such as truancy were considered normal growing pains that a child would, in all likelihood, outgrow. Recent research proves this point of view to be quite wrong (Achenbach 1981). Not all children experience serious emotional or behavioral problems, nor, we have come to learn, do those who experience problems in adolescence necessarily overcome their long-term effects. It is increasingly clear that serious adolescent difficulties and family dysfunction can seriously undermine a child's emotional and social development and have long-term negative consequences.

Yet the role of father absence in the development of emotional and behavioral problems in childhood and adolescence is not well understood. Clearly, a well-functioning two-parent family is the ideal family environment for a child, if only because of the financial security that such families typically enjoy. In addition, however, two competent parents can provide the emotional support and moral guidance that ease a child's transition to adulthood. But an ever-growing number of children do not grow up in such families, and many are placed at risk of serious emotional difficulties as a result. In what follows we summarize evidence concerning the impact

...her absence on children's mental health, but first we will summarize ...he recent data on the prevalence of mental illness among children and ...dolescents in the community to determine what sorts of problems children suffer from in general. It is only from this perspective that we can determine whether father absence has any unique effects on the mental health of children.

Several large-scale epidemiological studies that have been carried out in recent years reveal that as many as one in five children experience significant emotional or behavioral problems that have potential long-term consequences (Anderson et al. 1987; Bird et al. 1989; Boyle et al. 1987; Cohen and Brook 1987; Costello et al. 1988; Offord, Boyle, and Racine 1989; Costello 1989). Appendix 5.A summarizes several empirical studies that document the prevalence of mental illness and behavior problems in childhood and adolescence. Because minority group children are often exposed to serious psychological stresses associated with poverty, they are at particularly high risk of emotional and behavioral problems (Schwartz Gould, Wunsch-Hitzig, and Dohrenwend 1981; Zill and Schoenborn 1990). From this relatively hard data, we can conclude that there is a great deal of mental illness, and consequently of unmet need for mental health care services, among children in general and among poor minority group children in particular.

Although we do not have accurate estimates of mental health care use by poor and minority children, data for the general population suggest that most children in need of services never see a mental health professional. As is the case for adults, most children who receive any care at all for mental health problems are seen exclusively by general practitioners, primarily pediatricians (Costello 1986; Costello, Burns, and Costello et al. 1988; Starfield, Hankin, and Steinwachs et al. 1985). We have no idea, of course, what sort of treatment children with mental health problems receive from pediatricians. In all likelihood such treatment is inadequate, and we can safely assume that many children with serious problems would benefit from treatment by a mental health care specialist. It has been estimated that in the United States as few as one in five children with serious emotional problems ever receives treatment from a mental health care specialist (Costello 1986). A study in Canada showed similarly low rates of use of mental health services by children in that country (Offord et al. 1987). These figures dramatically emphasize the fact that most children with mental health problems do not receive professional care. For poor minority group children, among whom rates of psychopathology are high, the use of mental health services is even rarer.

One difficulty inherent in dealing with mental health problems in childhood is that the identification of mental health problems among children is a difficult task, primarily since there is little agreement as to what psychopathology means in childhood. Elane Gutterman, J. B. O'Brien, and J. G. Young (1987) note that "many diagnostic categories for children have a provisional quality, given rudimentary knowledge regarding the prognosis, prevalence, and etiologies of these diagnoses" (625). What these authors argue is that it is simply difficult to differentiate between the normal growing pains that accompany the difficult task of growing up and serious psychopathology.

Luckily, substantial progress in the development of structured diagnostic instruments for the estimate of the prevalence of specific emotional and behavioral problems in the community has been made in recent years (Costello 1989, Rutter 1989, Cantwell 1986). As yet, however, there are no large-scale studies of the role of family structure in the mental health of children in different racial and ethnic groups which use these structured diagnostic instruments. As a consequence, the little that we know of the role of family structure, especially as it interacts with race and Hispanic ethnicity to affect the mental health of children and adolescents, is based primarily on specialized studies that employ symptom checklists of the sort we discussed in chapter 4 (Achenbach 1981; Achenbach and Edelbrock 1978; Rutter and Tuma 1988; Quay and Werry 1986). Although such data do not allow us to make estimates of the prevalence of specific mental health problems in the community, they do provide important information on the role of family structure in childhood psychopathology.

As a consequence, in what follows we rely on parents' reports of emotional and behavioral problems in their children to examine the mental health consequences of father absence. We justify the use of such nonclinical assessments on the grounds that maladaptive behaviors and emotional problems that are not serious enough to qualify as full-fledged clinical entities can still cause serious lifelong problems for a child. Relatively few children suffer from autism, childhood schizophrenia, or other serious mental illnesses, but as the data we summarized above show, a much larger fraction suffer less serious psychopathology. In childhood, psychological problems often manifest themselves as emotional and conduct disorders since these are the primary avenues of self-expression available to children (Rutter 1980). Unfortunately, conflicts with parents, teachers, and other social authorities can have serious long-term consequences. Children whose behavioral and emotional problems interfere with their education and social development are at high risk of delinquency and of the long-term consequences of underachievement. Data on the adult impact of childhood maladjustment, for example, show that although most troubled adolescents grow up to be normal adults, the majority of adults with serious adjustment problems were troubled adolescents (Robins and Rutter 1990).

It is rather surprising just how early in life emotional and behavioral problems manifest themselves. In one study conducted in Rochester, New York, physicians found that among two-year-old children seen for well-baby checkups, a significant number had what their mothers described as behavioral problems (Nader 1975). The mothers rated their children's behavior on several dimensions including aggressive-resistant (disobedient, hits others, shows temper, stubborn, whining), dependent-inhibited (clings to mother, fearful, easily upset, seeks attention, shy), or friendly-outgoing (cheerful, curious, talkative, friendly, likes to be held). In terms of these behavioral dimensions, about 8 percent of toddlers had behavioral or emotional problems (Chamberlin 1975).

In another study, psychiatrists carried out evaluations of preschool age children to assess the number, duration, and severity of psychiatric symptoms the children manifested (Thomas and Chess 1977). By age five, 18 percent of the children in the study group had experienced a behavioral problem that was serious enough to require some form of therapy. Even fairly young children, therefore, can experience emotional and behavioral problems. Although we can assume that some, if not most, will outgrow these problems, others will not, and early difficulties may evolve into more serious problems later in childhood and adolescence. The task that remains for us as researchers is to determine whether father absence increases the occurrence of these emotional and behavioral problems in children.

Among school-aged children, the most frequently reported behavioral problems are those related to school. This is not surprising since education is a child's primary task and since school is a major source of frustration and socialization demands. In the study of children in Rochester, New York, that we just mentioned, the physicians reported that 25 percent of older children had some trouble with school work, were held back a grade, or had been suspended. Minority group status appeared to increase the occurrence of behavioral problems. Black children were almost twice as likely to have school problems as white children.

Although a few studies of this sort suggest that minority group children have more emotional and behavioral problems than majority group children, we have relatively little information on the differential prevalence of behavioral and emotional problems among different racial and ethnic groups. The few studies that do examine the impact of race on behavioral and emotional problems, like the Rochester study, suggest that black and Puerto Rican children experience more behavioral problems than white children (Patterson, Kupersmidt, and Vaden 1990; Canino, Earley, and Rogler 1988). This is hardly surprising in light of the socioeconomic disadvantage and discrimination that blacks and certain Hispanics experience in American society. As we showed in chapter 3, black children are much more likely than white children to live in single-parent homes and to have family incomes below the poverty line.

One major study that examined the impact of race and ethnicity on children's mental health was based on a large sample of children in New York City (Langner, Gersten, and Eisenberg 1974). This study revealed substantial differences among black, Hispanic, and non-Hispanic white children in the number and type of mental health symptoms reported by their parents. Black children were more likely than white children to experience delusions and hallucinations, and they were more likely than white children to have problems with memory, concentration, and speech. Black children were also more likely than white children to be delinquent.

This study revealed some other interesting differences among Hispanic, black, and non-Hispanic white children. Black children, for example, were more violent than Hispanic children but less violent than white children. White children were more likely than black children to feel depressed and to argue with their parents. Hispanic children had more organic developmental problems, including problems with memory and concentration and problems with toilet training, than non-Hispanic white children. Hispanic children were also more likely to suffer from repetitive motor behavior, delayed development, social isolation, dependency, and compulsivity. These data, then, show that many children and adolescents experience significant emotional difficulties, and they provide some evidence that the different economic and social situations in which black, Hispanic, and non-Hispanic white children find themselves influence the type of emotional and behavioral problems they manifest. Again, what remains to be done is to determine how father absence interacts with poverty and minority group status to influence the type and severity of emotional and behavioral problems children experience.

The family is a child's primary sources of physical and emotional support, and any disruption of this support system clearly has serious implications for his or her emotional well-being. Given the high rates of marital disruption among black and Hispanic families, these children are at very high risk of emotional illness. In what follows we summarize what little information is available on the impact of family structure on children's mental health and present the results of some of our own research dealing with the mental health of children in fatherless black, Hispanic, and non-Hispanic white families.

Family Structure and Children's Cognitive Functioning and Mental Health

The few scientifically sound studies that have been carried out are fairly consistent in showing that as we would expect in light of the economic, social, and psychological strains that they are subjected to, children in single-parent families have more emotional problems than children in two-parent families. These studies also show that these emotional problems can have long-term consequences. In a classic study carried out in St. Louis, Missouri, during the mid-1950s, researchers assessed the mental and social health of a sample of five hundred adults who had been seen thirty years earlier in a child guidance clinic.[1] Their mental health status was compared to that of a group of adults who were similar in terms of age, sex, race, social class, and IQ but who as children had not received counseling. Those adults who had grown up in broken homes had more antisocial personality disorders than those from intact homes.[2] In another study of adults who had attempted or actually committed suicide, researchers found that over half of those who had actually killed themselves and nearly two-thirds of those who had attempted suicide came from broken homes (Dorpat, Jackson, and Ripley 1965).

Children who grow up in fatherless families are also more likely to experience milder forms of psychiatric illness than children who grow up with both parents. Marion Caplan and Virginia Douglas (1969) compared depressed children in an outpatient psychiatric clinic in Montreal, Canada, to children on the waiting list who were not depressed and found that regardless of the type of separation (death, divorce, illness, or other reason), children with one parent were more depressed than those with both parents. James Peterson and Nicholas Zill (1986) studied the prevalence of childhood depression among 1,400 children in intact and disrupted families. After several important child and family characteristics were statistically controlled, they found that children living in female-headed families were more depressed than those in two-parent families.

Other researchers in Canada examined 1,800 families with children aged six to twelve to determine the extent of psychiatric disturbances among children in two-parent and one-parent households. They found that children who were living with only one parent were almost twice as likely as children living with both parents to have a psychiatric problem such as conduct disorder, attention deficit disorder with hyperactivity, or some other emotional disorder (Blum, Boyle, and Offord 1988). One interesting finding in this study, however, was that children who were living in conflict-ridden intact families were as depressed as children in disrupted families. Clearly, it is the emotional climate of the family that influences children's mental health (Peterson and Zill 1986).

In a classic two-year study conducted over twenty-five years ago at the University of Chicago Social Psychiatry Laboratory, researchers found serious social maladjustment among children who grew up in fatherless families.[3] The researchers were interested in how children felt about themselves and how teachers perceived the children's adjustment at school. The study revealed that children in fatherless families expressed high levels of psychological distress and were less socially adaptable than children in two-parent households. The children in fatherless families also experienced more psychological and emotional problems such as sadness, tension, and nervousness than children living with both parents. Moreover, many of the children in fatherless families manifested problem behaviors throughout the two-year period of the study, again suggesting that father absence has long-term mental health consequences.

These same patterns have been documented by several other researchers (e.g., Webster-Stratton 1989). Typically, children in fatherless families are more likely than children in intact families to experience depression and feelings of anxiety and to express hostility toward adults (Guidubaldi and Cleminshaw 1985, Koch 1961). These children's teachers report that they have more serious behavioral problems than children from two-parent households (Patterson, Kupersmidt, and Vaden 1990). These findings suggest, then, that children who grow up in single-parent households often receive less direction, supervision, and discipline than children in two-parent households and are therefore more likely to get into trouble and to suffer from low self-esteem.

In addition to playing an important role in a child's emotional and behavioral development, the literature clearly indicates that fathers also play an important role in young women's gender identity, personality development, and sexual adjustment (Fleck et al. 1980). Adolescent females whose fathers die often have trouble forming relationships with men when they reach adulthood, and girls whose parents divorce are more sexually promiscuous, precocious, and inappropriately assertive in their style of interactions with men than girls whose parents remain together (Hetherington 1972, Hetherington and Deur 1972).

As we noted earlier, emotional problems in childhood often manifest themselves as poor school performance. Several researchers have found that father absence reduces young children's school readiness. Patrick Fowler and Herbert Richards (1978) assessed the educational preparedness and academic achievement in a sample of black kindergartners from father-absent lower-class families. This study revealed that children from father-absent families were less advanced in reading, mathematics, and language arts when they entered kindergarten than children from intact families. Children born to teenage mothers, who are often unmarried, also do poorly in school, more frequently engage in delinquent behavior, and have higher dropout rates than the children of older mothers (Furstenberg 1976; Furstenberg, Brooks-Gunn, and Morgan 1987). Children in fatherless families have more learning problems, often have shorter attention spans, and are less able to act maturely in the classroom than children who live with both parents (Kellam, Ensminger, and Turner 1977).

As adolescents, the children of young mothers continue to experience difficulties in school (Furstenberg 1976). They run away from home, are adjudged delinquent, and are suspended from school more often than children born to older mothers (Brooks-Gunn and Furstenberg 1985). One of the reasons for this is that children from single-parent households are more susceptible to peer pressure to engage in deviant activities, such as vandalism, cheating on exams, and stealing, than children from intact families (Steinberg 1987). Once again, these data indicate that single mothers are often unable to provide the supervision, guidance, and discipline that adolescents need.

The effects of father absence early in life can apparently last throughout a child's school years. Brian Sutton-Smith, B. G. Rosenberg, and Frank Landy (1968) examined the effects of father absence during childhood on the intellectual abilities of college students enrolled in a psychology course. These researchers used the American College Entrance Examination (ACEE) test scores as an outcome measure. The father-absent sample had lower scores on both the quantitative and linguistic components of the examination. The effect of father absence was most dramatic for those students whose fathers were absent during both early and middle childhood.

Another researcher obtained similar results in a comparison of the cognitive performance of ninety-six college students from father-absent, stepfather, and intact families enrolled in an introductory psychology course (Chapman 1977). The students from nonintact families had lower Scholastic Aptitude Test (SAT) scores than children in two-parent households, and boys who were living with stepfathers had lower scores than boys living with their biological fathers. Although the exact mechanisms by which father absence exerts this effect are not clear, we can assume that the early deficits in school performance documented by the research we summarized earlier place young adults from fatherless families at a disadvantage throughout their educational careers. Since education is closely tied to occupational attainment, we can assume that for many children, father absence has serious lifelong effects.

The Mental Health Consequences of Divorce

One aspect of the phenomenon of father absence that has received a great deal of attention in recent years is the mental health consequences of divorce for children. The motivation for this research has clearly been the soaring divorce rate and the growing number of women who find themselves and their children having to deal with the economic, social, and psychological disruptions of marital dissolution. Of course, many of the investigators carrying out this research are themselves divorced, and it is clear that personal experience can serve as a major impetus to research. Whatever the motivations for this research, however, the findings of studies employing several different methodologies clearly show that the conflict and disruption of family life that precedes and accompanies divorce seriously affects children emotionally and often leads to serious behavioral problems (Hetherington 1989). Their parents' separation is usually preceded by a period of marital conflict that can be quite disturbing to children, and families that eventually disintegrate have often been dysfunctional from the start.

The negative mental health consequences of divorce have been documented by numerous researchers. E. Mavis Hetherington and her colleagues, for example, have conducted several studies that show that children whose parents divorce experience numerous emotional and conduct disorders immediately after the separation.[4] These children express feelings of anger, resentment, anxiety, insecurity, unhappiness, loneliness, and depression. These feelings persist, and even long after the divorce many children experience behavioral problems such as aggression, resistance to authority, and acting out (Hetherington, Cox, and Cox 1979, 1985; Hetherington 1989).

It is impossible, however, to attribute these negative outcomes solely to the divorce itself. They may, in fact, result from the family conflict that led to the divorce. There is evidence that children whose parents eventually divorce often exhibit problems long before the final breakup. One study, for example, conducted by psychologists at the University of California, Berkeley, found that for boys the family stress preceding divorce was associated with high rates of impulsiveness, restlessness, agressiveness, and stubbornness (Block, Block, and Gjerde 1986). In a carefully conducted study that employed two longitudinal data sets from Great Britain and the United States, researchers found that many of the adjustment problems that children experience after divorce were present prior to the divorce itself (Cherlin et al. 1991). Despite this evidence, however, we must point out that in addition to the emotional turmoil it entails, the divorce deprives a child of the emotional support and the role model that a father might provide and may, therefore, have subtle longer-term effects.

Clearly, many more studies will be needed before we begin to understand what effects different forms of father absence have on the emotional and social adjustment of children. Although almost all children who experience family disruption suffer some negative short-term emotional consequences, this magnitude varies greatly depending on the family's postdivorce situation. The departure of an abusive father can result in a less conflict-ridden home in which the children are better off, and if the family is able to maintain an adequate income, either through the mother's earnings or as the result of child support from the ex-husband, the children may be able to rebound from the emotional trauma of the divorce, especially if the father continues to interact with his children on a regular basis. However, if the problems that were part of the family's disruption persist, or if, as happens all too frequently, the children are abandoned by their father and the family experiences serious economic hardship, the children may suffer serious long-term physical and mental health consequences.

There is ample evidence that family disruption has long-term effects on children (Block, Block, and Gjerde 1986; Cherlin et al. 1991; Peterson and Zill 1986). In one study, adults whose parents had divorced or separated when they were children had higher rates of personality disorders than adults whose parents had died or had been institutionalized (Robins 1966). Judith Wallerstein and her colleagues have chronicled the long-term adjustment of children in the aftermath of divorce (Wallerstein and Kelly 1980). This research is based on in-depth interviews with 131 children and adolescents whose parents had divorced. The children were interviewed immediately after the divorce and then again several times over the next fifteen years. The interviews revealed that most of the children experienced serious emotional trauma at the time of the divorce and that more than one-third of them had clinical symptoms of depression and had problems even after five years.[5] Most of the children, however, adjusted adequately and had few long-term problems.

Wallerstein's research shows that the age of a child when the divorce occurs is an important factor in determining its long-term impact. After the divorce, preschool-age children initially have more fears than older children, but they are also more adaptable and rebounded more quickly than older children. It appears, then, that the timing of the divorce is an important factor in determining how it affects a child's health. Unfortunately, since Wallerstein's study did not include a control group of children whose parents had not divorced, it is impossible to tell whether these children's problems were substantially different from those of children from intact homes.

Clearly, divorce can have negative consequences for children. Unfortunately, studies of the impact of divorce on children's mental health tell us little about the consequences of fatherlessness for children who never have a father figure in the home. Again, in most studies of the impact of divorce on children's mental health, the effects of the emotional upheaval surrounding the disruption are confounded with the effects of the father absence that follows divorce. It is simply impossible to determine from these studies the independent effects of divorce and family structure. Findings from studies of the children of divorce, therefore, cannot be generalized to the children of never-married mothers; there are simply too many differences between these types of families. For example, for the children of divorced parents, the loss of the father's income can lead to poverty. This change in status, in conjunction with the emotional upheaval preceding the divorce, may contribute significantly to the emotional trauma they experience.

Families in which the father has never been present are often chronically poor, and it may be this poverty, rather than a rapid change in family structure or income, that accounts for any negative health consequences. Never-married mothers tend to be young and poor, and they are often ill-equipped to raise their children in an optimal manner. It is hard enough for an educated middle-class mother to deal with the burdens of raising a child alone. For a young woman with little education, few job skills, and no family support, the task can be truly daunting. The necessity of being both mother and father to her children while attempting to maintain a household beset by the disruptive forces of poverty can be an almost hopelessly difficult task.

We should note that a few studies find that father absence has no effect on children's mental health. In fact, in one study, adults who responded "No" to the question, "Did you live together with both your real parents up to the time you were 16 years old?" were less likely to have poor mental health than adults who grew up in intact families (Langner 1963).[6] In another study, researchers found no enduring effects of recent or earlier divorce on the self-esteem of a sample of adolescents (Mechanic and Hansell 1989).[7] Others researchers have reported similar nonfindings (Hanson 1986, Robertson and Simons 1989). Most of the studies, though, suffer from serious methodological limitations, including small samples, a reliance on retrospective data that is subject to serious recall error, and ambiguous measures of mental health. In our assessment, the preponderance of evidence clearly demonstrates that divorce has both short- and long-term negative mental health consequences for a large fraction of children.

However, determining the exact impact of father absence and divorce on the mental health of children is difficult as neither father absence nor divorce are simple situations. Families that eventually disintegrate were probably never warm and conflict-free. Growing up in a family headed by a poor never-married mother, who is herself often little more than a child, can easily cause feelings of insecurity. As we have suggested, father absence is associated with many other factors that may account for its negative mental health consequences. As yet, we can only guess about what these other factors might be or how they might work. Let us now turn to some of our recent findings concerning the impact of father absence on children's health.

Household Structure, Minority Group Status, and Health Care Utilization

In this section we present some original research in which we compare the mental and physical health of children in two-parent and female-headed families using three large, nationally representative samples: (1) the 1988 Child Health Supplement to the National Health Interview Survey (NHIS-CHS); (2) the 1984–1986 Hispanic Health and Nutrition Examination Survey (HHANES); and (3) the 1988 merged mother-child file from the National Longitudinal Survey of Youth (NLSY). We will briefly discuss each of these data sets when we present our findings.

We first examine patterns of illness from the 1988 NHIS-CHS, which contains 17,110 children six months to seventeen years of age (Dawson 1991). In this study interviews were conducted with mothers or with some other adult household member concerning the child's health, behavioral problems, medical care use, and sociodemographic background. Because this sample is large, it allows us to compare the mental health of black, Hispanic, and non-Hispanic white children in female-headed and intact families.

Table 5.1 presents information on behavioral and mental disorders and medical care use for non-Hispanic white, black, Mexican-American, and Puerto Rican children in two-parent and fatherless families. The information is presented separately for young children six months to eleven years old and for adolescents twelve to seventeen years old. This table reveals large differences between the two types of families in the mental health of both young and older children. In addition, it reveals various racial and ethnic differences. For example, regardless of race or ethnicity, a larger fraction of the single mothers of young children (top panel of table 5.1) report that their children need help for emotional problems than mothers in intact families. In addition, more single mothers than married mothers report that their children display behavioral problems, and a larger fraction of non-Hispanic white children in fatherless families have seen a mental health professional.

Table 5.1. Mental Health and Medical Care Utilization of Children in Two-Parent and Female-Headed Families by Race and Hispanic Ethnicity

	Non-Hispanic White		Black		Puerto Rican		Mexican-American		Other Hispanic	
	Two-Parent	Female-Headed	Two-Parent	Female-Headed	Two-Parent	Female-Headed	Two-Parent	Female-Headed	Two-Parent	Female-Headed
				CHILDREN 6 MONTHS–11 YEARS						
Ever Had Emotional Problems[a]	3.4	9.6**	0.9	3.4**	0.9	5.1	2.6	7.2*	1.7	18.0*
Often Experience at Least One Behavioral Problem[b]	28.5	36.7**	34.8	40.7*	41.0	42.6	35.8	44.8	31.8	51.8*
Ever Seen Psychotherapist[a]	3.3	9.2**	2.4	3.2	5.2	3.6	2.5	4.4	4.8	4.5
Past 12 Months Doctor Visit	84.5	81.7*	76.2	75.4	82.4	84.1	69.9	82.0	84.2	86.8
N (unwght)	(5,904)	(1,066)	(699)	(942)	(68)	(61)	(440)	(125)	(209)	(72)
				ADOLESCENTS 12–17 YEARS						
Ever Had Emotional Problems	7.1	14.6**	5.4	8.8	4.8	3.7	8.4	4.1	9.2	9.2
Often Experience at Least One Behavioral Problem	29.0	38.4**	29.5	39.4*	33.0	27.5	34.9	33.1	33.2	51.1
Ever Seen Psychotherapist	8.9	18.1**	4.7	7.5	7.4	4.8	2.2	4.7	4.4	22.1**
Past 12 Months Doctor Visit	75.2	78.7	62.3	63.6	68.2	85.3	55.0	63.3	70.0	74.0
N (unwght)	(3,262)	(664)	(431)	(531)	(29)	(35)	(198)	(62)	(97)	(55)

[a]Among children 3 years and older.
[b]Among children 5 years and older.
*Two-parent family is statistically different from female-headed family, p ≤ .05.
**Two-parent family is statistically different from female-headed family, p ≤ .01.

107

Despite the fact that black and Hispanic children in single-parent families have a greater number of serious emotional and behavioral problems than children in two-parent households, they are less likely than non-Hispanic white children in female-headed families to receive mental health care. It appears, then, that the children of single minority mothers need far more services than they are actually receiving. Although the children of single minority mothers are not receiving the mental health care they need, they see a physician as often as the children of married mothers. Clearly, Medicaid has been successful in providing the children of the poor and of single mothers access to physical health care. What remains a challenge for health care policy in the United States is a means for providing mental health care to children with serious emotional and behavioral disturbances (Zill 1988, Dawson 1990).

The second panel of table 5.1 provides information for adolescents. As was the case for young children, there are differences in emotional problems, behavioral problems, and mental health care use between adolescents in two-parent and single-parent families. Because they are older and have more opportunity to manifest behavioral problems, the rates for the adolescents are higher than those for younger children. Unfortunately, the number of Hispanic adolescents is small, and few of the differences between family types are statistically significant. Once again, though, as among younger children, a large fraction of black adolescents have behavioral problems and are much less likely than non-Hispanic white adolescents to have seen a mental health professional.

One intriguing aspect of this table is that although there are differences in the various measures between female-headed and two-parent Hispanic families, they are generally less dramatic than those between female-headed and two-parent non-Hispanic white families. For example, for Puerto Ricans, there are few differences between family types. Our suspicion is that because Puerto Ricans are likely to be poor regardless of family status, poverty outweighs the marital status of the family head in determining whether the children have behavioral and emotional problems. To a large extent, this is also true for blacks, but because of the large sample size, the differences between female-headed and two-parent black families are more often statistically significant.

Since, as we hypothesized earlier, we suspect that the negative effects of single motherhood are due less to the simple fact of father absence and more to the poverty and stresses that accompany single motherhood, we statistically control for a number of economic, demographic, and cultural factors in multivariate models predicting each of the health outcomes presented in table 5.1. These results are presented in Appendix 5.B. We will not discuss these results in detail but will only note that when all the control variables are entered into the model, single motherhood is only significantly associated with emotional problems but not visits to a mental health care professional, behavior problems, or visits to a doctor for physical problems. It appears, then, that other factors besides single motherhood itself are largely responsible for the problems that children in mother-only households experience.

Table 5.2 presents data on specific types of emotional disturbances manifested by children between the ages of five and eleven in female-headed and two-parent families. Table 5.3 presents the same data for adolescents aged twelve to seventeen. Each table presents seven problem areas that were identified in a factor analysis of specific behaviors and emotional problems that were part of the 1988 NHIS-CHS. The specific items and the factor loadings for these scales are presented in Appendix 5.C.

Table 5.2 shows that among young children, those in female-headed households experience more oppositional-defiant behavior, separation anxiety, and anxiety disorders. Once again, although the patterns hold generally for all racial groups, there are some differences, as shown in table 5.3. These data show that among adolescents, there are significant differences between female-headed and two-parent families. Adolescents in female-headed families manifest more anxiety, oppositional-defiant behavior, depressed mood, and attention deficits than adolescents in two-parent households. Unfortunately, our small sample of Hispanics once again keeps us from being able to make definitive statements concerning these groups. These data, however, are among the best that we have concerning the emotional health of children in different family types.

The data are fairly clear in showing that young children and adolescents in mother-only families have more behavioral and emotional problems than those in two-parent families. As we noted earlier, there is very little information on the impact of father absence on children's physical health primarily because of a lack of appropriate data. In addition, differences in physical health among children in different living arrangements are difficult to detect since in the United States, as in the developed world generally, even poor children are basically healthy, and any negative effects of father absence on physical health are likely to be subtle. Such subtle effects are unlikely to be detected using the relatively crude physical health measures that most community studies employ. Luckily, there is one special set of data that allows us to examine the impact of a mother's marital status on her child's health. These data are unique because they are based on an interview with the mother and include a physical examination of two large samples of children.

These surveys are part of the National Health and Nutrition Examination Survey series carried out by the National Center for Health Statistics

Table 5.2. Frequent Behavioral Problems of Children in Two-Parent and Female-Headed Families by Race and Hispanic Ethnicity (in Weighted Percentages)

	Non-Hispanic White		Black		CHILDREN 5–11 YEARS Puerto Rican		Mexican-American		Other Hispanic	
	Two-Parent	Female-Headed	Two-Parent	Female-Headed	Two-Parent	Female-Headed	Two-Parent	Female-Headed	Two-Parent	Female-Headed
Oppositional Defiant	15.8	22.7***	16.0	23.7***	16.5	19.0	19.9	24.0	15.5	31.8***
Separation Anxiety	7.4	13.6***	14.9	20.7**	23.5	5.5**	13.5	20.0	10.2	23.4**
Conduct Problems	1.2	4.1***	2.1	3.4	0.0	7.1	1.9	5.6	1.7	8.0**
Depressed Mood	3.4	6.7***	2.3	6.0**	6.8	5.4	3.9	8.6	0.8	13.1***
Attention Problems	8.8	11.5	12.8	11.5	10.8	8.8	11.0	18.1**	11.4	22.2**
Anxiety Disorder	11.3	16.1***	13.1	17.6**	21.9	9.4	18.3	24.0	16.3	22.2
Antisocial Behavior	2.2	3.7**	3.0	4.5	3.7	2.4	4.8	15.2**	0.0	14.4***
N (unwght)	(3,439)	(670)	(445)	(593)	(42)	(35)	(263)	(74)	(112)	(41)

Source: 1988 National Health Interview Survey–Child Health Supplement (CHS).

**p ≤ .05.
***p ≤ .01.

Table 5.3. Frequent Behavioral Problems of Adolescents in Two-Parent and Female-Headed Families by Race and Hispanic Ethnicity (in Weighted Percentages)

ADOLESCENTS 12–17 YEARS

	Non-Hispanic White		Black		Puerto Rican		Mexican-American		Other Hispanic	
	Two-Parent	Female-Headed	Two-Parent	Female-Headed	Two-Parent	Female-Headed	Two-Parent	Female-Headed	Two-Parent	Female-Headed
Anxiety	13.7	19.8***	14.9	23.5*	12.9	8.9	19.9	19.8	14.8	37.0***
Oppositional Defiant	16.5	23.4***	16.7	23.5*	23.7	15.3	23.0	26.0	18.0	33.4
Socialized Aggression	4.4	5.6**	7.6	8.9	5.0	2.5	5.6	7.6	11.1	24.8*
Peer Problems	1.7	3.7***	1.1	3.2**	0.0	0.0	4.6	0.0*	7.1	10.1
Depressed Mood	8.9	13.5***	9.3	13.2*	14.6	17.8	8.9	8.1	11.4	20.6**
Attention Deficit	8.9	14.8***	10.0	18.0*	22.2	8.2	13.6	14.2	9.2	29.4***
Nervousness	7.1	9.0	5.6	10.3	16.0	2.9*	9.4	3.3	13.1	18.2
N (unwght)	(3,271)	(665)	(432)	(535)	(29)	(36)	(198)	(62)	(95)	(55)

Source: 1988 National Health Interview Survey–Child Health Supplement (CHS).

*p ≤ .10.
**p ≤ .05.
***p ≤ .01.

(NCHS 1985: 131). Three surveys in this series have been conducted since the early 1970s. Here we employ the two most recent surveys, the National Health and Nutrition Examination Survey II (NHANES-II) conducted between 1976 and 1980 and the Hispanic Health and Nutrition Examination Survey, carried out between 1984 and 1986. The first of these two surveys consists of a representative national sample from which we draw a subsample of 5,995 black and non-Hispanic white children between the ages of six months and eleven years.

The second survey was carried out only among Hispanics in five southwestern states (Arizona, California, Colorado, New Mexico, and Texas), in the New York—New Jersey area, and in Miami, Florida. From this survey we draw a sample of 3,281 Mexican-American, Puerto Rican, and Cuban-American children aged six months to eleven years. Both the NHANES-II and the HHANES consist of a household questionnaire, a medical history designed to determine the presence of various chronic and acute conditions, and a physical examination that includes physiological measurements, blood and urine tests, and specific diagnoses of health problems recorded in terms of the International Classification of Disease (ICD) revision nine categories.

Table 5.4 presents information on the physical health of black, Mexican-American, Cuban-American, Puerto Rican, and non-Hispanic white children in two-parent and female-headed households. Since much of our prior work indicates that the language in which a questionnaire is administered has a large effect on parents' reports of their children's health, information for the three Hispanic groups is presented separately for those who were interviewed in English and those who were interviewed in Spanish (Angel and Worobey 1988*b*). This table reveals some complex interactions among race, ethnicity, and family structure in their impact on children's physical health.

Children in female-headed households have consistently poorer health than children in two-parent households, and a larger fraction of children in female-headed households have been hospitalized. For example, single mothers are significantly less likely to report their children's health as excellent than married mothers, tending instead to report more good and fair health. Single mothers also report that their children have more chronic physical health conditions.[8]

These data reveal some intriguing racial and ethnic differences in health status. Spanish-speaking Hispanic mothers report low rates of excellent and very good health and much higher rates of good, fair, and poor health, regardless of their marital status. Culture, then, at least measured in terms of language use, clearly influences a mother's report of her child's health (Angel and Worobey 1988*b*). These rather high rates of good, fair,

Table 5.4. Physical Health Characteristics of Children under 12 Years Old in Two-Parent and Female-Headed Households

| | Non-Hispanic | | | | Mexican-American | | | | Cuban-American | | | | Puerto Rican | | | |
| | White | | Black | | English Interview | | Spanish Interview | | English Interview | | Spanish Interview | | English Interview | | Spanish Interview | |
	Two-Parent	Female-Headed	Two-Parent	Female-Headed	Two-Parent	Female-Headed	Two-Parent	Female-Headed	Two-Parent	Female-Headed	Two-Parent	Female-Headed	Two-Parent	Female-Headed	Two-Parent	Female-Headed
Ever Had Asthma	5.6	5.9**	7.6	9.3	4.5	5.2	3.4	4.6	9.3	—	10.2	10.5	16.1	20.2	16.3	29.4**
Chronic Conditions	22.7	26.2**	18.4	20.7	18.5	23.2	14.5	15.9	23.3	—	24.4	23.1	30.1	30.1	23.4	39.1**
ICD Diagnosis	15.9	15.3	24.5	23.0	3.4	4.2	2.4	1.6	9.8	—	1.5	0.0	1.3	6.9	4.5	7.5
Self-Assessed Health:																
Excellent	59.1	46.1**	42.7	30.8**	41.4	31.1**	18.8	14.5	51.2	—	52.0	38.5	43.4	36.7**	33.7	20.2*
Very Good	25.3	28.0	26.0	27.8	25.2	31.7	15.4	11.3	20.9	—	15.3	14.7	21.7	12.3	20.4	19.0
Good	12.6	21.1	26.1	32.2	26.1	25.7	41.3	43.0	23.3	—	28.3	42.7	21.7	34.7	23.8	30.5
Fair	2.9	3.9	5.0	8.9	6.5	10.6	23.4	28.1	4.7	—	4.0	4.2	12.6	11.7	22.1	28.0
Poor	0.2	0.9	0.3	0.3	0.8	0.9	1.1	3.1	0.0	—	0.6	0.0	0.7	4.7	0.0	2.3
Ever Hospitalized	31.9	40.6**	31.6	36.2*	22.9	31.2*	17.2	17.5	32.6	—	28.3	36.4	32.2	45.5*	37.2	38.0
N (unwght)	(4,577)	(544)	(444)	(406)	(1,157)	(231)	(840)	(128)	(43)	—	(177)	(31)	(144)	(160)	(168)	(196)

Source: 1984–1986 Hispanic Health and Nutrition Examination Survey (HHANES) and 1976–1980 National Health and Nutrition Examination Survey-II (NHANES2).

*p ≤ .05.
**p ≤ .01.

113

and poor health are remarkable in light of the generally low levels of illness during childhood (Parmelee 1986).

One very intriguing finding is that although there are large differences between the various groups in mothers' assessments of their children's health, there are no significant differences in the proportion of children in single-parent and two-parent households with at least one diagnosis. In fact, doctors detected slightly more disease among non-Hispanic white and black children in two-parent households than in father-absent households. We must note that the much higher rate of diagnoses among non-Hispanic white and black children are, to an unknown degree, the result of the much more liberal diagnostic criteria used in the HANES-II. In the HANES-II acute conditions such as minor infections were recorded, but in the HHANES these were ignored. The only meaningful comparisons on this variable, then, are between female-headed and two-parent households within each racial and ethnic group.

These data suggest that single motherhood may have less of an effect on the child's actual health status and more of an impact on the mother's perceptions of it. It is, of course, possible that the mother is correct and that the doctor is not. The mother, after all, sees the child functioning in his or her family and social environment, and because she is a well informed observer, her assessment may be a better reflection of the child's overall physical and emotional well-being than that of the doctor who sees the child only briefly. Even if this is the case, though, it is clear that father absence does not cause serious physical health problems. These data appear to confirm our earlier speculation that since in the United States the physical health care needs of children are at least minimally met, father absence manifests itself more in terms of emotional and behavioral problems than as physical illness.

We employ one more national data set to assess the impact of a mother's marital history on her child's cognitive, socioemotional, and physiological development. The merged 1986–1988 child-mother file of the NLSY is a data set that contains over 7,000 black, Hispanic, and non-Hispanic children who were born to half of the original sample of 6,000 women who participated in the first survey of the study in 1979. The sample represents a cross section of American children in 1988. It captures approximately 60 percent of the mother's eventual reproductive experience. These data include considerable information pertaining to the child's family background, family employment, family structure, household composition, and prenatal and postnatal health care. We examine these variables in relation to the battery of age-appropriate tests that were administered to measure the child's intellectual and socioemotional development.

Table 5.5 presents five models that predict important aspects of the

Table 5.5. Determinants of Children's Development[a]

	Behavior Problems: TSS	Knowledge of Body Parts	PIAT Math: TSS	PIAT Reading: TSS	PIAT Comprehension: TSS
Intercept	95.84**	49.82**	104.96**	108.90**	117.23**
Age of Mother at Birth of Child	.12	.34	.13	.24	.38**
Hispanic	-1.77*	-14.51**	-4.10**	-2.63**	-1.92*
Black	-1.41*	-12.18**	-5.43**	-2.92**	-3.23**
Less than High School	3.28**	-10.82*	-6.20**	-7.15**	-4.24**
High School	3.21**	-5.93**	-3.47**	-3.95**	-2.86**
Unmarried	1.66*	-2.41	-.32	-.10	-.04
Unemployed	.28	.78	-1.46**	-1.17*	-1.28*
Number of Times Divorced	.82	2.42	.21	.70	.20
Income < $10,000	4.00**	-7.55*	-4.29**	-4.25**	-4.36**
Income $10,000–$24,999	1.78**	-7.00**	-2.94**	-2.72**	-2.87**
Missing Income	2.18**	-3.02	-2.55**	-2.87**	-2.92**
Number of HH Members Age 0–2	.86	-7.05**	-.51	-.57	-.34
Number of HH Members Age 3–5	.50	-3.6*	-1.50**	-.80*	.01
Number of HH Members Age 6–11	.08	-2.65*	-.73**	-1.54**	-2.16**
Number of HH Members Age 12–17	-.16	1.41	-2.15**	-2.87**	-1.40**
Rural	-.95	2.36	-1.02	-.94	-.98
Age of Child	.06**	.52**	.01	.00	-.11**
Adjusted R²	.04	.16	.13	.12	.21
Sample Size	(3,398)	(918)	(3,026)	(3,007)	(2,313)

Source: NLSY merged child-mother data.

*p < .05.

**p < .01.

[a]For the dependent variables, a higher score indicates (1) more behavioral problems; (2) a greater knowledge of body parts; (3) greater math skill; (4) greater reading ability; and (5) greater reading comprehension.

child's cognitive and emotional development: the behavioral problem index (BPI); the body parts recognition scale (BPRS); and three subtests of the Peabody Individual Achievement Test (PIAT), including mathematics, reading, and comprehension modules. Once again, the BPI includes questions pertaining to the frequency and type of problem behaviors that a child has demonstrated in the last three months in a variety of contexts, including school, the family, and the larger community. On this scale a child received a score of one if the parent reports the behavior to occur sometimes or often; otherwise, they receive a score of zero. The BPRS scale was developed by Jerome Kagan to measure infants' and toddlers' (1-through 3-year-olds) verbal and intellectual development (Baker and Mott 1989). Scores on this scale range from zero to ten. Finally, the PIAT measures mathematical and reading achievement and comprehension for children aged five and over (Baker and Mott 1989). These models reveal that even after sociodemographic and economic factors are statistically controlled, the children of unmarried mothers experience a greater frequency of behavioral problems than children in two-parent families. Again, being unmarried has no statistically significant impact in any of the other equations once other factors are controlled.

Since these data provide information on the mother's marital history, we can ask whether the number of times she has been divorced affects her child's cognitive and emotional development. These data indicate that this has no statistically significant impact on any of the outcomes. We should note that compared to children in families with incomes over $25,000 per year (the reference category that is omitted from the equations), children from families with incomes below $10,000 have many more behavior problems and are seriously cognitively disadvantaged. The income effects appear to be progressive since children from families with incomes between $10,000 and $25,000 do less well on these outcome measures than children from the richer families. In addition, larger family size is associated with poorer performance on many of the cognitive measures. Even after these factors are controlled, however, black and Hispanic children manifest more behavior problems and do worse on the cognitive assessments than white children.

These models suggest that the behavioral problems and cognitive deficits that children in father-absent households experience are almost entirely due to poverty and minority group status. The story we have told so far in this book is one in which father absence is associated with poverty, early fertility, and more children. The data we have just examined clearly show that poverty, large family size, and minority group status are major culprits in the cognitive disadvantage that some children experience.

The NLSY data allow us to examine other factors that we have shown to be important in determining children's health. Table 5.6 presents regression models that predict the probability of receiving a prenatal visit in the first trimester of pregnancy, the number of postnatal care visits a child has during the first year of infancy, and the probability of low birth weight (less than 2,500 grams). Again, we are interested in the impact of single motherhood on these variables, once we control for other health utilization-related factors. This table reveals that once other factors including income, minority group status, household size, and age of the mother at birth are controlled, unmarried mothers are less likely than married mothers to receive prenatal care during the first trimester.[9] Clearly, then, the low rates of prenatal care among single mothers are due largely to low income levels. The remaining models indicate that the mother's marital status has no statistically significant impact on either the number of postnatal visits a child receives or the probability that the child will be born prematurely. These data

Table 5.6. Determinants of Health Service Use and Child's Birth Weight

	Prenatal Care[a]	Low Birth Weight	Postnatal Care
Intercept	.83**	−2.42**	−5.82*
Age of Mother at Birth of Child	.05**	−.04*	−.07**
Hispanic	−.38**	.09	−.05
Black	−.06	.56**	−.25**
Less than High School	−.32*	.16	−.81**
High School	−.14	.23	−.25**
Unmarried	−.26**	.17	.15
Unemployed	−.06	.09	.09
Number of Times Divorced	.08	.05	−.19**
Income < $10,000	−.24*	.36*	−.56**
Income $10,000–$24,999	−.22*	.29*	−.53**
Missing Income	−.23*	.26	−.42**
Number of HH Members Age 0–2	.01	.12	−.11*
Number of HH Menmbers Age 3–5	−.07	−.08	−.44**
Number of HH Members Age 6–11	−.01	.00	.08*
Number of HH Members Age 12–17	−.01	.21**	−.17**
Rural	−.18*	.02	−.41**
Model Fit	5,610.3	3,499.74	.04
Sample Size	(5,480)	(5,841)	(6,120)

Source: NLSY merged child-mother data.

*p < .05.

**p < .01.

[a]For the first two dependent variables, the reference categories are (1) no prenatal care, and (2) normal birth weight. For the third dependent variable, a higher score indicates a greater number of postnatal visits.

also show that those black mothers who receive postnatal care are less likely to go as frequently for visits compared with non-Hispanic white mothers.

Conclusion

It is clear that the association between family structure and children's health is complex. Yet the preponderance of the evidence suggests that father absence results in fairly serious emotional and behavioral problems in children. Children in single-parent families suffer more psychiatric illness and are at a developmental disadvantage in comparison to children in two-parent families. These children have more problems at school, have less self-control, and engage in more delinquent acts than children who live with both parents. Children in father-absent families are more vulnerable to peer pressure and are more easily led to commit delinquent acts than children with a father present. A mother with no husband may often be a poor disciplinarian, and her children may seek moral authority from others. Often that source is their peers, and children who grow up in the streets are unlikely to be exposed to the best role models. The evidence also indicates that fathers are important for a girl's sexual development and her ability to form relationships with men. Taken as a whole, then, the research we reviewed indicates that father absence places both girls and boys at elevated risk of emotional, educational, and developmental problems.

The evidence for the impact of father absence on the physical health of children is mixed, however. Single mothers rate their children's health as generally poorer than do married mothers, and they report that their children experience more physical conditions and go to the hospital more often than do married mothers. But physicians' examinations reveal no large differences in the overall health levels of children in two-parent and single-parent households. This finding, in conjunction with previous work that we and others have carried out, suggests that a woman's marital status affects her perception of her child's overall well-being. Several researchers have found that a mother's own physical and mental health influences her perception of her child's health. It is very likely, therefore, that for many single mothers, their more negative perceptions of their children's physical health is at least partially a reflection of the increased emotional stress they experience as a single parent.

As we noted earlier, in the United States the low prevalence of serious illness in childhood means that the vast majority of children are healthy, and it is not surprising, therefore, that children in fatherless families have few physical health problems. These children, like most others, are for the most part generally healthy. It is possible that father absence and the poverty that it often entails increases the number of minor acute illnesses that children experience. These illnesses, however, are not associated with long-term handicaps and are, in any case, reported very unreliably in surveys.

In short, then, what we can conclude is that father absence places children at elevated risk of impaired social development, that it hinders their school performance, and, ultimately, that it can limit their chances for optimal social mobility. Clearly, if a child drops out of school, if he or she learns little while there, or if he or she is encumbered by a delinquent past, getting a good job and moving ahead in life may be difficult. Yet we must return to the point that we made in chapter 2, that father absence is only one risk factor for these outcomes. Most children who grow up without their fathers become productive and responsible adults. Perhaps most suffer some subtle psychological deficit, but in terms of overall functioning, they do well. Much more sensitive data than that currently available will be required to assess the subtler effects of father absence.

Finally, the data clearly indicate that the health risks associated with single motherhood are, for the most part, a function of family discord. The largest emotional and behavioral effects that have been identified are for the children of divorced parents. For these children the emotional upheaval and the loss of a parent cause serious problems of adjustment that have clear long-term implications. For the children of never-married mothers, who are typically quite young when they have their first child, any negative health effects are the result of poverty and the disorganized social environment in which they often live.

It is clear, then, that a family without a responsible and loving father does not provide an optimal family environment for children's development. Obviously, a child in a functional single-parent household is better off than one in a strife-ridden two-parent family. Yet we can say with great confidence that father absence is, at least in the United States, a mental health risk factor for children. The data clearly indicate that a healthy two-parent family optimizes both the economic well-being and the physical and mental health of children. Those public policies and programs that both encourage families to stay together and provide them with an adequate level of material well-being provide a high potential payoff in terms of children's health.

Appendix 5.A. Psychopathology in Childhood and Adolescence, Selected Studies

Author	Year	Measure	Percent	Male (%)	Female (%)	White (%)	Black (%)	Area	Age of Child
Krupinski et al.	1967	Diagnoses	—	16	19	—	—	Australia	Adolescent
Bjornsson	1974	Diagnoses	—	21	14	—	—	Iceland	13–14 years
Langner et al.	1974	Diagnoses	—	—	—	8–9	17–20	U.S.A.	6–18 years
Albert and Beck	1975	Diagnoses						Philadelphia	Early adolescent
Severe			2.2						
Mild			33.3						
Chamberlin	1975	Diagnoses	8.2	—	—	—	—	New York	1–4 years
Kellam et al.	1975	Behavior	20	—	—	—	—	Chicago	First Grade
		Diagnoses	4.6–6.9						
Rutter et al.	1975	Behavior						England	10 years
Teacher's Report		Behavior	10.6–19.1	13.8–24.5	7.1–13.2	—	—		
		Diagnoses	12.0–25.4	13.0–18.3	10.8–26.2	—	—		
Achenbach and	1981	Behavior	37	40	36	—	—	Virginia/D.C.	4–11 years
Edelbrock			35	35	37	—	—		12–16 years
Kandel and Davies	1982	Diagnoses	20	—	—	—	—	New York	14–18 years
Offer et al.	1983	Diagnoses	—	17	22	—	—	Chicago	Adolescent
Ostrov et al.	1984	Diagnoses	20	—	—	—	—	Chicago	Adolescent
Offord et al.	1987	Behavior/	18.1	—	—	—	—	Canada	4–16 years
		DMS III	—	19.5	13.5	—	—		4–11 years
			—	18.8	21.8	—	—		12–16 years

Appendix 5.B. Regressions of Children's Mental Health and Medical Care Use on Family Structure, Race, Hispanic Nationality, Comorbidity, and Selected Socioeconomic Characteristics[a]

	Psychiatric Visit	Emotional Problem	Behavior Problem	Doctor Visit
Single Mother	−.80**	.97**	.06**	−.01
Family Size	−.08	.06	.03*	−.06**
Birth Ordinal Position	−.10*	−.09*	−.03**	−.00
Black[b]	−.73**	−.64**	.01	−.05**
Puerto Rican[b]	−.01	−.29	.00	.02**
Mexican-American[b]	−.43	−.17	.01	−.02*
Other Hispanic[b]	−.50	−.08	.01	−.00
Mother's Education	.07**	−.03	−.10**	.02**
Mother Employed	.11	−.12	−.00	−.03**
Age	.13**	.13**	−.01	−.03**
Low Income	−.09	.07	.08**	.01**
Middle Income	.07	.22*	.05**	−.02*
Missing Income	−.34	−.50**	−.06**	−.03*
Health Insurance	−.05	n/a	n/a	.02
Asthma	.17	.36**	.03**	.11**
Food Allergy	.17	.37**	.02*	.05**
Other Respiratory	.28*	.24*	.01	.08**
Headaches	.10	.43**	.07**	.06**
Enuresis	.45**	1.39**	.09**	.00
Pneumonia	.22	.09	.01	.02**
Ear Infection	.24*	.37**	.07**	.09**
Behavioral Problem	.57**	n/a	n/a	n/a
	391.17[c]	620.24[c]	.050[d]	.074[d]
N	(8,579)	(14,638)	(10,220)	(14,566)

[a]Data from the 1988 Child Health Supplement to the National Health Interview Survey (NHIS-CHS).
[b]Reference category = Non-Hispanic white.
[c]Model chi-square.
[d]Adjusted R-square, standardized regression coefficients.
*p ≤ .05.
**p ≤ .01.

Appendix 5.C. Factor Analysis–Varimax Rotation–1988 National
Health Interview Survey, Child Health Supplement, Behavioral
Checklist

CHILDREN 5–11 YEARS (N = 5,187)

Factor 1–Oppositional Defiant

cheats or tells lies	.45
argues too much	.65
is disobedient at home	.67
is stubborn, sullen, or irritable	.61
has a very strong temper and loses it easily	.59

Factor 2–Separation Anxiety

clings to adults	.71
cries too much	.65
demands a lot of attention	.64
is too dependent on others	.68

Factor 3–Conduct Problems

is disobedient at school	.58
has trouble getting along with other children	.66
has trouble getting along with teachers	.72
is not liked by other children	.63

Factor 4–Depressed Mood

feels or complains that no one loves him or her	.52
feels worthless or inferior	.67
is unhappy, sad, or depressed	.67
is withdrawn, does not get involved with others	.45

Factor 5–Attention Problems

has difficulty concentrating, cannot pay attention too long	.75
is easily confused, seems to be in a fog	.66
is impulsive, or acts without thinking	.48

Factor 6–Anxiety Disorder

is rather high-strung, tense, or nervous	.66
is too fearful or anxious	.69
is restless or overly active, cannot sit still	.46

Factor 7–Antisocial Behavior

does not seem to feel sorry after he or she misbehaves	.55
is withdrawn, does not get involved with others	.48
breaks things on purpose	
deliberately destroys his/her or others' things	.63

ADOLESCENTS 12–17 YEARS (N = 5,010)

Factor 1–Nervousness

has sudden changes in mood or feelings	.63
feels or complains that no one loves him or her	.71
is rather high-strung, tense, or nervous	.53
is too fearful or anxious	.48

Factor 2–Oppositional Defiant

argues too much	.55
bullies, or is cruel or mean to others	.61
is disobedient at home	.53

Appendix 5.C. Factor Analysis–Varimax Rotation–1988 National Health Interview Survey, Child Health Supplement, Behavioral Checklist (*continued*)

ADOLESCENTS 12–17 YEARS (N = 5,010)	
does not seem to feel sorry after he/she misbehaves	.69
is sullen, stubborn, or irritable	.53
has a very strong temper and loses it easily	.49
Factor 3–Socialized Aggression	
cheats or tells lies	.48
is disobedient at school	.77
has trouble getting along with teachers	.73
hangs around with kids who get into trouble	.67
Factor 4–Peer Problems	
has trouble getting along with other children	.73
is not liked by other children	.75
feels others are out to get him/her	.49
Factor 5–Depressed Mood	
is unhappy, sad, or depressed	.49
is withdrawn, does not get involved with others	.53
is secretive, keeps things to him/herself	.72
worries too much	.54
Factor 6–Attention Deficit	
is easily confused, seems to be in a fog	.70
has difficulty concentrating, cannot pay attention for long	.75
Factor 7–Anxiety Disorder	
is rather high-strung, tense, or nervous	.46
is restless or overly active, cannot sit still	.74

6

Single Motherhood
Consequences for Women's Health

In this chapter we summarize what is known of the consequences of single motherhood for the physical and mental health of black, Hispanic, and non-Hispanic white women and investigate the sources of any negative health consequences we document. As we showed in chapter 3, single motherhood is a label that includes many different situations, each of which has different implications for the stresses a woman is exposed to. The common element in all of these situations is the absence of a husband and the presence of children. Beyond that similarity, however, single mothers are as different as anyone else. Because of this diversity, single motherhood is only a risk factor for ill health, most likely because of its association with poverty and the strains of unassisted parenthood. We will attempt to determine here which of these secondary aspects associated with single motherhood potentially affect the health of women.

We have seen that father absence has serious consequences for the emotional health of children. Children are particularly vulnerable to the conflicts accompanying divorce, and the evidence clearly shows that the emotional trauma of family dissolution increases their vulnerability to mental illness and social maladjustment even after they become adults. The emotional trauma of divorce has negative consequences for parents as well. One of the most consistent findings in the literature is that depressed children often have depressed parents (Dodge 1990; Fendrich,

Warner, and Weismann 1990; Trad 1987). Although this increased risk of depression for the children of depressed parents may be the result of some genetic vulnerability that both parent and child share (Weissman 1988), it is also likely that for both parents and children, depression is a response to family conflict. Because the family is such a close-knit and emotionally charged unit, the increased economic and emotional strains that often accompany single motherhood can easily lead to lower health levels for adults as well as for children (Belle 1990). In what follows we pull together the various strands of evidence that exist to provide some idea of how the physical and mental health of Hispanic, black, and non-Hispanic white women is affected by single motherhood.

The Transition to Single Motherhood

Marriage is one of the major life transitions of early adulthood, and although we often think of marriage as a single role, it really involves the adoption of several new identities (Cleary and Mechanic 1983, Pearlin 1983, Thoits 1986). For women, marriage brings with it the new roles of wife and, for most, of mother. Even though a couple may remain childless for some time after they are married, eventually the honeymoon ends, and, as parents, both husband and wife must deal with increased responsibilities and demands on their time (Aneshensel, Frerichs, and Clark 1981). A young mother must juggle the roles of confidante to her husband, of care giver to her children, and, for most women today, of wage earner. Conflicts among these various roles can lead to role strain and depression (Cleary and Mechanic 1983; Rosenfield 1989; Roberts and O'Keefe 1981; Kessler and Essex 1982; Gove and Geerken 1977; Pearlin and Johnson 1977; Radloff 1975).

Becoming a single mother is also a major life transition that involves the adoption of a new set of roles and the loss or redefinition of old ones. For a young unmarried woman, motherhood often means entering a stigmatized status that brings with it the economic and emotional burdens of caring for a child alone. Women who have children out of wedlock face society's disapproval as marriage before one has children is still the norm in our culture, even though extramarital fertility is increasingly common. Since for very young women the pregnancy is usually the result of impetuous and thoughtless behavior, it is often proof of the young mother's emotional immaturity and her lack of preparation for the responsibilities of parenthood. A young woman who drops out of school because of pregnancy abandons her role as student and, often, along with it her chances for a normal adolescence. The early exit from the typical roles of adolescence has long-term implications for a young woman's material welfare and often means that she misses the normal emotional and social experiences of young adulthood.

For a woman who becomes single as the result of divorce, there are many changes of a similar but also of a different sort. The divorce involves the loss of the role of wife and the loss of the husband's social network that, almost by definition, increases a woman's social isolation and reduces her social support (Fischer 1982). The divorce may be seen by the woman herself and by others as a failure on her part, and, almost inevitably, a divorced woman's income drops precipitously at the same time that her household and child-rearing burdens increase (Weitzman 1985). In addition, as we show later, the divorce itself has a serious impact on a woman's emotional health.

Whether as the result of an extramarital pregnancy or a divorce or widowhood, however, single motherhood brings with it stresses from several sources that can potentially affect a woman's physical and emotional well-being. The nature and impact of these stresses depend on factors that mediate their impact, including the presence of other adults in the household and the family's income. Once again, these mediating factors are influenced by the route a woman takes to single motherhood. Never-married mothers are typically young and poorly educated, they are often minority group members, and they are poorer on average than divorced mothers. Although divorced mothers are typically older and have higher incomes, they are still usually far from affluent and may experience serious emotional trauma as a result of the divorce itself and the loss of social status it often entails. Since, as we have shown, race and Hispanic ethnicity play an important part in determining the route to single motherhood, they may have important indirect effects on a woman's health.

The specific social and psychological mechanisms through which marital status affects a woman's health have been the object of a great deal of investigation. Over the last twenty years, a large literature dealing with the differential impact of marriage and work on the mental health of men and women has emerged (Cleary and Mechanic 1983; Rosenfield 1989; Roberts and O'Keefe 1981; Kessler and Essex 1982; Gove and Geerken 1977; Gove and Tudor 1973; Nathanson 1980; Pearlin and Johnson 1977; Radloff 1975; Krause and Markides 1985; Newman 1989; Verbrugge 1983; Weissman, Leaf, and Bruce 1987). This literature is far too extensive for us to summarize here, and we will confine our review to a summary of the most consistent findings. Perhaps the most consistent finding reported is that, with very few exceptions, women report higher rates of psychological distress and disorder than men. In addition, the majority of studies indicate that the stress a woman experiences increases as a function of the number of burdens she must bear and that this increased stress often leads to poor mental health. Among married women, the most stressed and unhappy are those who must both work and care for children (Cleary and Mechanic 1983). This is particularly true for women who do not want to work but who do so out of necessity. If, in addition to having to work, a woman is unhappy with other aspects of her life or her relationship with her husband, the impact is compounded and she can suffer serious depression. A short summary of some of the empirical findings concerning the negative mental health aspects of excess burden for women will help place our phenomenon in perspective.

Role Overload and Depression

Like any other organization, the family has certain maintenance tasks that must be carried out in order for it to function. Food must be purchased and prepared; children must be dressed, fed, and supervised; the household must be kept basically clean; and the various family members must be sent about their daily business. Although most people routinize these tasks and take them for granted, running a household requires a great deal of time and effort. Someone in the family, usually the wife, must take responsibility for seeing that these tasks are completed. Although many husbands help with household chores and child care, for the most part, women are responsible for the majority of household tasks even when they work (Voydanoff 1987, Vanek 1974).

Since everyone has a finite time budget (no one can work more than twenty-four hours a day), the more tasks a woman must perform and the more roles she must occupy, the greater the likelihood that she will suffer from what has been termed "role overload" (Pearlin 1983). Role overload refers to a situation in which a woman has more responsibilities than she can deal with and which, consequently, undermines her sense of well-being. Obviously, a woman who must combine the roles of wife, mother, and breadwinner and who finds the combination taxing is at greater risk of role overload than a woman with fewer demands.[1]

There is convincing evidence that such role overload leads to higher rates of depression and diminished life satisfaction (Cleary and Mechanic 1983, Pearlin and Johnson 1977, Rosenfield 1989). Women who feel overburdened, for example, are frequently dissatisfied with their roles as parents (Cleary and Mechanic 1983, Gove and Geerken 1977, Ross and Huber 1985). Responsibility is a part of life that is usually beneficial, but if one has too many responsibilities, it is difficult to devote enough time or energy to any particular one. Clearly, though, it is not simply the fact of having multiple roles or identities that leads to depression. Rather, it is the meaning that these various roles have for a woman and the social and economic context in which they must be carried out that determines their impact on her physical and mental health.

A woman who enjoys her work and who has a happy family life may well be exhilarated by the challenge of multiple role demands and gain a great deal of personal satisfaction in carrying them out.[2] Peggy Thoits very insightfully points out that "one's sense of self as a meaningful, purposeful entity is derived in part from the social roles one enacts (1986: 259)." She shows that occupying several meaningful roles can actually improve mental health rather than harm it. "Identity accumulation," as she calls it, can outweigh the negative aspects of multiple role demands by protecting one from social isolation (Thoits 1983). One's self-respect and sense of being a competent adult, after all, depend on living up to one's responsibilities and carrying out roles that society values.

But roles like mother, wife, or worker do not have a similar meaning for everyone, nor do they make up the same role packages. Motherhood is very different depending on the number and ages of one's children and whether or not one has a husband. Roles are social positions that actually comprise "role sets" with varying demands. The burdensomeness of these demands depends not only on the social context in which they are performed but also on the behavior of others. If a husband helps with household tasks, the burdens placed on a woman are lightened and she experiences less stress than a woman whose husband does not help her. Because single mothers have no husbands, they are at higher risk of role overload than are married mothers since unless they live with their own mothers or with someone else, they have sole responsibility for their own and for their children's care. The concept of role overload, then, is useful in helping us understand when and how single motherhood constitutes a health risk factor. Poor single mothers with several children and no help are at highest risk.

Since young minority group single mothers generally have low levels of education and few job skills, they are unlikely to qualify for the types of jobs that provide many intrinsic rewards. To be sure, single mothers who are able to support themselves and their children no doubt derive satisfaction from the simple fact of being self-sufficient and not dependent on welfare or on someone else. In fact, there are data to prove this. Single mothers who are able to support their children report a greater sense of personal control and self-efficacy than do single mothers who are unable to do so (Downey and Moen 1987). Work and role overload, then, are not synonymous; even low-paid work can provide psychological rewards. Nonetheless, the types of jobs that poorly educated single mothers are qualified for are less likely to provide them with either the economic self-sufficiency or the sense of autonomy that is possible for women with better educations and greater job skills.

It is clear, therefore, that role overload is not an inevitable consequence of single motherhood, nor is it a simple phenomenon. If a woman copes with multiple demands adequately and derives satisfaction from carrying out her various roles successfully, it makes little sense to speak of her as being overloaded. Role overload is subjective, and, as we noted, it implies an inability to cope with tasks that are perceived as burdensome. Only when role demands exceed a woman's material or emotional capacity to deal with them does role overload become a risk factor for physical or mental illness. Although most single mothers are adequate parents and cope well with the absence of a spouse, it is easy to see that they are at increased risk of role overload and its negative health consequence.

It is impossible, therefore, to treat social roles as if they are the same for everyone. Their personal meaning for a woman and their impact on her health depend not only on her personal resilience and psychological makeup but also on cultural and social class factors that determine the expectations that others have of her concerning how she should carry out her roles of wife, mother, and worker. The multiple roles that are forced on poor single mothers are unlikely to be psychologically beneficial, especially since some of those roles, like unwed mother or welfare recipient, are not socially valued and have negative personal connotations.

Unfortunately, with very few exceptions (e.g., Krause and Markides 1985), research on the mental health of women is based on non-Hispanic white samples, and it is impossible to know just how generalizable the findings are to black and Hispanic mothers. This research, like much other research from which universal human characteristics are inferred, is highly ethnocentric. Few of these studies tell us how the combination of multiple role demands, the lack of a spouse, and the increased risk of chronic poverty that often accompanies minority group status affects the mental health of black and Hispanic single mothers. Most of this literature ignores the cultural and social context in which single motherhood is experienced. Yet, the evidence we have presented in previous chapters concerning the impact of race, Hispanic ethnicity, and social class on income, family values, fertility behavior, and subjective well-being leads us to the inevitable conclusion that the assumption that single motherhood has the same mental health consequences for different social groups is probably wrong.

The Importance of a Confidant

As we noted briefly in chapter 4, there is a great deal of evidence that inadequate social support leads to poor health (House, Landis, and Umberson 1988). Unattached and unmarried people experience more mental and physical illness, engage in more maladaptive health behaviors, and, consequently, experience more illnesses and die more often than those with a confidant (Carter and Glick 1976; Glenn and Weaver 1979; Gove 1972, 1973; Kitagawa and Hauser 1973; Umberson 1987). The reasons for this are still a matter of debate. There may be something inherent in having an intimate relationship with someone else that protects a person from ill health, or it may be that healthy people are more likely than unhealthy people to attract a mate. Whatever the reason, though, the risk associated with the lack of a confidant clearly has implications for the health of single mothers.

Most unmarried and widowed women, of course, do not become seriously ill just because they lack a spouse. The absence of a confidant is only one risk factor among many others. In most cases, it is only when the absence of an intimate relationship occurs in conjunction with other predisposing psychological risk factors, such as poverty or having lost a parent in childhood, that it causes depression. In a very interesting study of depression among women in England, George Brown and Tirril Harris (1978) found that women who had lost their mothers before they were twelve years old and who as adults lacked a confidant were more likely to become depressed than women who either had not lost their mothers or had a confidant. Each of these factors greatly enhanced the negative mental health effects of the other.

Serious depression may even be the result of a genetic predisposition that, in conjunction with a traumatic event or chronic stress, leads to depression. As we said before, depression tends to run in families, and having a depressed parent may be a serious predisposing risk factor for children even after they become adults and move away from their depressed parent. When some traumatic life event occurs, or in the presence of some chronic stressor like poverty, these individuals may be the most vulnerable. These findings demonstrate that depression results from a combination of predisposing vulnerabilities, some of which may be biological, and various situational stressors to which single mothers are exposed. It is unlikely that by itself single motherhood causes either physical or mental illness. But for those women who are already at risk of ill health because of other predisposing factors such as having lost a mother in childhood or having a depressed parent, the loss of a spouse and the stresses of single motherhood may be the precipitating factors that finally bring on the depression.

The exact mechanisms through which marriage protects health are poorly understood. In all likelihood, the reasons for the association are quite complex, and social scientists are not very close to identifying them. For our purpose, it is enough to document the fact that inadequate social support is associated with poorer mental and physical health and that women who are not married and who do not have adequate social support from some other source are unhealthier on average than women who have adequate support. Nonetheless, before we proceed we must discuss two major possible explanations for the association between marital status and depression since they have different implications for the association between marital status and health.

Selection or Causation?

To begin to understand the mechanisms through which single motherhood affects the mental health of women, it is necessary to begin with the possibility that women who are highly vulnerable to depression are more likely to become single mothers than women who are less vulnerable to depression. If depressed women are more likely than nondepressed women to get divorced or to become pregnant out of wedlock because of a general lack of control over their lives, poorer mental health among single mothers would largely reflect the fact that many have poorer mental health to begin with. In this case, the poorer metnal health of the mother and her children would not necessarily be amenable to changes in the family's material welfare since it would be the result of innate predispositions. However, if mentally healthy women become depressed only after they become single mothers, we can assume that something about single motherhood itself, such as low income or the burdens of unassisted parenting, actually causes poorer mental health. If this were the case, improvements in the welfare of the family could improve the mental health of the mother and the well-being of her children.

It is very difficult to determine which of these two possibilities is the correct one, primarily because the sort of data that would be necessary are just not available. To be able to eliminate either selection or causation as an explanation for the impact of marital status on health, one would need a large long-term study of women in which their initial mental health is accurately recorded and changes in their subsequent marital status and mental health measured at various points over several years. One could then determine whether the mental health of women who become single mothers was worse initially or whether it deteriorated as the result of becoming a single mother. In the absence of longitudinal data with good mental health measures and adequate samples, researchers have made do with the data that are available. However, because of limitations in these data, the findings must be interpreted cautiously, but they do provide some fairly strong evidence that the stresses and social isolation of single motherhood actually cause decreased psychological well-being. Let us briefly review some of this evidence.

In a study that investigated the impact of single motherhood on a woman's psychological well-being over a one-year period, McLanahan (1985*b*) indirectly tested the selection hypothesis with data from a large representative sample of women. Pooling information for several years and controlling for the women's initial level of subjective well-being, she found that single mothers suffered a significant decline in their subjective well-being over the course of a year. Since the study controlled for the women's initial psychological state, the decline can be attributed to the strains of single motherhood. These data provided little support for a selection explanation of the poorer subjective well-being of single mothers. Unfortunately, the measures of psychological well-being that were employed in this study were fairly crude, and some of the characteristics of the sample make the findings tentative.

In another study, researchers recontacted a sample of predominantly black Chicago mothers ten years after these women had originally been interviewed (Thompson and Ensminger 1989). The purpose of the study was to determine how changes in women's marital status and living arrangements over the ten-year period affected their psychological well-being. The results were intriguing. Single mothers who were the only adult in the household at the beginning of the study and who were still the sole adult ten years later were at high risk of psychological distress. As in the McLanahan study, this was the case even for those mothers who were not distressed at the time of the original interview. This study, therefore, provides additional evidence that the stresses and social isolation of single motherhood actually cause poorer mental health.

The obvious question, then, is what is it about single motherhood that contributes to poorer mental health? Again, the data that might allow us to definitively answer the question do not exist, but one very interesting finding of the Thompson and Ensminger study suggests that it is not simply the lack of a spouse that leads to poorer mental health. In that study, other adults were able to compensate for the absence of a husband. When some other family member moved into the household, the single mother was no more likely to suffer negative psychological consequences than those mothers who were married throughout the study period. This evidence suggests that the presence of some other relative can serve as a functional alternative to a husband. Clearly, a grandmother or an aunt cannot perform all of the functions of a husband, but they can help with the housework and provide some emotional support. Single motherhood may be a situation in which some support may be a great deal better than none.

Mental Health and Single Motherhood: Empirical Findings

Although there are little data on how single motherhood itself affects physical and mental health, the large body of literature on multiple role demands provides some indirect evidence as to how the increased responsibilities and burdens of single motherhood might affect a woman's health. Unfortunately, most of this research is based on non-Hispanic white samples, and there are very little data that allow us to determine the health consequences of single motherhood for blacks and Hispanics. Later in this chapter we will present some new findings on the impact of single motherhood on physical health for these two groups, but first we review some of the major existing studies and summarize those findings that shed some light on the mental health consequences of single motherhood generally.

Much of the existing research examines the consequences of combining employment with motherhood. This literature clearly demonstrates that although mothers who work tend to do less housework than those who do not work, they still have the primary responsibility for housework and children. As a consequence, they get less sleep than nonworking mothers and spend a greater number of hours per week working and keeping house (Pleck 1985, Vanek 1974). Because of the constraints on their time, both single mothers and married mothers who work spend less time with their children than married mothers who do not work (Haveman et al. 1988). Although many women perform work and domestic roles voluntarily and gain satisfaction in successfully carrying them out, for some women the obligations of work and family increase levels of distress (Cleary and Mechanic 1983). Single mothers are particularly likely to experience overload and to report feeling depressed (Aneshensel, Frerichs, and Clark 1981; Guttentag, Salasin, and Belle 1980; Kandel, Davies, and Raveis 1985).

Child care is clearly one of the more time-consuming and demanding roles associated with motherhood, but if a husband helps with child care, the burden it places on a woman is greatly reduced. This help is particularly important for a working mother. Researchers at the University of Michigan found that the mental health of working married mothers is better than that of nonworking married mothers but only if their husbands share the responsibilities of child care (Kessler and McRae 1982). In this study wives who reported that their husbands helped with child care reported less anxiety than wives who received no assistance from their spouses.

Other researchers come to similar conclusions. Most find that those women whose husbands are unwilling or unable to help with child care or those who have difficulties in arranging child care are at increased risk of poor mental health (Ross and Mirowsky 1988; Ross, Mirowsky, and Ulbrich 1983). For a single mother who is the only adult in the household, the demands of child care are never-ending, and for many, the short respites from child care that even a fairly uninvolved husband might provide are rare. The maintenance of one's emotional health requires time to one's self, but such time alone is often a luxury for many of these women.

Several studies show that working women who have numerous responsibilities for child care and housework report a greater number of psychological symptoms and more feelings of dissatisfaction than working women with fewer family demands (Kessler and McRae 1982; Ross, Mirowsky, and Huber 1983; Krause and Markides 1985; Glenn and Weaver 1979). Employed married women with children are more likely to experience depression than mothers who remain at home (Cleary and Mechanic 1983). For working mothers, it appears that any psychological benefits they might gain from working are often negated by the burdens of raising children, especially if they have little income.

Yet, as we have noted before, it is not just the multiple demands that place a woman at risk for depression. For women with multiple demands, a subjective sense of mastery and personal control protects them against feelings of anxiety and depression (Rosenfield 1989). Unfortunately, because they in fact have less control over their lives, many poor single mothers feel oppressed and unable to affect their environments. This sense of helplessness produces anxiety and limits a woman's capacity to deal with daily problems (Thoits 1987, Kohn 1972). Because young, poorly educated, minority mothers are less likely to have power and autonomy in their jobs than women with more education, they are clearly at elevated risk of depression. We can see, then, how single mothers are subject to multiple disadvantages that place them at risk of poor health: they lack a confidant, experience increased role demands, and lack power and autonomy in work or family life.

Although, by itself, role overload places a woman at elevated risk of depression, we must keep in mind that a lack of economic resources increases the likelihood of depression (Warheit et al. 1976). Role overload often occurs in conjunction with poverty, and, as we have shown, minority women in the United States are at very high risk of both role overload and poverty. As a consequence, black and Hispanic single mothers are also at particularly high risk of depression and other negative mental and physical health consequences (Dohrenwend and Dohrenwend 1969, Dohrenwend et al. 1980). Clearly, the interaction of economic strain and personal values concerning work, family, and parenting is an important factor that helps to account for the negative psychological effects of single motherhood.

Culture and Social Support: Implications for Health

The impact of culture on the extent of the role overload that single mothers experience is demonstrated by one of the few studies of employment and psychological well-being among Mexican-American mothers (Krause and Markides 1985). In a study carried out in San Antonio, Texas, researchers found that it was not simply a matter of working or not working that affected the health of single mothers. Rather, it was the women's expectations concerning motherhood that affected the meaning of work and her sense of subjective well-being. Divorced and separated Mexican-American mothers suffered more depression if they worked but had nontraditional sex-role orientations than single mothers with more traditional orientations, especially if they had young children.

Although they had no proof, the authors speculated that traditional sex-role orientations are part of a cultural package that includes extended and supportive kin networks. These women may receive more help with child care than less traditional women, who are less likely to be part of an extended kin network. The reasons for the increased distress among nontraditional women, then, may be a lack of instrumental social support. This study shows that culture, which among Hispanics is associated with familism, influences the meaning and the actual burdensomeness of the roles a single woman occupies.

This body of research, then, suggests that mutually supportive kin networks and extended households containing grandmothers, aunts, or other women may be a functional alternative to the two-parent nuclear family. If the institution of marriage is becoming less viable for certain groups in our country, extended living arrangements may take its place (Angel and Tienda 1982, Tienda and Angel 1982). Consequently, cultural or social class factors that influence the probability of extension potentially affect the health and well-being of both single mothers and their children.[3] We know, in fact, that black and Hispanic female-headed households often include nonnuclear kin, and there is evidence to suggest that this doubling-up is, at least partially, an attempt to deal with the economic hardships that minority female-headed households face (ibid.). Culture and social class interact to determine living arrangements, and, in turn, living arrangements affect a single mother's economic well-being as well as her social support and her mental health.

The importance of such doubling-up and the sharing of resources is dramatically illustrated in a fascinating ethnographic study of black single mothers and their families carried out in an urban midwestern neighborhood by Carol Stack (1974). The women Stack studied had adapted to the serious poverty in which they lived by developing patterns of exchange, coresidence, and child rearing that involved several households. Because of the high unemployment among men in the community, few women married before becoming pregnant, and pregnancy among adolescents was a normal occurrence. Children were cared for by a large network, and child rearing in the neighborhood involved a great deal of informal and temporary adoption.

Stack clearly showed that these adaptations were a necessary and rational response to poverty. In the absence of the exchange networks with their elaborate rules of reciprocity that governed exchanges of money, goods, and services between members of kinship networks, the burdens of poverty would have been crushing. Stack notes, however, that although this intense interdependence among network members was adaptive, the norms governing sharing and the dependency on welfare made saving money almost impossible and discouraged marriage. Mutual dependence, therefore, was both a salvation and a trap for these poor families. This study proves that fatherlessness is not a new phenomenon and that it is the economic situation in which a group finds itself, as well as the lack of employment possibilities for men, that leads to the formation of female-centered families and the separation of reproduction from marriage.

This is exactly the pattern that Wilson (1987) has documented on a much larger scale among the contemporary underclass. He notes that the increase in fatherlessness among the poor is a result of the fact that in the United States the labor market has changed and has left many black and Hispanic men outside of the employable labor pool. When men, whether because of discrimination or the lack of salable skills, cannot find work, they cannot contribute to family welfare, and women are forced to adopt patterns of mutual exchange, coresidence, and support that stretch their limited resources as far as they will go. These are adaptations that, as Stack notes, many middle-class Americans view disparagingly and that are frequently seen in moral terms as the decline of the family.[4]

Others have documented the importance of kin networks among the minority poor (Jewell 1988; McAdoo 1978, 1981; Gibson and Jackson 1989; Hogan, Hao, and Parish 1990; Casas and Keefe 1978; Krause and Markides 1985). Such networks are not only economic adaptations to single parenthood but psychological ones as well. Harriet McAdoo (1981) finds that single black mothers who live in extended households experience less stress than those living alone or with nonrelatives. Preliminary evidence from the Better Babies Project being carried out in one Washington, D.C., neighborhood shows that the functioning of black single mothers is enhanced if they are well connected to their own mothers, sisters, and friends and if they use these social resources to solve problems (Coates 1989). Among these single mothers, those who have supportive relatives feel more hopeful and positive about their futures than those who do not.

As the traditional husband and wife family becomes less common, other family forms emerge to take its place. In many of these men play no active or ongoing role, and in their absence women are forced to rely on one another. The evidence we have cited suggests that the negative consequences of single motherhood are not primarily a function of the absence of a husband and that if the situation is normalized, or even only partially normalized, as with the addition of some other relative to the household, the husband may not be missed. Even the negative consequences of divorce for mothers and children are not inevitable. Although the conflict and disruption of family life immediately surrounding the separation causes both parents and children a great deal of emotional distress, if after the divorce family life is relatively peaceful and free of conflict, both mothers and children are able to recover within two or three years (Hetherington 1988*b*).

Unfortunately, for many families the stresses surrounding divorce are compounded by other economic and psychological stresses, and the negative consequences of the family disruption can persist for some time. As one might expect, both the mother's and the children's emotional and behavioral states are affected by whether or not the mother remarries. Mothers who do not remarry are more dissatisfied with their lives and experience more emotional problems than mothers who remarry. After the divorce, a mother's relationship with her children is often affected, and even as long as six years following the divorce mothers tend to have difficulty in their relationships with their sons (Hetherington 1988*b*). To a large extent, these negative consequences are reversed when the mother remarries, although a whole new set of issues relating to the children's adjustment to the new family arise.

In light of these findings concerning the impact of social support on health, it is easy to see how cultural and social class factors that affect the probability of becoming a single mother or that influence the size and composition of a woman's extended social network can affect health. Cultural values and practices that increase the size of families and encourage nonnuclear family members to live together also increase the chances that a single mother will have other adults present to compensate for the lack of a husband. The demographic mechanism of extension operates throughout the life course, and, as we shall show in chapter 7, older black women are more likely than non-Hispanic white women to live in multigenerational female-headed households (Worobey and Angel 1990*a*). Once again, this pattern appears to be a response to poverty. As marriage becomes less of a realistic option for many poor women, multigenerational extended female households play an increasingly important role throughout the family life cycle.

The Physical Health of Single Mothers

As is the case for children, then, the data show that the strains of marital disruption and single motherhood have negative mental health consequences for women. We might ask whether those same stresses have negative consequences for physical health. Unfortunately, there are very little data on the physical health consequences of marital disruption or single motherhood for women. Again, as is the case for children, in the United States relatively few young adults suffer serious physical health problems (National Center for Health Statistics 1989). Infectious illnesses do not kill many young adults (although the AIDS epidemic may once again make infectious illness the killer of young adults that it was in previous centuries), and the life-threatening chronic conditions, like heart disease and cancer, that eventually kill their victims are the result of aging.

We would not expect marital disruption, therefore, to lead to serious physical health problems, just as we would not expect it to result in serious psychoses. Rather, as in the case of mental health where marital disruption and stress result in emotional difficulties, the physical health consequences of single motherhood are likely to be more subtle and result in more acute illness or in a generally diminished physical vitality. Such problems may not be life-threatening or even detectable in community surveys, but they can have important consequences for a woman's ability to deal with the burdens of single motherhood. Unfortunately, there are very little reliable data on rates of acute illness by marital status in the United States.

In the absence of such data, the study of the physical health consequences of single motherhood must be based on more general assessments of health status. In the few studies that exist, single mothers report poorer physical health than married mothers. In one study single mothers reported more chronic conditions, more functional disability, poorer health, and feeling more bothered by health problems than married mothers (Berkman 1969). In another study that was based on data from a large, nationally representative sample, female heads of families reported poorer overall physical health and more illness behaviors, like visiting the doctor, staying in bed because of illness, and going to the hospital, than women living with their husbands (Anson 1988).

These studies are suggestive, but as we pointed out in chapter 4, self-reports of physical health are complex entities. They are heavily influenced by one's psychological status, and they must be interpreted as reflecting both physical and mental health (Angel and Gronfein 1988, Angel and Guarnaccia 1989, Angel and Thoits 1987). As we showed above, single mothers have ample reason to be distressed, and their reported poorer physical health may be a reflection of their emotional state. This characteristic of self-assessments makes them troublesome for some purposes and useful for others. As clinical assessments, they are imprecise. In making a diagnosis, a physician certainly takes the patient's assessment into account, but he or she also relies on more objective tests and measurements.

But for the general comparison of the overall health levels of large groups of people, self-assessments are useful. We, for example, are not necessarily interested in the occurrence of specific health conditions among single mothers. Rather, we want to know how marital disruption affects health more generally. For this purpose a clinical assessment may be too narrow and the individual's own global assessment more meaningful. Global assessments of health are a good reflection of an individual's level of functioning in her social environment. In what follows we employ data from several sources to produce a composite picture of the physical and mental health of black, Hispanic, and non-Hispanic white single mothers.

Some New Findings

The research that we have reviewed allows us to fairly confidently say that, in general, single mothers have poorer physical as well as mental health than do married mothers. Unfortunately, the existing research tells us little about health differences among black, Hispanic, and non-Hispanic white single mothers. Here we present some new findings on the health of single black and Hispanic mothers and compare them both to married mothers of their own race and ethnicity and to married and unmarried non-Hispanic white mothers. All of what we present refers to mothers between the ages of eighteen and forty-four. What these findings show is that although single motherhood has negative mental health effects for all groups, these effects are more serious for black and Hispanic single mothers. Since we must rely on several data sources that contain different information and since, as we have argued, mental and physical health measures do not clearly distinguish mental from physical illness, we discuss mental and physical health simultaneously and treat them as measures of general subjective well-being.

Table 6.1, which is based on information concerning physical and mental health collected from a large sample of black and white respondents, shows that single mothers feel more distressed than married mothers and that a large fraction have visited a doctor for a mental health reason.[5] The table also reveals racial differences. Black single mothers have a higher average chronic condition score than black married mothers, and, in general, black mothers worry more about their health and assess their health as poorer than white mothers. Unfortunately, these data do not contain enough Hispanics for us to compare them to blacks and non-Hispanic whites. To do so, we employ two other nationally representative data sets.

Table 6.2 presents data on physical health for four Hispanic groups as well as for blacks and non-Hispanic whites. These results are based on a nationwide sample of mothers from the 1985 Health Interview Survey, a large health survey of over one hundred thousand people conducted annu-

Table 6.1. Psychiatric and Physical Morbidity of Unmarried and Married Mothers by Race

	White		Black	
	Unmarried	Married	Unmarried	Married
Health Problem Worry[a]	40.1	39.6	53.6	52.1
Chronic Condition Score[b]	14.8	13.8	13.0	10.8*
Functional Disability Score[c]	4.4	4.5	3.8	4.3
Self-Evaluation of "Fair" or "Poor" Health	8.5%	8.1%	27.3%	23.5%
Distress Score[d]	32.0	26.9**	32.1	26.4*
Proportion with at Least One Mental Health Visit[e]	40.8%	36.0%	23.2%	24.0%
N (unwght)	(196)	(934)	(69)	(104)

Source: Rand Health Insurance Experiment (HIE), 1974–1982.

*$p \leq .05$.

**$p \leq .01$.

[a]A higher score (range 0–100) indicates a greater tendency to worry or be concerned about personal health.

[b]A higher score (range 0–58.6) indicates a greater number of chronic conditions.

[c]A higher score (range 0–5) indicates an overall ability to perform self-care, mobility, and physical activities.

[d]A higher score (range 0–100) indicates a greater tendency to be distressed.

[e]A mental health visit was based on at least one of the following criteria: (1) use of a mental health service, such as therapy, (2) receiving a psychiatric diagnosis, (3) visit to a mental health care provider, or (4) prescription of psychotropic medication.

ally by the National Center for Health Statistics (National Center for Health Statistics, Kovar, and Poe 1985). The table reveals several differences in the physical health of non-Hispanic white, black, and Puerto Rican, Mexican-American, and other Hispanic mothers in two-parent and female-headed families. In general, although the associations are not always statistically significant, single mothers report poorer health, more disability, and more chronic and acute illness than married mothers.

Regardless of marital status, however, black and Hispanic mothers are in poorer health than non-Hispanic white mothers. Marital status and ethnicity, therefore, form two independent dimensions of vulnerability. In health, as in economic well-being, single motherhood is not the same for everyone. For blacks and Hispanic women, it has more serious mental health consequences. This table shows, however, that even though they are in poorer health, unmarried mothers do not go to the doctor any more often than married mothers. Only black single mothers are more likely to have visited a doctor in the past year. These data indicate that even though they are exposed to more objective and emotional stress than mar-

Table 6.2. Physical Health and Medical Care Utilization of Mothers in Two-Parent and Female-Headed Households by Race and Ethnicity

	Non-Hispanic White		Black		Puerto Rican		Mexican-American		Other Hispanic	
	Two-Parent	Female Headed	Two-Parent	Female-Headed	Two-Parent	Female-Headed	Two-Parent	Female-Headed	Two-Parent	Female-Headed
Self-Evaluation of "Fair" or "Poor" Health	4.9	7.7**	11.5	21.3**	15.5	17.9	9.3	24.4**	7.3	28.6**
At Least Some Functional Disability	7.5	12.7**	7.5	13.5**	12.7	11.5	7.3	12.7	6.5	18.0*
Past 12 Months Doctor Visit	80.7	81.2	81.4	85.8*	85.5	88.4	70.9	77.5	82.6	84.2
At Least One Chronic Condition	39.9	51.7**	34.7	47.0**	42.9	37.8	29.6	49.0**	33.4	49.7*
At Least One Acute Illness	6.9	10.9**	5.0	7.3	8.8	7.9	7.3	7.5	2.4	9.0*
N (unwght)	(7,078)	(886)	(901)	(868)	(71)	(52)	(369)	(78)	(206)	(57)

Source: 1985 National Health Interview Survey (NHIS).

*p ≤ .05.
**p ≤ .01.

141

ried mothers, single mothers do not receive the help they need in dealing with their emotional distress.

Recall, though, that single mothers differ in more than race and ethnicity; as we showed in chapter 3, the various routes to single motherhood, either through divorce or through never having been married, have different implications for a woman's economic well-being. They may also have an impact on her health. In table 6.3, we compare the physical health of black and non-Hispanic white divorced, never-married, and widowed or separated single mothers to that of married mothers. Since divorced mothers tend to be older than never-married mothers and since any differences in health might be due to age differences, the proportions presented in table 6.3 are age adjusted. The most dramatic finding is that all of the single mothers are in poorer health than married mothers, but, except for income, there are essentially no differences among divorced, never-married, and separated mothers. These data suggest, therefore, that the negative health consequences of single motherhood are the result of being single and not of one's prior marital status.

It appears that some factor associated with single motherhood itself is the cause of these women's poorer health. Again, the one factor that many single mothers have in common is economic insecurity, and it may be poverty that accounts for their health deficits. To test for this possibility we examined the association between three of the health measures (self-assessed health, chronic conditions, and disability) and various sociodemographic, economic, and family characteristics as well as previous marital

Table 6.3. Proportion of Non-Hispanic White and Black Mothers with Poor Physical Health and Disability by Marital Status (Age adjusted)

	Married	Divorced	Widow/Separated	Never Married
	NON-HISPANIC WHITE			
Health (Fair or Poor)	4.8	7.4**	9.5**	7.9
Acute Illnesses (1 or More)	6.9	13.2**	5.0	9.9
Chronic Illnesses (1 or More)	40.0	53.5**	47.2**	50.3*
Disability (At Least Some)	7.6	12.2**	13.5**	16.8*
	BLACK			
Health (Fair or Poor)	12.7	14.9	22.7**	24.8**
Acute Illnesses (1 or More)	5.1	5.6	8.0	6.1
Chronic Illnesses (1 or More)	34.9	41.1*	46.0**	47.2**
Disability (At Least Some)	7.9	12.1	15.4**	14.8**

Source: 1985 National Health Interview (NHIS).

*p ≤ .05.

**p ≤ .01.

status. These multivariate models, which are presented in Appendix 6.A, give us some idea about the impact of previous marital status, independent of its association with these other health risk factors.

In the text we only highlight the results and refer the interested reader to the Appendix. What the models tell us is that income has a significant independent impact on self-assessed health and disability, but it does not totally account for the negative health consequences of single motherhood. Even after we control for various health risk factors like age, education, the number of children, employment status, race, and ethnicity, single mothers report poorer health on all three measures. Thus, the stresses of single motherhood appear to be more than economic.

The differences in health between majority and minority group mothers are intriguing and call for further explanation. In the United States minority group status is associated with large cultural differences as well as with large income differentials. As we showed in chapter 4, culture influences self-assessments of health and is associated with other important health-related characteristics, like education and income. Consequently, it potentially has both direct and indirect effects on health. Unfortunately, we know next to nothing about the health consequences of single motherhood for minority group women. In what follows, we present some of the only findings that have been reported.

In table 6.4, we compare the mental and physical health of Mexican-American, Cuban-American, and Puerto Rican single mothers. These analyses are made possible because of a new and unique data set, the Hispanic Health and Nutrition Examination Survey (National Center for Health Statistics 1985), one of the few large data sets on Hispanic health in

Table 6.4. Psychiatric and Physical Morbidity of Unmarried and Married Hispanic Mothers

	Mexican-American		Cuban-American		Puerto Rican	
	Un-married	Married	Un-married	Married	Un-married	Married
Distress Score[a]	11.2	8.5**	9.7	5.9	15.5	11.3**
Self-Evaluation of Fair or Poor Health	31.1	30.2	35.4	21.4	44.5	31.1
Physician Assessment of Fair or Poor Health	3.8	3.1	0.0	0.8	4.0	3.9
N (unwght)	(229)	(824)	(34)	(123)	(191)	(191)

Source: 1984–1986 Hispanic Health and Nutrition Examination Survey (HHANES).
**$p \leq .01$
[a]Based on the Center for Epidemiological Studies Depression Scale (CES-D). A higher score (range 0–60) indicates a greater tendency to be more distressed.

Single Motherhood

the United States. In this survey, which was conducted between 1984 and 1986 and which included approximately 12,000 Hispanics, the participants provided a complete medical history and were given a rather thorough physical examination. The participants also completed a twenty-item questionnaire designed to measure their emotional well-being.[6]

Table 6.4 shows that among all three Hispanic groups, single mothers are more emotionally distressed than married mothers, and although the differences are not statistically significant, a larger fraction of single than married Cuban-American and Puerto Rican mothers report their health to be only fair or poor. Although they are more depressed and perceive their own health to be poor, the physicians who examined these women found them to be, for the most part, healthy. The generally poor self-assessments of physical health by the single mothers, therefore, may reflect the increased stress they experience. Whether or not these physical health measures reflect actual physical illness, the results clearly show that the single mothers' subjective well-being is undermined.

As we did earlier for blacks and non-Hispanic whites, we might ask whether there are significant differences between Hispanic single mothers depending on their previous marital status. In table 6.5, we present the various health measures, again age adjusted, separately by prior mari-

Table 6.5. Proportion of Hispanic Mothers with Poor Physical Health and Average Depression Score by Marital Status (Age adjusted)

	Married	Divorced	Widowed/Separated	Never Married
		MEXICAN-AMERICAN		
Health (Fair or Poor)	28.7	25.0	38.6	35.2*
Depression	8.6	11.3*	11.7**	9.5
Physician's Examination (Fair or Poor)	2.8	3.5	4.8	1.9
		CUBAN-AMERICAN		
Health (Fair or Poor)	19.9	30.2	40.5	39.0
Depression	6.3	10.1	10.1	6.8
Physician's Examination (Fair or Poor)	1.0	0.0	0.0	0.0
		PUERTO RICAN		
Health (Fair or Poor)	32.0	47.6*	39.9	43.8*
Depression	12.9	15.7	15.9	16.1
Physician's Examination (Fair or Poor)	3.8	4.5	1.0	4.1

Source: 1984–1986 Hispanic Health and Nutrition Examination Survey (HHANES).

*$p \leq .05$.

**$p \leq .01$.

tal status for the three Hispanic groups. What we find is that the various nation of origin groups differ greatly in their health levels but that only among the Mexican-Americans are divorced and widowed or separated mothers significantly more depressed than married mothers.

Widowhood is fairly infrequent in the contemporary United States, and the widowed and separated category is made up primarily of separated individuals who are, for all practical purposes, similar to divorced women. Among the Puerto Ricans, divorced and never-married mothers report poorer self-assessed health than married mothers, and although the differences are not statistically significant, single Puerto Rican mothers have very high depressive affect scores. Many researchers who use this particular scale consider scores of sixteen or higher to be evidence of potentially major depression.

These associations are intriguing. Once again, single mothers are clearly under great economic and emotional strain, and these data show that the various stressors in their lives affect their subjective well-being. Our discussion of role overload leads us to expect that both poverty and the emotional burdens of single motherhood contribute to poor subjective health. As we did in our analysis of the health of black and non-Hispanic white single mothers, we performed multivariate analyses and statistically controlled for the impact of various health-associated characteristics to determine the independent effect of previous marital status on the physical and mental health of Hispanic single mothers. The results are presented in Appendix 6.B. Again, we only highlight the major findings in the text and refer the interested reader to the Appendix.

These multivariate models show that after we control for income and other health-related variables, marital status has no independent impact on either the physician's assessment or the woman's own subjective assessment of her health. However, divorced and widowed/separated single mothers continue to be more depressed than married mothers, but never-married mothers are no more depressed than married mothers. Unfortunately, this data set contains no mental health information for blacks or non-Hispanic whites, so we are unable to compare the Hispanics to these other two groups.

At least for Hispanics, then, divorced mothers appear to be more depressed than never-married mothers. In the multivariate analyses, low income accounted for the lower self-assessed physical health reported by Hispanic single mothers, but it did not account for their increased depression. These findings are consistent with the finding we reported in chapter 5 which showed that the children of divorced parents suffer serious emotional and behavioral problems, but that whatever impact divorce has on physical health, it is too subtle to detect with these sorts of measures.

These results also suggest that there are important cultural differences in the meaning of single motherhood and its impact on women's health. The general neglect of race and ethnicity in the literature dealing with social support and health may misrepresent reality. The meaning of social support is defined largely by an individual's cultural and social context. Race and ethnicity are clearly politically charged topics, and as we showed in chapter 1, potential accusations of blaming the victim lead many social scientists to avoid the topic. Yet in the United States, race and Hispanic ethnicity cannot be ignored; they are too intimately tied up with our system of social stratification and, consequently, with differential health risks. Single mothers are disproportionately black and Hispanic, and studies of the health risks faced by single mothers and their children must take culture and social class into account.

Conclusion: Is Single Motherhood Bad for Health?

After having reviewed the rather extensive research on marital status and women's mental health and after having presented our own findings, we end this chapter by asking what we can really say about the impact of single motherhood on health and of the role of race and ethnicity in mediating this impact. For one thing, we can fairly safely say that the role overload associated with single motherhood adversely affects the subjective well-being of women, especially for those who have few other social or economic resources at their disposal. We can also say that there is a great deal of variation in emotional resilience among single mothers; most do not experience serious role overload, nor are they depressed. A woman's emotional response to single motherhood depends both on her own psychological makeup and on the economic and social resources at her disposal. In this chapter, we have identified a set of vulnerabilities that in the contemporary United States place single mothers, especially black and Hispanic single mothers, at increased risk of poor health. The data clearly show that race and ethnicity place a woman at increased risk of poverty and role overload, and this combination often undermines her subjective well-being.

Perhaps the major mental health vulnerability that single mothers face is poverty. Poverty is not just a lack of money, however. It also means social and political powerlessness. The poor are not only denied many of the basic necessities of life and most of its luxuries but they often lack the basic sources of self-esteem. Many of the roles that single mothers occupy, like unwed mother, welfare recipient, or charity case, are stigmatized. They are not the sort of roles that are likely to enhance one's sense of mastery and control over one's environment. Single mothers must often bear the burden of such stigma alone. Although the poverty that single mothers experience in the United States is not as serious as that of the poor in the Third World, it is serious enough (especially in relative terms), and given the increasing hostility of middle-class taxpayers to programs for the poor, it is hard to imagine that the situation will change greatly in the future. Single mothers will not only increase as a percentage of all mothers but they will comprise an ever-growing percentage of the population in poverty.

One consistent finding that emerges in the literature is that both men and women who lack a confidant are at elevated risk of poor health. Obviously, for single mothers, the lack of a spouse increases the risk of poverty, but there appears to be something beyond the mere material aspects of marriage that accounts for the fact that married mothers tend to have better health than single mothers. There appears to be something about an intense relationship in and of itself, perhaps the emotional support or the companionship, that protects people from both physical and mental illness. Even as divorce rates have increased in recent years, people tend to remarry and apparently overwhelmingly prefer to live with an intimate other.

One of the most significant findings of our research is the importance of culture in determining both the risk of single motherhood and the effect it has on a woman's health. Minority group status places a single mother at greatly elevated risk of poverty. In addition, the data clearly show that blacks, Hispanics, and non-Hispanic whites cope with poverty in culturally specific ways. Blacks and Hispanics are more likely than non-Hispanic whites to resort to extended living arrangements. The anthropological evidence reveals that black and Hispanic women employ elaborate systems of exchange and reciprocity, in addition to coresidence, to deal with a serious shortage of marriageable males. The data suggest that these extended living arrangements serve partially as a functional alternative to the two-parent family both economically and psychologically. As the single-parent household becomes an ever-larger fraction of families, minority group women are forced by necessity to develop alternative forms of family life.

As with children, we found essentially no objective physical health differences between single mothers and married mothers. Of course, we really do not have the sort of data we need to assess the subtle physical health consequences of spouselessness. In the United States we have eliminated most of the large social class differences in mortality, and few young adults die of infectious disease. Any physical health effects of single motherhood, therefore, are likely to be subtle and are perhaps restricted to acute illness. Yet the elevated mortality rate of single adults means that the question remains open. Our data show that single mothers assess their physical health as poor more often than do married mothers. We suspect that these negative self-assessments are as much a reflection of the women's emotional status as of their actual physical health. Nonetheless, they cannot be trivialized. They clearly indicate that a single mother's subjective well-being can be undermined by the stresses of single motherhood. This diminished well-being undermines the quality of a woman's life and can easily affect the family environment, thereby affecting the health of her children as well.

Conceivably, research in immunology and other areas of medicine may one day identify some impact of depression on the immune response and provide some insight into the mechanisms through which social support affects mortality. At present, however, we can only say that spouselessness undermines many single mothers' overall sense of well-being. Before we can definitively go beyond this broad generalization, we will need much better data. Since single mothers are becoming such a large part of our

Appendix 6.A. Regressions of Mother's Health on Selected Socioeconomic Characteristics, 1985 National Health Interview Survey (NHIS)

	Self-Assessed Health[a]	Chronic Conditions[b]	Functional Disability[b]
Divorced[c]	−.02*	.50*	.31*
Never Married[c]	.00	.40**	.29*
Separated/Widowed[c]	.01	.35**	.36*
Black[d]	−.20**	−.17	.04
Mexican-American[e]	.13**	−.37**	−.31
Puerto Rican[e]	.03**	−.24	−.10
Age	.08**	.01**	.06**
Number of Children under 6 Years	−.04	−.05	−.18**
Number of Children in Household	.01	−.00	−.04
Low Income[f]	.07**	.03	.63**
Middle Income[f]	.09**	.05	.45**
Missing Income[f]	.03**	−.17*	.07
Education (in years)	−.20**	.00	−.05**
Employed	−.06**	−.15**	−.77
N = 10,476			
R	.322	.083	.231

[a]Ordinary least squares equation.
[b]Logistic regression equation.
[c]Reference category = Married mothers.
[d]Reference category = Non-Hispanic white.
[e]Reference category = Other Hispanic.
[f]Reference category = High income.
*Significant at ≤ .05.
**Significant at ≤ .01.

population, perhaps we will see more research on their health and the health of their children in the future. The data we have are sufficient, however, to say with some certainty that social welfare programs that support single mothers and their children are crucial to maintaining their health. In the next chapter, we examine the health consequences of spouselessness for mature women.

Appendix 6.B. Regressions of Mother's Health on Selected Socioeconomic Characteristics, 1984–1986 Hispanic Health and Nutrition Examination Survey (HHANES)

	Physician's Examination	Self-Assessed Health	Depression
Divorced[a]	−.02	.02	.06*
Never Married[a]	.03	−.00	.02
Separated/Widowed[a]	−.01	.02	.05*
Age	.19**	.07**	−.02
Family Size	.05*	.01	.04
Low Income[b]	.04	.10**	.12**
Middle Income[b]	.04	.12**	.09**
Missing Income[b]	−.02	.05*	.04
Education	−.09**	−.25**	−.01
Employed	−.04	−.04	−.07**
Mexican-American[c]	−.06	.05	.05
Puerto Rican[c]	.25**	.07*	.18**
Spanish Interview	.07*	.09**	.04
Physician's Examination			.09**
Adjusted R²	.169	.143	.095
N = (1,795)			

[a]Reference category = Married mothers.
[b]Reference category = High income.
[c]Reference category = Cuban-American.
*Significant at ≤ .05.
**Significant at ≤ .01.

7

Single Women in Mature Adulthood
A Health Research Agenda

In the last two chapters, we documented the negative health consequences of father absence for children and of the lack of a confidant for
mothers. Here we focus on the potential health consequences of long-term
single motherhood for women in middle and late adulthood. Because
there is almost no data on the impact of a woman's marital and fertility
history on her health in later life, our discussion in this chapter is more
speculative than in the last two, and we focus more on the development of
a theoretical model of the association between a woman's family situation
and her health. To do so, we draw on a large literature dealing with the
comparative health of blacks, Hispanics, and non-Hispanic whites, as well
as the literature on depression among the elderly, to begin to understand
the impact of single motherhood on the health of women in middle and
late adulthood.

As is the case among younger age groups, poverty among the elderly is
concentrated among blacks and Hispanics as well as among female-headed
households. Differences between racial and ethnic groups in educational
and occupational opportunities early in the life course translate into large
differences in wealth in later life. After a lifetime of asset accumulation,
most middle-class elderly individuals are fairly well off (Crystal and Shea
1990); by the time they are ready to retire, most middle-class married couples have retirement income, they have usually paid off their mortgages,

and a large number have saved at least some money in interest-bearing investments. These material assets, in conjunction with the guarantees of Social Security, mean that for the middle-class elderly, retirement is an economically secure time of life (Myles 1984). When a woman in such a marriage becomes a widow, her income certainly drops, but she retains the couple's assets and, usually, at least a portion of her husband's pension. These assets, in conjunction with her own Social Security and retirement income, mean that although she may not have as much as she had been used to, her income remains at least adequate.

For black and Hispanic elderly women, retirement is less often an economically secure time of life. Since one's economic situation in later life is based on the compounded gains of earlier years, the economic disadvantage faced by young and middle-aged minority workers means that, on average, they accumulate fewer assets than middle-class individuals over the life course. Consequently, when an older black or Hispanic female becomes widowed, she often inherits little property. But since a large fraction of minority women are single, for those women, even that small amount often does not exist. Obviously, not all minority group members are in this position; middle-class minority retirees are as well off as anyone else, and the expansion of Supplemental Security Income in recent years has eliminated much of the most serious poverty even among single black and Hispanic elderly women. Nonetheless, because of racial and ethnic differences in education, occupational attainment, and asset accumulation, elderly minority women are at high risk of poverty.

As important as material assets are in old age, after a woman retires or becomes widowed, her physical and psychological well-being is largely determined by her social network. People, whether children, other relatives, friends, or formal care givers, form the core of a woman's social support system at a time in life when both instrumental and emotional support are particularly important. Although there is a growing literature documenting the importance of social support for the mental health of the elderly, we have little data on how a woman's marital and fertility history affects either her social support or her health in later life, nor do we have good data on differences in levels of social support or the comparative health of older Hispanics, blacks, and non-Hispanic whites. Yet, from what we know concerning the impact of poverty, the burdens of unassisted parenthood, and the lack of a confidant on health generally, we suspect that a woman who experiences long periods of single motherhood faces serious physical and mental health risks that may manifest themselves later in life. At the very least, we know that in middle and later adulthood minority and single women are disproportionately poor and, consequently, at risk of such health problems as diabetes and hypertension that are associated with poverty. Whether long-term single motherhood adds to the negative health consequences of poverty and minority group status is something about which we can, as yet, only speculate.

In addition to poverty, many poor single grandmothers have additional burdens to bear. In middle and late adulthood, a growing number of these women find themselves responsible for the daily care of their grandchildren because the children's mother, either because of youth, incarceration, or drug addition, is unable to do so herself. These increased family burdens, in conjunction with the disintegrating family and social environment that often accompanies them, can result in stresses that undermine the senior woman's health.

For numerous reasons, therefore, we expect to find substantial differences in the physical and mental health of single women in later life, and we expect these differences to be influenced by a woman's previous marital and fertility history as well as by her race or ethnicity. In what follows, we develop a theoretical model and research agenda that is based on existing research on the impact of race, Hispanic ethnicity, living arrangements, and social support on the health of middle-aged and older women. The dramatic post-World War II decline of the traditional family that we documented in earlier chapters means that more and more women will spend a large fraction of their lives as single mothers and will find themselves alone or responsible for children and grandchildren in later adulthood. Because of the precarious economic situation in which many of these families will find themselves, it is likely that both adults and children will suffer negative health consequences. Since the family is a tightly knit unit in which the mental health of one member affects the health of other family members, it is imperative that we begin to understand the situation of mature women and not focus solely on mothers and children as we have in the past. We begin our examination of health in later life by characterizing the situation of women to whom we apply the label "new grandmothers."

The New Grandmotherhood

One of the most interesting and potentially significant demographic developments of recent years is the growth in the black population of the number of extended family households containing grandmothers. In 1969, 11 percent of unmarried black women lived with their grandchildren; but by 1984, this proportion had grown to one quarter of all black women (Beck and Beck 1989). Because many of these grandmothers had children early in life and because the daughters of adolescent mothers are themselves likely to become pregnant early, many of these grandmothers are quite young.

This family life course is illustrated by pattern IIIc of the theoretical model of the life course of the female household that we elaborated in chapter 1. In this pattern, fertility is highly accelerated in each generation, and it is quite common for a woman to become a grandmother in her forties or even earlier. As we document below, this early grandmotherhood is often part of a package that includes truncated educational opportunities, long-term single motherhood, and poverty for two or more generations.

Becoming a grandmother under these circumstances places a woman in a rather different situation than that we imagine as the role of the traditional grandmother. Our usual view is of a woman whose place in the family has changed from one of daily responsibility for the care and rearing of children to one in which she has intimate, yet more casual and less burdensome child care responsibilities than those associated with the role of mother. This idealized role is enviable, since such a grandmother can enjoy the company of her grandchildren when she desires it and send the little dears home to their parents when she has had enough of them. After a lifetime of dawn-to-dusk responsibility for child rearing, she achieves a new and esteemed status in which she enjoys the love and affection of her children and grandchildren without having to bear the day-to-day responsibility for their welfare.

Such an idealized role, like most idealizations, has never been quite accurate for most women. For many poor women, it is not even a close approximation of reality; for them, the transition to grandmotherhood does not bring with it disengagement from the taxing responsibilities of child rearing, nor does it necessarily occur in later adulthood. For poor women, the transition to grandmotherhood increasingly represents an extension of the more burdensome aspects of motherhood with the added responsibilities of caring for grandchildren. At a time in their lives when they should ideally be disengaging from the more immediate responsibilities of child rearing, older minority group females often find themselves caring for two younger generations, frequently in dire socioeconomic circumstances. The responsibilities that accompany caring for both children and grandchildren under these conditions may significantly increase the stresses these women experience, especially since a large fraction of lower-class female-headed households are plagued by problems of unemployment, drug abuse, and family disorganization (Bohlen 1989; Gross 1989, 1991). It is rather easy to imagine how the stresses accompanying such living conditions might adversely affect the mental and physical health of older females.

This scenario places the older woman in the role of care giver and matriarch of the family. For many older women, however, living with one's family is the result of economic dependency and, often, of poor health. Many older women need care themselves once their health begins to decline, and in these situations the multigenerational household may be the only option available. For all practical purposes, institutionalization is not an option for older blacks or Hispanics (Gibson and Jackson 1989; Worobey and Angel 1990*a*, 1990*b*). Elderly minority women who experience serious functional declines may simply have no choice but to remain with their families. Among the poor, therefore, the extended female-headed household may serve two purposes: it may be the only option available to young adult children who are unable to set up their own households, but it also may be the only alternative available to older minority women in poor health.

Obviously, extended living arrangements in later life are determined by many factors other than the economic need of either the younger or older generations. Cultural factors, such as the supposed familistic orientation of Hispanics, influence the living arrangements of older women. In the following discussion, we assess the relative impacts of poverty and health on the formation of female-headed households in later life and attempt to understand how they affect the health of middle-aged and older women. We begin by reviewing the literature on depression among the elderly and then proceed to a discussion of the association between social support, living arrangements, and health.

Depression and the Elderly

In the last few years, a rather large literature dealing with the mental health of the elderly has appeared.[1] In this chapter, we focus primarily on studies of depression because depression is perhaps the most common mental illness among all age groups and also because it is clearly affected by social factors, such as the loss of a spouse, as well as by changes in physical health. The elderly are certainly at elevated risk of organic brain syndromes, such as Alzheimer's disease, that are quite devastating and even life-threatening, but these are less obviously caused by specific life events or chronic stressors than is depression. Here we are only interested in those conditions that are likely to be caused by external events or living conditions. In the next section, we will examine the co-occurrence of depression with the physical health conditions that afflict the elderly.

In modern American society, we have conflicting impressions of the emotional situation of the elderly. As in the case of the idealized grandmother, we often conceive of senior citizens as a revered and privileged group who are enjoying the fruits of their labor in close and intimate contact with their families. We are frequently reminded, however, that many elderly are isolated and lonely and find it difficult to live on their small retirement incomes. Clearly, mature adulthood can be either happy or sad, depending on one's economic and social circumstances. One reason that the elderly are often seen as vulnerable to depression is that growing old inevitably invovles both physical and emotional losses. Because the old must endure such losses as the death of a spouse and friends and because they must give up important social and occupational roles, it is easy to imagine that they are more frequently depressed than other age groups. Yet, there is actually little convincing evidence to support this view. The elderly are neither substantially more nor less depressed than younger age groups, and the different ways in which mental illness is measured, as well as a lack of comparability between the samples employed in different studies, make any differences that are found between rates of depression for older and younger age groups suspect (Feinson 1985, Newman 1989).

As with other characteristics like income, the variation in depression among the elderly appears to be greater than differences between the elderly and younger age groups. Some elderly cope well with the difficulties they encounter, while others are overwhelmed by them. Most older individuals adapt adequately to the changes that accompany biological aging and the loss of social roles that are an important part of one's identity in earlier years (Idler and Angel 1990*b*). Nonetheless, the rather dramatic changes that result from the loss of occupational roles through retirement, the loss of a spouse, and the loss of friends and other relatives require a great deal of adaptation by older people, and some find that adaptation more difficult than others (Butler and Lewis 1977, Blazer 1982).

Perhaps the most difficult change that an older woman must deal with is the loss of a spouse. The death of one's husband means not only the loss of one's life companion but the loss of his social network. The research clearly shows that newly bereaved widows are at high risk of depression (Newman 1989; Blazer 1982, 1989). Women who enter mature adulthood never having been married or those who divorced their husbands earlier in life are spared this trauma, but they must bear other burdens, often including the absence of adequate social and emotional support. Prior marital history, therefore, is an important factor in determining a woman's emotional health in middle and late adulthood. Because of the property and retirement income they acquired while married, widows can be better off economically than divorced or never-married women, but they may suffer more emotional trauma and social isolation as a result of the loss of their husbands. Never-married women, who were never dependent on a spouse for emotional or social support, may be better off emotionally in later adulthood since they may have developed alternate social support networks, but they may suffer greater economic deprivation.

Clearly, there are numerous theoretical mechanisms through which a woman's marital and life histories can affect her emotional well-being in later life. Without data on the marital and fertility histories and on the mental health of large samples of women from different racial and ethnic groups, however, the emotional consequences of the loss of a spouse as well as the impact of living arrangements on their physical and mental health cannot be unambiguously determined. Individual differences in emotional resilience and physical vitality may well outweigh any systematic effects of the loss of a spouse. It would be useful, however, to summarize the major findings concerning the predictors of depression among older age groups.

The literature on age differences in depression, like the literature on gender differences, is immense, and it would be pointless for us to attempt a comprehensive review.[2] We will, however, mention some of the better-known studies of the association between age and depression. Some of the most recent evidence on depression among the elderly comes from a large study that attempted to estimate the prevalence of specific psychopathologies in community samples.[3] One part of this study was carried out in New Haven, Connecticut, and included more than 1,300 adults sixty years of age and older. Of the 27 percent of these older individuals who reported depressive symptoms, 19 percent were found to be suffering dysphoria, a mild form of depression, 4 percent had moderate depression, and only eight-tenths of 1 percent had major depression based on rigorous psychiatric criteria (Blazer, Huges, and George 1987). Relatively minor depressive symptoms, then, appear to be as common among the elderly as they are among younger age groups. In only a few cases are these symptoms associated with serious mental illness.

In another study of elderly individuals carried out in 1972 in Durham, North Carolina, researchers found that nearly 15 percent of a sample of 997 elderly people had what they considered to be significant depressive symptomatology (Blazer and Williams 1980). Fewer than 4 percent of this sample had symptoms of major depressive disorder, however, and for a large fraction of those with depressive symptoms, these were associated with poor physical health. As we will show in greater detail below, it is well known that physical illness has a negative impact on one's sense of well-being at any age. This study also confirmed what other studies show among younger groups, that the lack of a confidant and a limited social network leave one vulnerable to depression. Widowed individuals and those with few material or social resources were at highest risk of depression.

Depression among the elderly, therefore, appears to be brought on by the same factors that cause depression among younger individuals. These include stressful life events, the loss of physical vitality, and a lack of social support (Phifer and Murrell 1986; Norris and Murrell 1984; Aneshensel,

Frerichs, and Huba 1984; Gurin, Veroff, and Feld 1960). The major difference between the old and the young in their vulnerability to depression
arises from the fact that the old experience more losses as a consequence
of the aging process. Again, as among younger age groups, the research
shows that among the elderly, the separated and divorced, in addition to
the widowed, are at particularly high risk of depression (Bellin and Hardt
1958). The old, therefore, are not all that different from the young, and, as
is the case for younger people, the data indicate that adequate social support protects the elderly from depression (Goldberg, Van Natta, and
Comstock 1985; Gallagher et al. 1983; Lopata 1979).

Obviously, because aging eventually involves the loss of significant others, one of the major emotional problems of old age is loneliness. Although loneliness is certainly not a mental illness in and of itself, social
isolation is associated with an elevated risk of depression, and even when
it does not cause full-blown depression, severe loneliness can undermine
a woman's sense of well-being and diminish the quality of her life. Several
studies have found that the unmarried elderly are lonelier than those who
live with a spouse (Essex and Nam 1987, Gubrium 1976; Longino and
Lipman 1982). One interesting finding in this literature is that the never
married report feeling less lonely in old age than the formerly married
(Essex and Nam 1987). Evidently, those individuals who never marry are
spared the trauma of losing a spouse, and since they never had a spouse,
they have developed ways of coping with loneliness.

In light of the evidence showing how important a confidant is to mental
health at any age, it is hardly surprising that the loss of a confidant and life
companion results in a grief reaction that is often characterized by such
symptoms of depression as sleep disturbances and excessive crying
(Blazer 1982; Butler and Lewis 1977; Gallagher and Thompson 1989;
Seeman et al. 1987). Grief, like loneliness, is not a mental illness; rather,
it is a perfectly normal reaction to loss. However, when the grief reaction
continues past a certain period and threatens the quality of the surviving
spouse's life, it can be considered pathological. We should not find it particularly surprising that the availability of other sources of social support,
such as children and friends, can help moderate this grief reaction. Widows who have few friends and those who feel distant from their children
are at higher risk of emotional problems than women who have more satis-
fying social relationships (Goldberg, Comstock, and Harlow 1988).

Although many individuals remain vital and active well into their eight-
ies and nineties, the aging process invariably leads to physical decline.
Tissues age and lose elasticity, muscles lose tone and strength, and major
organs become less efficient. As scientists have developed vaccines and
antibiotics to combat the acute illnesses that killed many individuals in

their prime not that many decades ago, the chronic diseases of old age have emerged as the major causes of illness and death in the developed world. If one lives long enough, one will almost inevitably develop one of the major conditions of old age, such as cardiovascular disease, arthritis, or cancer. Unlike acute illness, chronic diseases are not self-limiting, nor are they necessarily curable. For the most part, they can only be controlled and, often, lead inexorably to death. As we mentioned above, the loss of physical vitality is one of the major causes of depression, and because chronic diseases are so prevalent in later life, we spend some time addressing the issue of the association between physical illness and depression.

Physical and Mental Comorbidity Among the Elderly: Cultural and Social Factors

One of the most serious problems that the elderly face is the accumulation of illness conditions. As the body ages, many organ systems cease to function optimally, and the aging individual is often plagued by multiple recurring health problems. It is certainly not an overstatement to say that the loss of health is analogous to the loss of a spouse in its impact on mental health. A serious decline in health, after all, represents the loss of self in much the same way as the death of a spouse represents the loss of a significant other. As does the death of a spouse, therefore, the loss of one's physical vitality often leads to severe depression. The elderly are at particularly high risk of serious declines in health and functional capacity from multiple sources. It is difficult enough to have to deal with one illness condition, but as conditions become compounded, especially as they begin to interfere with one's functioning, illness begins to dominate one's existence. This loss of vitality and social involvement, and the changing concept of the self from that of a healthy and involved person in life to that of an unhealthy person approaching death, can lead to serious depression.

Depression can also exacerbate existing physical conditions. Previous research indicates that one's mental status alters the impact of physical illness on one's functioning and even on the probability of death. In one longitudinal study of the impact of depression among elderly patients, for example, those individuals who were depressed had a higher mortality rate over a four-year period than a control group who were not depressed (Murphy et al. 1988). In our own previous research involving a sample of adults with arthritis, those individuals who had fewer symptoms of depression reported less pain and better overall health than individuals who reported more symptoms of depression (Idler and Angel 1990*b*, Mechanic and Angel 1987). Of course, without longitudinal data it is impossible to know which came first, the physical illness or the depression, but it is clear that the two often occur together.

The elderly, therefore, are at higher risk of what we term "comorbid" physical and mental conditions, and the combination of depression and physical illness compounds the impact of each, further undermining an individual's overall well-being. It is easy to imagine that a physical illness can worsen and even result in death if, because of depression, an individual fails to follow a medically recommended regimen. Since the topic has such clear relevance to the elderly, before proceeding we will speculate a bit about how mental illness and physical illness are related and how they affect functioning in old age.

We suspect that one of the major mechanisms through which physical illness causes depression is its impact on physical and social functioning (Idler and Angel 1990*a*, 1990*b*; Berkman et al. 1986). The inability to perform customary roles or to care for oneself usually signals the beginning of serious physical decline that requires a reevaluation of one's capacities and of one's future, and without hope for the future, life can seem quite meaningless. For most people, social health is a major component of overall health. If because of physical incapacity an older person loses the ability to maintain emotionally supportive social bonds, her mental health may suffer. A large number of studies have documented a great deal of psychiatric morbidity in the population at large as well as in general medical care settings (e.g., Shepherd 1987; Hankin and Oktay 1979; Wilkinson 1985; Institute of Medicine 1979; Goldberg and Hutley 1980; Schulberg and Burns 1987; Goldman et al. 1980; Myers et al. 1984; National Institute of Mental Health 1987). Although specific estimates of the proportion of patients in general medical care who have mental health problems vary greatly, there can be little doubt that a large fraction of patients who see primary care physicians suffer significant mental or emotional comorbidity (Shapiro et al. 1984, 1985; Wells et al. 1987; Regier, Goldberg, and Taube 1978). Since the elderly use general medical services far in excess of their population proportion, they are overrepresented among this group.

The literature on mental and physical comorbidity is far too extensive to review here (see Katon and Sullivan 1990 for a recent review), but it can be summarized as convincingly showing that depressive states are common among patients with various chronic physical illnesses (Wells, Golding, and Burnam 1988; Katon and Sullivan 1990). Arthritis, cancer, chronic lung disease, neurological disorders, and heart disease have all been shown to be associated with depression (ibid.). The evidence for an association between other chronic diseases such as diabetes, arthritis, and depression is mixed and illustrates the methodological difficulties in determining the direction of causality between mental and physical states (Helz and Templeton 1990; Creed, Murphy, and Jayson 1990).

The fact that older single women are disproportionately exposed to multiple stressors, including poverty and the responsibility for younger generations, places them at risk for such comorbid conditions. Because of poverty, we know that such women are already at elevated risk of certain health conditions, including cancer and heart disease (Perales and Young 1988, Worobey and Angel 1990*a*). Once such conditions manifest themselves, their impact on functioning can only be exacerbated by the chronic stresses a poor woman is exposed to. In a situation in which she can least afford it, a single woman's physical and emotional health may be harmed, thereby undermining her ability to function optimally. Functional capacity, therefore, has particular significance in the study of the health of the elderly, and below we focus on the importance of social networks in maintaining the physical and mental health of the elderly. Because one's living situation significantly influences one's social network, we also examine the association between living arrangements and older unmarried women's functional status.

Social Networks, Living Arrangements, and Health

In old age, social assets are every bit as important as material wealth in preserving an individual's physical and mental well-being. The evidence we have reviewed consistently shows that the loss of a spouse, declines in physical health, and social isolation place elderly women at elevated risk of depression (Bellin and Hardt 1958, Blazer 1982). Social networks, consisting of children, other relatives, friends, and fellow church members, are particularly important in maintaining the health and social functioning of elderly women. Cultural and social class factors that influence the size and functioning of a woman's immediate network, therefore, play an important role in determining her health and welfare.

Factors that reduce the size of a woman's social network or that interfere with the interactions she would like to have with others can lead to demoralization. Many grandmothers live far from their families and often have little active involvement with their grandchildren. These women are deprived of a potential source of emotional satisfaction, and many feel unhappy, bitter, and discontent (Kivnick 1985). Grandmothers who interact with their grandchildren on a regular basis are happier and report higher levels of life satisfaction than grandmothers who are unable to do so because of reasons such as declining health or distance (Cherlin and Furstenberg 1986). Several qualitative studies reveal that unfulfilled expectations concerning the role of grandmother place a woman at high risk of depression (Cherlin and Furstenberg 1986, Kivnick 1985, Robertson 1977). A woman can feel deeply disappointed if she expects to have frequent contact with her grandchildren but cannot because they live far away.

Not surprisingly, children are among the most important people in an older person's social network, and as we documented earlier, black and Hispanic women are more likely than non-Hispanic whites to live with their children. Whether this means they have more supportive interactions with them is, of course, impossible to tell. For blacks and Hispanics, extended living arrangements are often involuntary and the result of economic need, and they may, consequently, not be as emotionally fulfilling as voluntary arrangements might be. Nonetheless, they provide an older woman with potential social support and protect her from social isolation. Existing research suggests that among blacks and Hispanics, social networks provide not only material aid but important emotional and instrumental support.

A common theme in the social sciences, as well as in the popular media, is that modern industrial society undermines individuals' intimate social networks and increases their vulnerability to mental illness.[4] This belief has been expressed in various forms by such classical theorists as Emile Durkheim and Ferdinand Tonnies as well as by such contemporary social critics as Christopher Lasch (1977). According to these theorists, the family has been weakened as its functions have been taken over by formal organizations. Those who hold this view believe that the human ties that form the basis of our emotional support system have been undermined by the atomistic and specialized nature of modern life.

These formal theories of the decline of community are part of a widespread perception in the modern world that individuals are no longer part of supportive social networks that cushion them from the emotional traumas that are an inevitable part of life. In our increasingly individualistic, mobile, and atomistic society, older individuals whose children live far away can easily find themselves without someone from whom they can receive emotional and instrumental support. Although critics of modern life often romanticize life in earlier times, it is impossible to doubt that the highly mobile nature of modern society has an important impact on the availability of kin for many elderly people (Litwak 1985). The empirical evidence shows that while modern life does indeed reduce the intensity of interactions with close kin, at least among highly educated and geographically mobile professionals, ethnic groups differ significantly in terms of residential proximity to family and in their patterns of interaction with kin

(Fischer 1982). We briefly highlight what is known about the social support networks of blacks and Hispanics and their impact on health and
well-being in later life.

In the American melting pot, even when ethnic groups retain much of
their cultural identity, there is inevitably a great deal of within-group variation in the extent to which individuals take on the appearance, language,
culture, and beliefs of the larger society. Many Hispanics, for example, are
essentially indistinguishable from members of any other American ethnic
group, and except for the color of their skin, middle-class blacks are no
different in their family structures, behaviors, and social interactions than
similar whites. It is impossible, therefore, to characterize the members of
any one ethnic group in terms of common preferences or practices. At the
very most, we can talk of general cultural tendencies, realizing that some
individuals manifest these to a greater degree than others. Having made
this point, then, we ask how race, Hispanic ethnicity, and social class interact to influence an older woman's social support network.

Several researchers have provided evidence that among elderly blacks,
informal support from family and friends improves levels of functioning
(Gibson and Jackson 1989; Taylor 1985, 1986). It is clear, therefore, that
social class and cultural factors that influence the size and composition of
an older woman's immediate social network are potentially important indirect determinants of her mental health (Litwak 1985). Groups that encourage high fertility and close family ties provide older women a greater number of potential social supports.

Mexican-Americans have often been characterized as familistic, with a
highly developed sense of loyalty to parents, children, and other relatives
(Grebler, Moore, and Guzman 1970; Gilbert 1978). Again, one has to be
cautious in making such generalizations, since many writers doubt that
Hispanics are in fact any more familistic than other groups.[5] Nonetheless,
many researchers find that Hispanic elderly are more likely to live with
family and less likely to live alone than are non-Hispanic whites (Mindel
1985, Markides and Mindel 1987, Lubben and Becerra 1987). Not only
are the Hispanic elderly more likely to live with family than are non-
Hispanics but they engage in the exchange of mutual aid among a larger
extended kin network than is typical of non-Hispanic whites (Mindel
1980). The Hispanic elderly also appear to rely more exclusively on kin for
emotional support than non-Hispanics, who seek emotional support from
a wider range of individuals (Mindel 1980, Lubben and Becerra 1987).

As are the Hispanic elderly, black elderly are actively invovled with
their families (Stack 1974). A large body of literature shows that blacks
have more contact with kin than do non-Hispanic whites; their social networks also include a larger number of nonnuclear relatives (e.g., Hogan,

Hao, and Parish 1990; Aschenbrenner 1975; Stack 1974; McAdoo 1978; Pearson et al. 1990).[6] These extended networks respond to the increasing need for instrumental aid by the elderly as they age (Litwak 1985, Taylor and Chatters 1986a). It is important to note, however, that these exchanges are reciprocal; among blacks, adult children provide both instrumental and material assistance to their elderly parents, and grandparents provide essential domestic services, such as child care, to the younger generations. In many cases, the grandmother steps in to replace the mother when she is unable to care for her child, and even when the mother is present, grandmothers engage in many parenting activities (Pearson et al. 1990).

Several studies show that older blacks, like older Mexican-Americans, are not only more likely than non-Hispanic whites to live near their children but they also interact with children and grandchildren more frequently than do non-Hispanic whites. They also report that they feel very close to their families and that they receive adequate support from family and friends (e.g., Taylor 1985, 1986; Gibson and Jackson 1989). Elderly black females are very often the focal individuals in the black extended family (Aschenbrenner 1975; Stack 1974; Shimkin, Shimkin, and Frate 1978). These women are particularly well integrated and play a very important role in the family. The nuclear family and the extended network of which it is a part, therefore, are clearly very important in maintaining the health of elderly black women (Lopata 1978).

There are numerous, often contradictory, findings concerning the role that friends and distant relatives play in the social support of elderly blacks.[7] Such factors as social class, religion, and marital history influence the number of these individuals who are available. In the black community, the church has always been a vital part of life, and it clearly serves as an important source of support for the black elderly (Taylor and Chatters 1986b).

In general, then, we can say that elderly blacks appear to be well integrated into functioning social networks that provide both instrumental and emotional support. This mutual dependence between generations is largely a response to the discrimination and restricted employment opportunities that blacks have historically faced in the United States. They have simply had to rely on one another and on an extended network in the face of hostility from white society. The existing research clearly demonstrates that the nuclear and extended families are crucial to the well-being of elderly blacks and Hispanics. Without these sources of social support, an older individual would be truly alone and would have to rely on the generosity of strangers.

One of the major determinants of one's social support, as well as of one's welfare in old age, is one's living arrangement. Individuals who live with family are in a very different situation from those who live alone. Because of this, and because the elderly often change living arrangements, the living arrangements of elderly women have received a great deal of attention. Below we briefly summarize the literature on the association between living arrangements and health among the elderly and then present the results of our own research on the association between health and living arrangements for elderly Hispanics, blacks, and non-Hispanic whites.

Living Arrangements and the Health of Unmarried Older Women

One of the most dramatic demographic trends that has occurred in the United States since the 1950s is the growth in the number of older individuals who live alone (Kobrin 1976, Wolf and Soldo 1988). The post-World War II boom in the American economy resulted in a dramatic growth in the nation's housing stock and a rapid decline in average household size. The increasing availability of housing, in conjunction with the greater economic security of the elderly, has allowed most older persons to exercise their apparent preference to live alone (Worobey and Angel 1990*b*). If behavior is a reflection of preferences, as at least economists believe it to be, most women prefer to live alone with their husband while he is alive but to live alone after he dies. Only a small fraction of widowed women live with their children. However, although this is true generally, there are large differences in the proportion of single black, Hispanic, and non-Hispanic older women who live with their children, and we show below that the health of these women differs from that of single older women who live alone.

The greater tendency for older black and Hispanic women to live with their children may, at least to some degree, reflect culturally influenced preferences, but it is to a much larger degree a matter of economic necessity (Angel and Tienda 1982; Tienda and Angel 1982; Mutran 1985; Worobey and Angel 1990*b*; Stack 1984). Elevated rates of adolescent pregnancy, a higher prevalence of fatherless families, and high poverty rates mean that black and Hispanic single mothers and grandmothers who might prefer to live alone may be forced to double up and form extended households.

As we have documented, however, the growth in the number of households containing grandmothers is not a single phenomenon, and there are large differences in the economic well-being of such households depending on whether or not the grandmother herself is the head of the household. Those households headed by single grandmothers are similar to other female-headed households in their economic profiles. Table 7.1

Table 7.1. Economic Characteristics of Single Grandmothers in Multigenerational Family Households

	Non-Hispanic White		Black	
	Head	Non-Head	Head	Non-Head
Total Income				
Amount $	2,052	3,460	1,227	2,223
AFDC[a]	21.8	2.7	54.1	5.1
Amount $	257	284	303	308
Social Security[a]	54.0	87.8	41.8	42.4
Amount $	482	455	393	314
SSI[a]	9.1	11.5	18.9	23.7
Amount $	246	285	265	358
Unemployment[a]	0.6	0.4	3.2	0.0
Amount $	196	340	186	-0-
Food Stamps[a]	0.7	0.7	53.1	25.9
Amount $	143	243	184	148
Transfers[a]	34.5	18.8	64.3	28.8
Amount ($)	292	229	385	349
N (unwght)	(62)	(71)	(69)	(24)

Source: 1984 Survey of Income and Program Participation (SIPP) Wave III.
[a]Percent reporting receiving cash payment or welfare benefit.

shows that they have low incomes and rely heavily on means-tested benefits such as AFDC, food stamps, and other transfers, including energy assistance and housing subsidies.

These data indicate that, as among younger women, there are two dimensions of disadvantage among households containing older women, family headship status and race. Over half of black grandmother-headed families receive AFDC, food stamps, and other transfers, while only one-fifth of non-Hispanic white grandmother-headed households depend on these sources of support. In contrast, households that contain a grandmother but in which she is not the head are much better off. A large fraction of these households are headed by a couple and represent situations in which an aged parent has moved in which her children. Since these households usually contain one or more working adults, they are better off economically than households maintained only by unemployed or underemployed women. Grandmother headship, therefore, is a major dimension of disadvantage, especially for blacks. Since children who are forced to live with their parents are, almost by definition, unable to support themselves independently, they usually contribute little to the aggregate income of the household, and the household's income consequently remains low at the same time that there are more mouths to feed.

Understanding the physical and mental health consequences of these various family situations for older women is clearly important. Unfortunately, although there is a large literature on age differences in depression, there has been little research comparing the physical and emotional health consequences of the lack of a spouse or of living arrangements for older women from different racial and ethnic groups. Below we will provide evidence from some of our own research that provides at least a glimpse of how marital status, race and ethnicity, and living arrangements operate singly and together to affect the health of middle-aged and older women.

Several studies of the living arrangements of elderly females show that elderly white single women who are in poor health are more likely than those who are in better health to live with others than to live alone (e.g., Beland 1984; Shanas 1962; Soldo, Sharma, and Campbell 1984; Schwartz, Danzinger, and Smolensky 1984; Tissue and McCoy 1981). Widowed elderly white women appear to prefer to live alone as long as their health will allow. They move in with others only when their functional capacity declines to a level at which they are unable to live independently (Worobey and Angel 1990*b*).

For black women, however, health has less of an impact on living arrangements. Older black women are more likely than whites to live with others regardless of health status (Bachrach 1980; Bishop 1986; Wolf 1984; Wolf and Soldo 1988; Worobey and Angel 1990*a*). For white widows, then, becoming ill often involves a change from independent to joint living arrangements or institutionalization, but for black elderly females, poor health less often results in such a change. Since fewer unmarried elderly black women than white women live alone, those who become ill continue to live in the family situation that preceded the illness (Worobey and Angel 1990*b*). Economic and social disadvantages restrict choices in living arrangements for older black women, just as they do for young black and Hispanic mothers who often have no choice but to remain in their own mother's home.

We know relatively little about the relationship between health and the living arrangements of elderly Hispanic women, but our knowledge is beginning to increase (Burr and Mutchler 1992). Our lack of knowledge is due to the fact that few large-scale national data sets include sufficient numbers of older Hispanics. Some initial evidence, however, suggests that very old Hispanics are more likely than non-Hispanics to live with family regardless of their health status (Worobey and Angel 1990a). These preliminary findings suggest that culture may affect preferences for coresidence and also influence norms concerning family responsibility to care for aging parents (Thomas and Wister 1984). As we noted above, Hispanics are typically considered to be more familistic than non-Hispanics, and this may increase the likelihood of older parents living with adult children.

Figure 7.1 summarizes how race and ethnicity interact with social class to influence a woman's family status and living arrangements in mature adulthood and old age. The broken two-headed arrow at the left indicates that race and ethnicity are correlated with socioeconomic status. Although there is tremendous within-group variation, blacks and Hispanics are, on average, poorer than non-Hispanic whites. In this conceptualization, race, ethnicity, and socioeconomic status influence living arrangements. Black and Hispanic elderly women are more likely than non-Hispanic white elderly women to live with others (Worobey and Angel 1990a). In turn, living arrangements determine the role strain and stress that an older woman experiences as well as the social support that she has at her

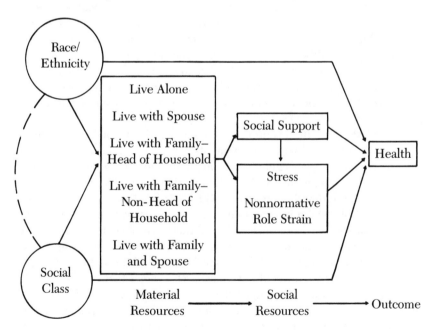

Figure 7.1. Conceptual Model of Health Consequences of Living Arrangements of Older Women

disposal, both directly and through association with socioeconomic status. Once again, blacks, Hispanics, and non-Hispanic whites differ in the size and composition of their social networks (Casas and Keefe 1978; Taylor 1988; Gibson and Jackson 1989; Angel and Tienda 1982). These various factors, therefore, have both direct and indirect effects on health.

This model emphasizes the fact that role overload and its associated stresses for older females results from poverty and, for single grandmothers, from the increased domestic responsibility for younger generations. Older single women lack the emotional support of a spouse, and as we showed in chapter 5, the lack of a confidant places one at risk of depression. The role of the older single female, then, often entails the double jeopardy of increased responsibility for family and inadequate social support. At a time in her life when she should be disengaging from the more immediate tasks of child rearing, she often finds herself burdened wtih the responsibility of caring for an extended family, and the consequent role strain may have a serious impact on her health.

Although living arrangements may influence health, health can clearly affect living arrangements. Poor health increases stress and potentially affects the amount of social support a woman has at her disposal. Becoming ill often means that a single older woman can no longer maintain social contacts. For older single women, living with family can mean increased responsibility at the same time that it provides potential sources of emotional support. Although much of this conceptual model must remain speculative since we do not have the data to test it, below we examine the association between living arrangements and functional capacity for elderly black, Hispanic, and non-Hispanic white women using some recent data.

In the last part of this chapter we examine the association between functional capactiy and living arrangements for black, Hispanic, and non-Hispanic white women aged fifty-five to ninety-nine. To do so, we use two national data sources[8] to compare the functional capacity of single older women and grandmothers who live with their families as head of household to that of women in two other situations: those who live with family but are not the head of household, and those who live alone. Table 7.2 shows that among the elderly, unmarried black and Hispanic women are nearly three times more likely than non-Hispanic whites to live with children as the head of household. This table also shows that, in general, elderly Hispanic women are most likely to live with their children both when they are married and when they are unmarried, reflecting the greater familistic orientation among Hispanics that many writers have commented on (Casas and Keefe 1978, Gratton 1987).

Table 7.3 presents information on the sociodemographic characteristics

Table 7.2. Household Living Arrangements of Elderly Women 55 and Older by Race/Ethnicity (Unweighted N's in Parentheses)

	Head of Household Live with Children	Non-Head of Household Live with Children	Married Live with Children	Live with Spouse Only	Live Alone
Non-Hispanic White	5.4	3.8	10.2	46.7	33.9
	(432)	(354)	(589)	(3,357)	(2,974)
Black	15.1	6.2	11.7	29.2	37.8
	(88)	(47)	(57)	(169)	(253)
Hispanic	15.5	8.7	17.4	33.2	25.3
	(28)	(19)	(29)	(66)	(52)

Source: 1984 National Health Interview Survey (NHIS)—Supplement on Aging (SOA).

of single elderly women in three living arrangements: (1) unmarried and living with family as the head of household; (2) unmarried and living with family, not as the head of household; and (3) living alone. As was the case for households headed by single mothers, this table reveals two dimensions of disadvantage: race and headship status. For all three racial and ethnic groups, a larger fraction of households headed by older women have incomes below the poverty line, but the combination of female headship and race and Hispanic ethnicity leads to even greater disadvantage. As among younger women, nearly half of black and nearly one-third of Hispanic female-headed households are poor. This table shows, however, that those women who live alone are the most likely to be poor.

Table 7.3 reveals other interesting differences between family households headed by older women and other household types. These are largely a reflection of the fact that elderly women who head their own households are younger, on average, than those who live alone or than those who live with family but are not heads. Women who are heads of household are less well educated than those who live with their children but are not the head of the household. However, they have more education than those who live alone. These patterns result from the fact that household headship among single elderly women, especially among minority single women, is associated with early fertility and low education. Because households in which the elderly female is not the head of household are often headed by a married couple with children, these households are larger, on average, than those headed by the older female.

Table 7.4 presents data on the health status of the unmarried elderly female, including problems with activities of daily living (ADLs),[9] self-assessed general health, the presence of one or more chronic health condi-

Table 7.3. Sociodemographic Characteristics of Unmarried Elderly Women in Family and Nonfamily Households by Race and Hispanic Ethnicity[a]

	Live with Children Head of Household			Live with Children Non-Head of Household			Live Alone		
	Non-Hispanic White	Black	Hispanic	Non-Hispanic White	Black	Hispanic	Non-Hispanic White	Black	Hispanic
Mean Age	68.5	65.2	64.6	76.7	74.1	72.2	72.0	69.6	66.5
Mean Education	12.6	10.8	10.5	13.3	12.7	12.2	10.9	7.9	7.8
Mean Family Size	2.5	3.2	3.4	3.6	4.2	4.6	1.0	1.0	1.0
Percent Below Poverty	13.4	45.8	29.3	5.1	34.6	23.2	25.6	65.0	39.8
Percent 1 or More Grandchildren	12.9	33.1	36.6	41.1	58.3	56.5	0.0	0.0	0.0
N	(432)	(88)	(28)	(354)	(47)	(19)	(3,032)	(256)	(54)

Source: 1984 National Health Interview Survey (NHIS)—Supplement on Aging (SOA).

[a]Weighted percentages, unweighted N's in parentheses.

Table 7.4. Health Characteristics of Unmarried Elderly Women in Family and Nonfamily Households by Race and Hispanic Ethnicity[a]

	Live with Children Head of Household			Live with Children Non-Head of Households			Live Alone		
	Non-Hispanic White	Black	Hispanic	Non-Hispanic White	Black	Hispanic	Non-Hispanic White	Black	Hispanic
ADL									
Percent 1 or more	22.7	28.3	20.4	45.5	56.7	27.8	22.8	29.6	21.0
Medical Conditions									
Percent 1 or more	67.7	61.9	74.9	80.7	87.7	90.6	72.1	79.0	74.7
Percent Hypertension	47.5	67.9	41.2	49.5	61.8	31.9	46.1	65.1	51.7
Self-Assessed Health (%)									
Excellent/Very Good	49.2	36.5	22.8	54.6	46.9	65.9	59.4	51.4	47.4
Good	41.0	49.1	62.6	37.6	37.7	11.1	31.3	32.5	38.3
Fair/Poor	9.7	14.4	14.7	7.8	15.4	23.0	9.4	16.1	14.4
N	(432)	(88)	(28)	(354)	(47)	(19)	(3,032)	(256)	(54)

Source: 1984 National Health Interview Survey (NHIS)—Supplement on Aging (SOA).
[a]Weighted percentages, unweighted N's in parentheses.

tions,[10] and hypertension. The first row shows the proportion of women in each living arrangement who report that they have trouble with at least one activity of daily living. As in the previous table, these data reflect two dimensions of disadvantage, race and household type. A larger proportion of older black women than non-Hispanic white women report some functional disability. In general, women who are the heads of household report the lowest levels of functional disability, again reflecting their younger age. Conversely, largely because they are older, those women who live with family but who are not heads of household have the highest levels of functional disability.

To determine what other factors might influence the association between living arrangements and health, we performed a multivariate analysis in which we predicted the extent of functional capacity as a function of various living arrangements, while controlling for the impact of various sociodemographic, economic, and cultural characteristics. These results are presented in Appendix 7.A and show that after all the other factors are taken into account, blacks are no different from non-Hispanic whites in terms of functional capacity. However, Hispanics are less likely than non-Hispanic whites to be disabled. In addition, those women who live with family but are not the head of household are more likely than women who live with their spouses to report a disability. Clearly, then, family living arrangements interact with race, ethnicity, and income to affect health.

The statistics for chronic conditions and for hypertension in table 7.4 also reflect the different ages among women in the various living arrangements. In general, largely because they are younger, women who head their own households have fewer chronic conditions and report less hypertension than either women who are not heads of households or women who live alone. Older black women have consistently higher rates of hypertension than the other two groups regardless of household type, a finding that is universal in the literature.

The final dimension of health in table 7.4 is a subjective evaluation of one's overall health status. Even though black and Hispanic women who are heads of household reported fewer functional disabilities and fewer medical conditions than their white counterparts, they report poorer self-assessed health. Over 14 percent of women in both groups report only fair or poor health, and a much smaller fraction report excellent and very good health than do non-Hispanic white heads of household. The fact that this global assessment is inconsistent with the more objective indicators, functional capacity and chronic conditions, is intriguing and suggests that even though they are in relatively good physical health, the stresses associated with the responsibility of managing a household lead to poorer subjective well-being among older women. As we showed in chapter 4, such global assessments of physical health largely reflect one's psychological status, and we can assume that a good number of these women are stressed.

If, in fact, heading one's own household is stressful, why would one do it? As we noted earlier, the formation of extended households is largely a response to need. Because she has no job skills, a young mother may simply have no choice but to move in with her own mother. Conversely, a destitute or ill older woman can either enter a long-term care facility or move in with her family. Table 7.5 gives us some idea of the reasons for extension among the various racial and ethnic groups. It compares responses to the question, "What is the main reason you are now living together [with family]? Is it for health, finances, or some other reason?" The responses show that black and Hispanic elderly women are much more likely to live with family for economic reasons than are non-Hispanic whites. In contrast, all three groups are similar in the proportion reporting health as the reason for living together. These results show that, in fact, economic need is a major motivation for extended living arrangements among black and Hispanic elderly women.

To examine what other factors might influence the association between income and living arrangements, we performed several multivariate analyses. These are reported in Appendix 7.B. They show that even after controlling for age, education, region of the country, and central city versus rural residence, both income and health remain highly significant predictors of living arrangements. Women with low income are more likely to live alone, and women with a greater number of functional disabilities are less likely to live alone. Even after controlling for those factors, race and Hispanic ethnicity continue to be significant predictors of extended living arrangements. Blacks and especially Hispanics are more likely than non-

Table 7.5. Reasons for Living with Family by Race and Hispanic Ethnicity[a]

Reason	Non-Hispanic Whites	Blacks	Hispanics
Economic Need	25.5	40.1	40.9
	(339)	(73)	(29)
Chi-Square = 23.339, p = .000			
Health Problems	23.5	28.6	28.2
	(313)	(52)	(20)
Chi-Square = 2.827, p = .243			

Source: 1984 National Health Interview Survey (NHIS)—Supplement on Aging (SOA).
[a]Weighted percentages, unweighted N's in parentheses.

Hispanic whites to live with others. Clearly, then, health, income, race, and Hispanic ethnicity are all important determinants of the living arrangements and well-being of elderly females.

One other available data set allows us to examine the impact of single motherhood and divorce on a woman's health. These data come from the 1988 National Survey of Families and Households (NSFH), which contains information on the health and economic characteristics of over 13,000 American families (Sweet, Bumpass, and Call 1988). For our analyses, we selected a subsample of 2,106 women fifty-five years of age and over who were of either non-Hispanic white, black, or Hispanic origin. We were interested in the long-term effects of single motherhood on the health of women in later life. Appendix 7.C documents the fact that after we controlled for age, education, race/ethnicity, income, marital status, and number of children, the length of time a woman has spent as a single mother has no effect on the four health outcomes. These measures of physical and mental well-being are defined in terms of how she perceives her life in general; how she evaluates her own health in general; the number of physical disabilities in caring for her daily needs; and her own level of psychological distress (CES-D). What does seem to be an important determinant of a woman's health in later life, however, is the number of times she has been married. The more times a woman has been married, the greater number of psychological symptoms she reports. What these results show is that the amount of time a woman spends as a single mother is not associated with poor health, but as in children, marital disruption has serious mental health consequences for women in late adulthood.

Social Support, Health, and Functional Capacity: A Theoretical Model

We began this chapter with the promise that we would develop a theoretical model of the association between a mature woman's family situation and her physical and mental health. In what follows, we summarize the results of a number of studies of the association between marital status, social support, and living arrangements and their impact on health among the elderly. None of the data we summarized, however, provided an unambiguous answer to the question of how a woman's marital and fertility history in early and middle adulthood affects her physical and mental health in mature adulthood. A definitive answer to the question will have to await longitudinal data on large samples followed over a lifetime. Such a data set may never become available. The research we reviewed here, however, allows us to make a plausible inferential case concerning the impact of race and Hispanic ethnicity, as well as marital and fertility history, on an older woman's well-being.

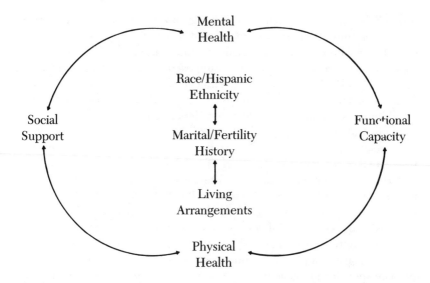

Figure 7.2. Theoretical Model of the Interdependence of Dimensions of Health in Later Life

Figure 7.2 presents our final inductively derived theoretical model of the association between social support, race and Hispanic ethnicity, living arrangements, marital and fertility history, and health in mature adulthood. This model identifies key associations, but because of the complex interactive nature of the various dimensions of physical, mental, and social health, it does not propose simple one-way linkages between the various domains. In fact, on the basis of the research we reviewed in this and previous chapters, it is clear that when we are dealing with social support, mental and physical health, and functional capacity, clear delineations between dependent and independent variables are somewhat artificial. A lack of social support, for example, can undermine health, but poor health can make the maintenance of social interactions difficult, thereby leading to a reduction in social support. Poor mental health can make it difficult to maintain social contacts, and it can undermine physical health. Conversely, a lack of social support or poor physical health can result in depression.

Most of the associations between the health constructs we have discussed are of this interactive sort, and our inability to clearly distinguish between them may not simply be a matter of inadequate measures; these outcomes may, in fact, be manifestations of a common underlying entity, something we might label general health or well-being. In chapter 4 we showed that at the experiential level, mind and body are inseparable and that the experience of self is influenced by various cultural and social factors. Global concepts, such as well-being, are troublesome in empirical science because they are imprecise and difficult to operationalize and quantify. As empiricists, our instincts and training lead us to dimensionalize such concepts into their supposed constituent elements. Although it is clearly possible and even necessary for research purposes to treat social support and other measures of health as distinct entities, we should not lose sight of their clear interdependence.

To illustrate the interdependent nature of our health outcomes, in figure 7.2, social support, functional capacity, mental and physical health are placed in a circle to signify that each affects the other simultaneously. Race and Hispanic ethnicity, marital and fertility history, and living arrangements are at the center of the circle to illustrate that, as we have documented, they influence each of the health outcomes. We also wish to emphasize the centrality of culture and group differences in family structure to the determination of health in the broadest sense. This conceptual model is clearly complex, and from a research perspective, it is only heuristic. The specification of actual research models requires a clear identification of dependent and independent variables. We hope that this conceptual model and the research we have summarized in this chapter will motivate future research into the impact of marital and fertility history, family structure, and living arrangements on the health of older women.

We can conclude that at the very least, single grandmotherhood, when it occurs in conjunction with poverty and a disorganized social environment, harms an older woman's physical and emotional health. We can also confidently say that the availability of alternative forms of social support, such as children and fellow church members, can protect a single woman from many of the negative health consequences of spouselessness. We should not end here, though. A better understanding of the factors that affect the health of elderly single women is important for numerous reasons. In the latter half of the twentieth century, a growing number of poor minority women find themselves single through all or much of their reproductive lives, and as a result, we should be prepared for an increase in the number of multigenerational female-maintained households. The growth in the number of female-headed households is a significant factor in the rise in chronic poverty, and if current trends continue, an increasing number of minority families will become part of a social order in which men are peripheral to the household throughout the family life course.

In this chapter we also documented large differences in the association between health and living arrangements among Hispanic, black, and non-Hispanic white elderly women. Our research and the research of others, much of it of a qualitative sort, show that among blacks and Hispanics, the extended family serves as an important source of social support for older women and that, in large part, it appears to be a demographic response to the restricted economic opportunities faced by minority males and females in American society. Relatively few blacks or Hispanics enter nursing homes, and, unfortunately, we know little about how individuals who have been subjected to the lifelong health risks of poverty cope with diminished health in the later years of life. Both the existing literature and our data indicate that minority group elderly females have limited options in the event of poor health and that minority families are more active in the care of the infirm elderly than are non-Hispanic white families.

As the female-headed household supplants the husband-wife family, poor women increasingly enter middle age and the later years of the life course burdened with responsibilities for young children as their own daughters have children and continue to need support. Since these women lack the financial, instrumental, and emotional support of a spouse, the entire burden of a household beset with the problems of poverty falls on their shoulders. It would be surprising if such increased burdens were not to adversely affect the mental and physical health of older women. Since the family is an interdependent entity in which the health of one member affects the health of others, the stresses faced by poor female-headed households may undermine the health of all generations.

Many writers have noted that Hispanic culture has strong norms concerning responsibilities toward the elderly that increase the likelihood that an older person will continue to reside with his or her family even after becoming infirm (Gratton 1987, Sena-Rivera 1979). Whether Hispanics are more or less familistic than non-Hispanics in the contemporary United States is an open question. However, it is clear that as Hispanics migrate to the inner city, they take on many of the characteristics of the black urban underclass, including high rates of poverty and female-headed households (Moore 1989, Wilson 1987). Regardless of the culture of origin, the disruptive aspects of inner-city life and the lack of occupational opportunities for men forces women to rely on one another. In years to come we are likely to see a large increase in the number of female-headed households among Hispanics, and we can expect this phenomenon to be part of a growth in chronic poverty among these groups.

We should end by noting that although we have chosen to focus on those black and Hispanic older women at greatest risk of poverty and ill health, the majority of older women are not at elevated risk of either. The elderly, in fact, have been among the best served by our social welfare state. John Myles (1984) has labeled the welfare state in the United States an "old-age welfare state." This label is intended to convey the fact that most of what we spend on social welfare goes to the elderly. As we show in the next chapter, by far the majority of funds spent by government on programs that ensure the health and welfare of citizens go to the elderly. SSI was one of the few welfare programs that was not cut but actually expanded during the early years of the Reagan administration. As a consequence, in recent years the extent of poverty among the elderly has dropped dramatically (Children's Defense Fund 1990).

For the vast majority of older Americans, therefore, late adulthood is not a problem-ridden time of life but rather a secure and potentially productive one. As we noted in our discussion of single mothers in chapter 6, there is no inherent reason why female-headed households should be harmful to health. The same is true for grandmother-headed households. In the absence of males, this family form is a perfectly reasonable way for women and children to provide practical and emotional support to one another. Unfortunately, as with female-headed households generally, those headed by an older female are at high risk of poverty and its associated health threats. For these households, a welfare system geared toward the alleviation of transitory poverty may be inadequate. The reality of modern American urban life is that because of the multiple disadvantages that minority group single women face throughout life, in the absence of relatively generous governmental support, these families would almost certainly face serious deprivation.

In previous centuries, elderly individuals remained with their families until death. For blacks and Hispanics, certain elements of this pattern continue to hold today. Few blacks or Hispanics enter nursing homes, and as our data show, they remain with their families even when they suffer fairly serious declines in functional capacity. As the number of older individuals increases, in years to come the extended minority family will play an increasingly important role in the care of the infirm elderly. Although in the future a greater number of black and Hispanic elderly persons will no doubt enter nursing homes, an alternative option would be to provide the extended family help in caring for their aging relatives at home. Hispanics, who have higher fertility than non-Hispanics and who appear to be culturally attuned to caring for the elderly at home, may be very receptive to this option. We end this chapter by noting simply that, whatever policy options we choose, it is clear that the phenomenon of female-headed households containing older women is increasing and that many of these households will require ongoing assistance. In chapter 8, we review the development of policy toward female-headed families over the last two decades and provide an outline of current and future options for their support.

Appendix 7.A. Standardized Coefficients for Pooled and Separate Regressions of
Functional Capacity among Non-Hispanic White, Black, and Hispanic Elderly Women

| | | Non-Hispanic | | |
	Pooled	Whites	Blacks	Hispanics
Sociodemographic				
Age	.22**	.22**	.19**	.27**
Education	−.07**	−.06**	−.10*	−.01
Culture[a]				
Black	.02			
Hispanic	−.03*			
Cuban-American				.07
Puerto Rican				.18*
Income[b]				
Low Income	.09**	.09**	−.06	.07
Middle Income	.01	.01	−.04	−.00
Headship[c]				
Live alone	−.03*	−.03*	.04	.02
Live with Nonrelative	.03*	.03*	.04	−.02
Married–Live with Family	−.02	−.04*	.06	.17
Unmarried–Live with Family (Non-head of household)	.10**	.08**	.19**	.12
Unmarried–Live with Family (Head of household)	−.01	−.01	.06	.04
Daughters	.05**	.06**	−.01	.06
Son	.04**	.06**	−.04	.02
Adjusted R²	.105	.105	.099	.052
	(7,627)	(6,853)	(592)	(182)

Source: 1984 National Health Interview Survey (NHIS)–Supplement on Aging (SOA).

Note: Variables are continuous unless otherwise indicated. Reference categories for dummy variables are described below.

[a]Non-Hispanic white.

[b]High income.

[c]Live with spouse only.

p < .05.

**p* < .01.

Appendix 7.B. Logistic Regressions of Household Extension on Income and Health
Controlling for Sociodemographic and Structural Characteristics

	Model 1[a]			Model 2[b]		
	Pooled	Black	White	Pooled	Black	White
Sociodemographic						
Age	−.01*	.02	−.01*	−.04**	−.11	−.04**
Education (in years)	−.16**	−.07*	−.17**	.09**	.06	.10**
Culture[c]						
Black	1.05**			.24		
Hispanic	1.18**			−.09		
Economic[d]						
Low Family Income	−3.03**	−3.17**	−3.00**	1.54**	2.70**	.10**
Middle Family Income	−1.22**	−.32	−1.31**	.78**	2.68**	1.47**
Structural						
North Central[e]	−.35**	.01	−.37**	−.11	.30	−.16
South[e]	.22*	.42	−.28*	.11	1.19	.05
West[e]	−.51**	.33	−.55**	.20	2.19	.01
City[f]	−.10	−.23	−.05	.25	−.36	.26
Rural[f]	.12	−.07	.15	.13	−1.17	.20
Health						
ADL	.09**	.05	.10**	−.06**	−.07	−.06**
R²	.210	.166	.204	.115	.207	.099
N	(3,922)	(384)	(3,439)	(1,112)	(157)	(902)
Proportion in Category 1	(28.4)	(40.9)	(26.2)	(56.7)	(68.8)	(54.8)

Note: Variables are continuous unless otherwise indicated. Reference categories for
dummy variables are described below.
[a]Live alone.
[b]Live with family not as head of household.
[c]Non-Hispanic white.
[d]High income.
[e]East.
[f]Suburb.
*$p < .05$.
**$p < .01$.

Appendix 7.C. Determinants of Health among Older Women[a]

	Things in General	Self-Evaluation	Physical Disability	CES-D Score
Intercept1	.30	−3.61**	−3.68**	14.69**
Intercept2	—	−2.39**	—	—
Intercept3	—	−.56	—	—
Intercept4	—	1.77**	—	—
Age	−.01*	.01*	.05**	.03
Education	−.08**	−.14**	−.11**	−.58**
Number of Times Married	.07	.12	.13	1.82**
Black	−.20	.29*	.23	−1.92*
Hispanic	−.41	−.01	−.46	−1.67
Months Single Mother	.00	.00	.00	.00
Divorced	.53**	.23	.38*	1.93
Widowed	.47**	−.10	.19	.79
Never Married	.13	.38	.69*	1.44
Number of Children	−.05*	.02	.04	.06
Income $0–$9,999	.12	.52**	.67**	1.20
Income $10,000–$19,999	.18	.35*	.18	.03
Income $20,000–$29,999	−.31	.40*	.61*	.26
Income–Missing	.11	.53**	.36	.56
Sample Size	(2,106)	(1,989)	(2,103)	(2,106)

Source: National Survey of Families and Households (NSFH), 1988.

*p < .05.

**p < .01.

[a]The first three dependent variables refer to (1) being satisfied with life in general; (2) reporting less than excellent health; and (3) reporting at least one physical disability. The fourth dependent variable refers to greater psychological distress.

8

Single Motherhood, Health, and the
New American Political Reality

Convention dictates that we come to some overall conclusion regarding the impact of single motherhood on the health of women and children and make some suggestions about what might be done to address their health care needs. In this chapter, therefore, we provide a summary assessment of the magnitude of the health consequences of single motherhood for women and their children, examine state differences in the response to the health-related needs of single-parent families, review recent trends in funding levels for nutritional and health programs, and offer some informed suggestions concerning potential alternatives for addressing the health care needs of fatherless families. We also summarize recent important reforms in Medicaid that clearly benefit single mothers and their children, and we examine the question of just how far toward a federally financed and sponsored national health insurance scheme, perhaps like the current Canadian system that provides comprehensive physician and hospital insurance to all citizens, the United States could or should move in the future.

In the preceding chapters, we reviewed a great deal of evidence showing that a woman's marital status, her living arrangements, and her fertility history influence her health and her children's health in often subtle, sometimes dramatic, ways. What is particularly intriguing is the possibility that these factors influence physical and mental health across the life course. The data clearly show that father absence has negative emotional and behavioral health consequences for children. For young women, single motherhood and the lack of a confidant often undermine emotional well-being, and for many older women, spouse absence is often accompanied by depression and social isolation. Unfortunately, since most of the available evidence is based on cross-sectional data, we cannot be certain how the health consequences of single motherhood at different ages are interconnected.

What we would like to know is whether father absence has long-term health consequences for children and whether single motherhood has long-term health consequences for women. We would also like to identify the mechanisms through which any negative physical or mental health effects operate. Unfortunately, a more detailed understanding of these mechanisms must await longitudinal data on marital status, fertility, and health. We can be fairly certain, however, that any negative health consequences of single motherhood for children or for adults result from complex interactions among poverty, emotional stress, and such factors as low education and inadequate social support. What remains for future research is to disentangle these complex interactive relationships and to identify those factors that are most responsible for any health deficits that single mothers and their children suffer.

Let us begin our look toward the future by asking if it is possible to provide a brief summary of the impact of single motherhood on the health of women and children. Obviously, simple characterizations misrepresent much of the reality that affects the lives of women and children in fatherless families and also gloss over the great heterogeneity among single-parent families. Nonetheless, a summary of general differentials in health is certainly possible, even desirable, as a point of departure for assessing the health care needs of these families. Perhaps the least debatable conclusion that we can draw from the vast amount of information we have reviewed is that the health problems of single mothers and their children are different today than they were in the past. As for all segments of the population of the developed world, acute infectious illness has become a minor problem for single mothers and their children. Unfortunately, the recent increase in the proportion of inadequately immunized children and the growing AIDS epidemic may quickly render this statement untrue. Nonetheless, as we have doucmented, although the children of the poor are far worse off economically than the children of middle-class Americans, they do not suffer the serious physical health afflictions that were common earlier in the century and that kill millions of children and adults in the Third World today. To be sure, infant mortality rates in the United States remain shockingly high for certain groups, and in some of our major urban centers black infant mortality rates approach those of the Third World. But for the most part, the programs of the welfare state have had their intended effect, and today the vast majority of Americans live physically healthy and disease-free lives.

Yet we have hardly achieved a health care utopia. What we have done, in fact, is to exchange one set of health problems for another. Although children no longer suffer from the more serious physical health problems of previous centuries, the evidence we reviewed clearly demonstrates that both single mothers and their children are at high risk of emotional and behavioral problems as the result of the conflict surrounding family disruption, unassisted parenthood, inadequate adult supervision, and poverty. Additionally, many children born to single mothers experience educational deficits that can have serious long-term consequences. These emotional, behavioral, and educational deficits are particularly worrisome because, at least for the foreseeable future, a large fraction of children, especially among blacks and Hispanics, will grow up in poor single-parent families where they will be at elevated risk of these outcomes.

Although these problems, like the growing problems of family violence and drug abuse, are not medical in a strict sense, they affect the health of millions of American children and adults. Our health and welfare policy, therefore, must address these issues since they threaten the social and emotional well-being of millions of children and could ultimately undermine the very social fabric of our nation. Unfortunately, dealing with these massive social problems in a period of economic stagnation and growing voter hostility to programs for the poor will prove particularly difficult. Let us briefly examine the social and political context within which the response to the health problems of single mothers and their children is being shaped.

A New Health Policy Agenda

As we noted in chapter 2, in the developed world family support policies are crucial for ensuring the good health of single mothers and their children. Most developed nations provide some support, including health care, to all families with children. The United States has no such universal program, and government sponsorship of health care is directed toward the elderly and the poor. Yet over thirty-five million Americans are not covered by any form of health insurance. This incomplete system of insurance coverage is one of the major social problems facing our nation as we approach the end of the twentieth century. To understand the sources of this gap in health insurance, we must understand the larger economic, political, and social forces that shape family and health care policy in the United States and that limit the possibilities for change.

Unemployment and underemployment, of course, lie at the basis of the problem of poverty and, consequently, of poor health and the lack of access to medical care for the poor in the United States. Almost by definition, a good job is one that provides adequate income and benefits like health insurance. Unfortunately, because a large fraction of jobs are in marginal service industries that offer few benefits, many workers have no health insurance and yet have inadequate income to purchase private health insurance. Since whatever growth in employment we can expect for at least the next decade will occur in the low-paid service sector, the number of individuals without employment-based health insurance can only increase. There seems little choice but some form of federally mandated health insurance, perhaps as a state-sponsored and subsidized employment benefit. Ultimately, however, the insurer of last resort must be the federal government.

If we wished to think in terms of utopian solutions to the health problems of single mothers and their children, we could suggest radical solutions that would go directly to the source of the problems associated with poverty. Obviously, the negative consequences of poverty could be best addressed by a full employment policy that would ensure everyone who is able to and wants to work a job with adequate pay. If young minority men were self-supporting, young minority women would no longer face a disappearing pool of marriageable males, and families would be less likely to disintegrate. We might offer training and employment opportunities to single mothers so that they could eventually provide for themselves, and we could ensure that all families, regardless of income, have adequate child care, health insurance, transportation, housing, and other support services.

Clearly, the best health policy would be an employment and income support policy that would make everyone self-sufficient and ensure adequate nutrition and health care on a nonstigmatizing basis. Unfortunately, the sort of full employment policy that would make those single mothers who are currently unemployable self-supporting strikes us as neither politically nor economically realistic. Radical solutions to the problems of poverty that include restructuring the labor market and adopting something like the more advanced family support systems of Western European countries are unlikely in the United States at this point in our history. Large-scale experimentation with programs to enhance the employability of poorly educated adolescents and adults during the 1960s and 1970s met with very limited success (Danziger and Weinberg 1986), and it is simply unclear that even with the best of intentions, it would be possible to provide adequate employment to everyone who might want it in the private sector. Many single mothers are simply too young or too poorly educated to be employable. These women and their children, therefore, will remain dependent on the state for basic welfare and medical care, and the dependency burden that they represent will in all likelihood increase in the future.

We might ask whether any significant expansion in welfare or health care programs for the poor is likely to accompany the growth in the number of fatherless families in the United States during the next few years. Although no one can foretell the future with certainty, given our current political climate, such an expansion seems unlikely. Of course, expenditures for welfare, including those for health care, will inevitably increase simply as the result of the growth in the number of eligible families, but in all likelihood the value of the overall package of goods and services that single mothers and their children receive will remain much the same as it is today. A relatively stagnant economy, the absence of effective political coalitions advocating the extension of welfare, the declining political influence of labor, and the growing racial antagonisms in American society are only some of the factors that, in our opinion, make the development of a European-style paternalistic welfare state that would provide cradle to grave income and health services for all Americans rather unlikely.

Perhaps future changes in the economy and labor force, in conjunction with the aging of the baby boom cohorts, will force a refocusing of our basic welfare philosophy toward a more comprehensive and egalitarian system, but for the immediate future we can be fairly sure that things will continue as they are. Today, the expansion of welfare programs, including those that provide medical care to fatherless families, is simply not at issue; retaining existing funding levels will be difficult enough. The task at hand, therefore, is to identify those programs that are most important to the health and welfare of single mothers and their children and to determine how the health care needs of fatherless families can be addressed in an economically and politically realistic manner. Our dilemma involves finding ways of controlling the cost of health care for the poor at the same time that we ensure that the medical care they receive is of adequate quality.

State Differences in the Magnitude of the Problem

The possibilities for reform, of course, are limited by the nature of our political and economic institutions. One of the major obstacles to radical change in the way health care is financed and delivered to the poor is the fact that our health care system, like our state–federal government system generally, is among the least centralized and coordinated in the world. The lack of a central coordinating capacity results in large state differences in health care availability to the poor. Although the federal government establishes certain minimal criteria that states must meet if they are to participate in programs such as Medicaid, the determination of eligibility for these programs is left up to the states. Such a system results in serious inequities, since similarly needy families receive much more in some states than in others. Such differences far exceed any differences in the average cost of living. A brief examination of basic state differences in indicators of the severity of the problem of adolescent pregnancy and unemployment, as well as differences in the proportion of the potentially eligible population covered by social welfare and health-related programs, readily illustrates the point.

Table 8.1 shows large interstate differences in four social indicators associated with poverty and single motherhood: adolescent pregnancy rates, the proportion of births to unmarried women, high school graduation rates, and youth unemployment rates. In our nation's capital, over 17 percent of pregnancies are to adolescents and 21 percent are to unmarried women. This phenomenon is part of a package of social problems that includes high rates of school dropout and youth unemployment. In Washington, D.C., only half of all children graduate from high school, and one-fifth of young people are unemployed. The situation is particularly serious in the South. In Mississippi, for example, over 35 percent of births are to unmarried women, one-third of adolescents fail to graduate from high school, and nearly one-third of young people are unemployed.

Table 8.2 presents information on state differences in participation in programs on which single-parent families rely. Once again, we can see that states differ greatly in the extent of coverage. In our nation's capital, fewer than two-thirds of mothers receive early prenatal care; 80 percent rely on WIC; more than one quarter are enrolled in Head Start; one out of five eligible children receives child support from the absent parent; and in only one out of five extramarital pregnancies can paternity be established. Of course, states differ greatly in the number of children in need, and program enrollment statistics reflect this fact. For example, In Mississippi, over half of poor children are enrolled in Head Start, while in Alabama, an equally poor state, only 16 percent of poor children are enrolled.

These statistics illustrate one of the major dilemmas that is an almost inevitable consequence of maximizing local control in a large federally organized nation with large regional differences in income, employment opportunities, and health care needs. Some states have both the resources and the desire to provide more welfare and health care to fatherless families than others. Since the 1980s, the federal government has restricted its

Table 8.1. Problems Associated with Single Motherhood

Region of U.S.	1987 Proportion of All Births to Adolescents[a]	1987 Proportion of All Births to Unmarried Women[b]	1987 High School Graduation[c]	1988 Youth Unemployment[d]
New England				
Connecticut	8.6	23.5	80.5	5.5
Maine	10.6	19.8	79.3	10.6
Massachusetts	8.3	20.9	76.5	9.7
New Hampshire	7.8	14.7	72.7	10.0
Rhode Island	9.8	21.8	69.4	9.7
Vermont	8.0	11.1	78.0	5.5
Mid-Atlantic				
Delaware	13.3	27.7	70.1	10.0
District of Columbia	16.3	59.7	55.5	20.0
Kentucky	17.3	20.7	67.4	20.6
Maryland	11.4	31.5	74.5	15.6
New Jersey	9.2	23.5	77.2	10.4
New York	9.4	29.7	62.9	13.9
Pennsylvania	10.9	25.3	78.7	13.9
Virginia	11.4	22.8	74.0	12.9
West Virginia	17.0	21.1	76.2	26.8
North Central				
Illinois	12.4	28.0	75.7	16.3
Indiana	13.9	22.0	73.7	12.0
Iowa	9.3	16.2	86.8	15.2
Michigan	12.3	20.4	62.4	17.5
Minnesota	7.5	17.1	90.6	10.2
Missouri	13.3	23.7	74.4	20.0
Nebraska	8.9	16.8	86.7	13.4
North Dakota	7.6	24.9	88.4	11.7
Ohio	13.2	24.4	82.8	15.6
South Dakota	10.4	29.0	79.7	11.0
Wisconsin	9.7	20.7	85.4	6.5

Table 8.1. Problems Associated with Single Motherhood (*continued*)

Region of U.S.	1987 Proportion of All Births to Adolescents[a]	1987 Proportion of All Births to Unmarried Women[b]	1987 High School Graduation[c]	1988 Youth Unemployment[d]
West				
Alaska	9.3	23.0	66.6	17.9
California	10.8	27.2	66.1	15.7
Hawaii	9.8	21.3	70.8	10.7
Idaho	11.1	13.0	78.8	15.3
Montana	10.1	19.4	86.2	16.8
Nevada	11.7	16.4	72.1	13.3
Oregon	11.4	22.4	72.8	13.6
Utah	9.5	11.1	80.6	12.2
Washington	10.4	20.8	77.8	16.7
Wyoming	11.2	15.8	89.3	13.8
Southwest				
Arizona	13.9	27.2	64.4	17.4
Colorado	10.6	18.9	73.7	18.4
Kansas	11.4	17.2	82.1	13.0
New Mexico	15.3	29.6	71.7	24.5
Oklahoma	16.0	20.7	72.6	14.8
Texas	15.0	19.0	65.1	21.8
South				
Alabama	17.4	26.8	70.2	17.6
Arkansas	18.8	24.6	77.5	21.0
Florida	13.5	27.5	58.6	19.0
Georgia	16.6	27.9	62.5	18.5
Louisiana	16.8	31.9	60.1	28.9
Mississippi	20.1	35.9	64.8	27.4
North Carolina	15.7	24.9	67.8	12.4
South Carolina	16.4	29.0	66.9	13.1
Tennessee	16.8	26.3	67.8	21.8
U.S. Total	12.4	24.5	71.1	15.3

[a]From Children's Defense Fund (1990*a*): 161.
[b]Ibid., 160.
[c]From Children's Defense Fund (1990*b*): 92.
[d]Ibid., 93.

Table 8.2. State Response to Problems Associated with Single Motherhood by Region

U.S. Region	1987 Early Prenatal Care[a]	1989 Eligible WIC Population Served[b]	1985 Head Start Enrollment[c]	1988 Child Support[d]	1987 Paternities Established[e]
New England					
Connecticut	85.7	76.5	25.3	59.3	35.4
Maine	83.5	39.7	18.2	17.9	28.5
Massachusetts	83.3	56.3	19.7	23.4	39.9
New Hampshire	83.4	57.6	26.8	22.8	7.8
Rhode Island	83.8	59.2	18.8	51.6	19.6
Vermont	79.0	80.1	23.1	24.9	74.8
Mid-Atlantic					
Delaware	77.7	57.0	18.6	30.0	68.1
District of Columbia	60.5	83.5	27.6	16.8	16.8
Kentucky	75.9	58.0	22.5	12.7	36.4
Maryland	80.5	48.4	20.1	26.9	28.5
New Jersey	80.5	50.9	17.4	25.9	52.3
New York	71.4	66.7	12.1	32.5	22.8
Pennsylvania	78.6	67.9	16.0	53.3	36.9
Virginia	80.9	55.8	14.5	31.3	13.0
West Virginia	70.3	43.4	13.7	19.0	6.1
North Central					
Illinois	78.5	61.0	15.5	41.7	41.1
Indiana	77.9	56.4	13.7	—	20.7
Iowa	85.4	54.0	11.1	13.6	27.1
Michigan	80.8	65.8	18.2	19.6	63.6
Minnesota	80.4	67.3	13.4	36.4	34.7
Missouri	80.3	53.0	16.8	11.2	—
Nebraska	82.4	46.5	12.2	14.9	17.7
North Dakota	82.1	65.0	11.3	40.4	79.4
Ohio	81.9	57.8	19.2	20.1	23.3
South Dakota	74.3	53.5	13.1	15.8	24.8
Wisconsin	83.3	62.8	17.2	—	59.5

Table 8.2. State Response to Problems Associated with Single Motherhood by Region
(*continued*)

U.S. Region	1987 Early Prenatal Care[a]	1989 Eligible WIC Population Served[b]	1985 Head Start Enrollment[c]	1988 Child Support[d]	1987 Paternities Established[e]
West					
Alaska	76.4	61.7	19.5	16.9	14.2
California	75.9	59.2	11.7	20.3	20.4
Hawaii	76.8	35.4	15.6	20.1	26.7
Idaho	74.9	40.9	10.5	15.3	18.5
Montana	77.2	44.4	12.6	8.1	—
Nevada	73.2	75.2	7.5	16.3	19.4
Oregon	73.7	61.6	12.7	16.2	21.9
Utah	82.2	48.6	13.1	21.5	32.9
Washington	77.1	45.5	11.5	14.6	27.8
Wyoming	79.4	74.8	15.2	6.2	8.8
Southwest					
Arizona	70.1	62.1	9.9	35.5	5.9
Colorado	77.4	66.5	18.7	15.3	12.7
Kansas	80.7	55.0	17.9	13.6	16.9
New Mexico	56.4	52.7	16.7	18.6	5.1
Oklahoma	73.0	48.9	19.7	13.9	5.2
Texas	67.3	59.0	10.7	10.8	1.2
South					
Alabama	73.6	54.7	15.7	33.5	43.9
Arkansas	68.6	49.6	16.0	20.4	62.7
Florida	69.4	57.6	11.6	19.2	26.5
Georgia	72.4	72.0	14.8	17.9	49.3
Louisiana	75.4	68.4	13.9	33.1	12.4
Mississippi	76.5	70.1	55.8	13.3	12.7
North Carolina	77.6	61.4	18.7	28.7	42.6
South Carolina	66.3	65.1	16.1	45.2	26.1
Tennessee	75.8	60.8	15.4	32.3	42.8
U.S. Total	76.0	59.6	15.5	23.4	27.3

[a]From Children's Defense Fund (1990*b*): 84.
[b]Ibid., 96.
[c]Ibid., 97.
[d]Ibid., 99.
[e]Ibid., 89.

role in providing welfare and health care to the poor and has increasingly turned this responsibility over to the states, many of which have introduced innovative changes into their Medicaid programs. We will discuss these innovations below. This trend toward greater state control in determining program content and eligibility may result in even more exaggerated differences in levels of support for fatherless families depending on their state of residence. As we explain later in our discussion of national health insurance, a more centralized system of health care financing might eliminate some of these inequities between states—but only at the cost of decreasing local control. A philosophy of state autonomy is such a central aspect of American political culture that it would be hard to overcome. We must keep in mind, however, that this adherence to a philosophy of state control is one of the major factors limiting the possibilities for change in the way health care is provided to the poor.

Rather large state differences in problems associated with single motherhood and in levels of support, therefore, are central features of our health care system. They must be understood, however, in light of the general stagnation in levels of welfare and health program participation since the 1980s. Table 8.3 presents information on recent national trends in participation in various health-related programs. This table reveals that except for WIC, the expansion in programs that ensure the nutrition of women

Table 8.3. Trends in Federal Food Program Participation, 1975–1987

Year	Food Stamps	NSLP[a]	Breakfast[b]	WIC[c]
1970	4.3	22.4	0.5	—
1975	17.1	24.9	1.8	0.5
1980	21.1	26.6	3.6	2.0
1981	22.4	25.8	3.8	2.2
1982	21.7	22.9	3.3	2.3
1983	21.6	23.0	3.4	2.7
1984	20.9	23.4	3.4	3.2
1985	19.9	23.6	3.4	3.3
1986	19.4	23.7	3.5	3.5
1987	19.1	24.0	3.6	3.6

Source: U.S. Bureau of the Census, *Statistical Abstract of the United States: 1989.* 109th ed. (Washington, D.C., 1989). Table no. 601.

[a]National School Lunch Program. Data are based on the month in which most pupils participated nationwide. The program covers public and private elementary and secondary schools and residential child care institutions.
[b]School Breakfast. Based on nine-month average daily meals served divided by the ratio of average daily attendance to enrollment.
[c]Women-Infant-Children. Covers special supplemental food program and commodity supplemental food program.

and young children came to an end in the early 1980s. Participation in the food stamp program, for example, peaked in 1981 and has declined since then. Participation in the school lunch program has declined since 1980, and participation in the school breakfast program has remained the same. In the future, large increases in funding for programs such as Medicaid and WIC will most likely not come from the federal government. If they expand at all, the funds must come from the states, giving us further reason to anticipate that current state differences in the situation of fatherless families may become even more exaggerated.

Prevention versus Cure

We might think of nutrition programs such as WIC and school lunch as prevention programs. Children who are adequately nourished are less likely to become ill, they are more attentive at school, and, consequently, they have better long-term developmental outcomes. Prevention of this sort addresses many health problems before they occur. Immunization against childhood illness is also prevention, as are measures to stop adolescent pregnancy. Unfortunately, prevention is one of the least-developed aspects of the current publicly funded health care system for the poor. Perhaps this is not surprising, since our medical care system is generally more focused on cure than prevention. Nonetheless, we suspect that substantial long-term savings could be had by even a modest increase in funding for such preventive services. Let us give some examples.

Most of the studies that we reviewed in previous chapters documented the fact that the most seriously disadvantaged fatherless families are those headed by adolescents. Teenage pregnancy frequently ends a young woman's education, thereby undermining her employability and placing her and her children at elevated risk of poverty. Almost all observers agree that the most rational approach to teenage pregnancy is prevention (Hayes 1987, Kammerman and Kahn 1988). If an adolescent female was to postpone childbearing for even a few years, the potential payoff for herself, for her children, and for society at large would be significant. Although there is nearly universal agreement that teenage pregnancy should be prevented, there is little agreement on how this objective should be accomplished. The social, biological, and psychological forces that lead young people to engage in high-risk sex are just too powerful to be countered by persuasion alone, and providing contraceptives to children offends the moral sensibilities of a large number of Americans. As a result, since the vast majority of adolescent mothers keep their babies, the problems of single mothers and their children can only get worse in years to come.

When a conception cannot be prevented, the objective of intervention must be the prevention of pregnancy-related health problems for the mother and of birth defects for the infant. Table 8.4 presents statistics related to prenatal care and to birth outcomes for blacks and whites. It reveals large racial differences in prenatal care and infant health problems. Nearly a quarter of all black births are to adolescents, and twice as many black as white infants are underweight. The problem of adolescent pregnancy is again illustrated in the third panel of table 8.4, which shows that almost one quarter of low birth-weight births among blacks are to adolescents. Even among whites, a large fraction of underweight infants are born to adolescent mothers. This table also reveals rather large differences between blacks and whites in the proportion of mothers who receive prenatal care. Fewer blacks than whites receive prenatal care, and the situation is even worse for adolescent mothers. One out of ten black women either never received prenatal care or their care began in the last trimester. Only 73 percent of white pregnant women and 50 percent of

Table 8.4. Proportion of Births to Adolescent Mothers, Low Birth-Weight Infants, Women Receiving Prenatal Care, and Infant Deaths by Race in 1987

Health and Medical Care Outcome	White	Black
Births to Women 19 and Younger (% of all births)	10.4	22.6
Percent of Births that Were Low Birth Weight, All Women	5.7	12.7
Low Birth-Weight Births (% of all low birth-weight births) 19 and Younger	14.2	23.5
Prenatal Care (began care in the first trimester), All Women	79.4	61.1
Prenatal Care (began in the third trimester or not at all), All Women	5.0	11.1
Infant Deaths		
Total	8.6	17.9
Neonatal	5.5	11.7
Postneonatal	3.1	6.2

Source: Children's Defense Fund (1990a): 66.

black pregnant women received what we might consider adequate prenatal care (Children's Defense Fund 1991).

These differentials in prenatal care are reflected in birth outcomes. Black infants are twice as likely as white infants to die in the first year of life. Black neonatal mortality rates (within the first month) and postneonatal mortality rates (after the first month but within one year) are twice those of whites. Table 8.4 shows that prenatal care is effective in reducing both infant mortality and the proportion of children born underweight. Even though health programs like WIC and early pregnancy intervention are clearly effective, they reach only a portion of those eligible to receive such services. In 1988, for example, only 38 percent of those below the official poverty line were covered by Medicaid, and less than half of those eligible participated in WIC (Grad 1988).

These statistics reveal the extent of unmet need for preventive prenatal and early infant services. They also illustrate the serious health risks faced by blacks. For both adolescent pregnancy and the health problems of children, the data clearly demonstrate that an ounce of prevention is worth a pound of cure. If a young women avoids early pregnancy, she is more likely to complete her education and to become employable, and when she eventually has her children, she is better prepared to provide both material and emotional support. There can be little doubt that a mother who is herself little more than a child cannot provide an optimal home environment for her child's development. For these young women who do become pregnant, early intervention is the best guarantee of a favorable birth outcome. In either case, prevention and early intervention are the key.

Childhood Immunization

One of the most significant medical contributions to children's health has been immunization. Since the advent of mass immunization, diseases like diphtheria, pertussis, polio, measles, and tetanus have nearly disappeared. In spite of this general success at ensuring the health of children, however, serious shortcomings remain (Children's Defense Fund 1987, Miller et al. 1986). In recent years the number of children who are fully immunized against the major childhood diseases has decreased, largely as the result of the freezing of federal immunization funds. Between 1984 and 1985, the number of cases of measles in the United States more than doubled from fewer than 3,000 to more than 6,000 (Children's Defense Fund 1987). The lowest immunization rate is among preschool-aged children and children from poor families (Miller et al. 1986). These statistics

Table 8.5. Proportion of Immunized Children in the United States, 1985, by Race and Place of Residence

				Type of SMSA[a]	
				Central	
Vaccination	White	Black	Suburbs	Cities	Rural
1- to 4-year-olds					
Polio (3+ doses)	77.5	61.5	79.6	68.9	75.9
DTP[b] (3+ doses)	88.5	75.2	89.7	79.6	88.6
Measles	78.1	67.2	76.7	73.5	79.0
Mumps	77.1	62.7	76.8	70.5	77.0
Rubella	75.0	64.1	75.0	70.4	75.0
5- to 6-year-olds					
Polio (3+ doses)	88.6	76.5	91.0	81.6	86.7
Polio (4+ doses)	73.2	54.5	74.2	63.8	72.4
DTP (3+ doses)	94.3	85.9	96.5	87.5	93.5
DTP (4+ doses)	86.6	71.8	88.5	77.1	86.0
Measles	90.0	80.0	90.7	81.6	91.2
Mumps	89.7	80.4	90.6	81.4	90.7
Rubella	85.9	74.1	88.7	75.0	85.9

Source: Congress of the United States, Office of Technology Assessment, *Healthy Children: Investing in the Future* (Washington, D.C.: U.S. Government Printing Office, 1987): 143.

[a]Standard Metropolitan Statistical Area.
[b]DTP refers to diphtheria, tetanus, and pertussis vaccine.

are disturbing, since the costs of fully immunizing children against childhood diseases are small relative to the potential lifelong health deficits that can result from childhood illnesses (Hinman and Koplan 1984).

Table 8.5 shows that black children are less likely than white children to be adequately immunized against polio, diphtheria, tetanus, pertussis, measles, mumps, and rubella. Central-city children, who are disproportionately black, Hispanic, and poor, are less likely to be adequately immunized than children who live in suburban communities or rural areas. We can only imagine that the problem of inadequate immunization is made worse by the presence of the children of illegal immigrants, who do not have equal access to medical care. The 1986 Immigration Reform and Control Act (PL 99-603), which provides access to health care for illegal immigrants, may increase immunization levels for children in central cities.

There is little doubt that investments in prevention, health, and nutrition programs for mothers and children are cost-effective and have greatly increased the quality of life for millions of Americans. Programs that provide prenatal care are more than cost-effective; they have a human payoff that is almost immeasurable. For this reason, conflicts in the financing of health programs for the elderly and those that affect the health of children have particularly tragic implications. At a time when we are able to extend the lives of poorly functioning and sick elderly individuals for a few years through the use of expensive medical interventions, we may be squandering our future and condemning millions of children to lifetimes of poverty and dependency because of a lack of relatively inexpensive, effective prenatal and preventive services (Hewlett 1991).

Children whose health is damaged by poverty are more likely than healthy children to be dependent on society for their entire lifetimes, and they are less likely to contribute productively to the community. These children are also likely to pass these handicaps on to their own children. It is a well-documented fact that the absence of prenatal care doubles a woman's chance of giving birth to a low birth-weight child, and the immediate cost of caring for these children can easily exceed $100,000 (Smythe 1988). In addition, such children often suffer lifelong disabilities, including cerebral palsy, seizure disorders, blindness, mental retardation, and behavioral and learning problems. If greater access to prenatal care improves the birth outcome of even a fraction of these children, it would be worth the investment on the basis of any criteria we might imagine. Health is the most basic aspect of one's human capital. Without it, an individual has little chance of taking advantage of other opportunities, such as education, or of gaining true economic independence.

For every dollar spent on prenatal care, as much as $3.38 is saved in care for low birth-weight infants, and for every dollar spent on the Childhood Immunization Program, $10 is saved in other medical costs (Smythe 1988, Grad 1988). Programs like WIC, immunization, and the Maternal and Child Health Services Block Grants (MCH) are crucial to our efforts to ensure the health of our population and increase the quality of life for the most vulnerable members of our society. Budget cuts that diminish these already minimally funded programs are short-sighted, since the immediate savings they represent are trivial and may be purchased at the long-term costs of the seriously diminished functional capacity of millions of children.

Mental Health Care for Children

Our findings indicate that in terms of physical health, the United States has achieved rough equality between the children of the poor and the children of the middle class. Despite the shortcomings of the health and nutrition programs that were documented above, universal immunization and nutrition programs have virtually eliminated the infectious diseases that killed and maimed so many children only a few decades ago, and Medicaid has ensured at least general equity in medical care to the poor and their children. When it comes to mental health care, however, the situation is very different. Here we have not achieved anything like equity between the children of the poor and the child of the middle class. The data we presented in chapter 5 showed that the children of the poor and children in single-parent households are less likely than children in two-parent households to receive mental health care, in spite of the fact that they experience more emotional and behavioral problems. Because their mothers are little more than children themselves and because single mothers often have little time to devote to their children and are highly stressed by the demands of unassisted parenthood, many of these children do not receive the emotional support and supervision that they need to develop into healthy adults.

There are few publicly funded programs that provide mental health services to children. The federal government's involvement in mental health services is limited to such efforts as mandating that states provide mental health services to the children of drug-addicted mothers, to physically and sexually abused toddlers, and to handicapped children under provisions of the 1986 amendments to the Education for All Handicapped Children Act (Children's Defense Fund 1990). Certain states have responded with innovative programs. Maine, for example, has developed a program to improve the coordination and delivery of existing mental health care services. As part of this program, a multidisciplinary team evaluates the seriousness of a child's mental health problems and evaluates his or her family situation so as to help parents make decisions about which of the available options and support services they should use.

As part of Maine's program, children may receive treatment from a number of mental health professionals, including home visitors, child development specialists, social workers, nurses, psychologists, and doctors. In addition, special education teachers employ a specially designed curriculum for preschool children with developmental disabilities, and families are encouraged to involve their children in extracurricular activities. The goals of this combined effort are to help parents cope with the difficulties involved in caring for a mentally handicapped child, to facilitate family interaction, and to enhance the quality of family life.

Clearly, Maine's program is a model of the best sort of mental health care intervention for children. Yet even this program reaches only a fraction of those children who might benefit. Few states have gone even this far, and extending such services to all children in need would obviously be a very expensive proposition. For the most part, poor children's emotional problems simply go unaddressed or are dealt with outside the mental health care system. The Children's Defense Fund (1990*a*) estimates that 70 to 80 percent of the approximately 7.5 to 9.5 million American children and adolescents with emotional problems are not getting the help they need.

Health care for the poor, therefore, is directly affected by changes in basic welfare policy. As we mentioned earlier, since the 1980s, the federal government has withdrawn from direct involvement in determining eligibility for participation in health and welfare programs. What has happened is that the funding for many programs has been combined and distributed to the states in the form of categorical block grants, and the states have been given a freer hand in setting eligibility criteria for the various programs. The federal government establishes minimal criteria for coverage, but the option to provide additional coverage is left up to the individual states. Many have introduced reforms in the way eligibility for Medicaid is determined and in the way health care is provided to pregnant women and children. Many of the innovations in programs such as Medicaid introduced by progressive and concerned states promise to greatly improve health care for fatherless families and to serve as an example for less progressive states. Of course, no programs can succeed completely, but for at least the next few years, the states will be the source of innovative health care for single mothers and their children. Although we reviewed recent changes in Medicaid in chapter 3, it would be useful here to describe some of the more important reforms in prenatal care, infant care, and mental health care that we can expect in the coming years.

Recent Changes in Medicaid: Cost versus Quality of Care

Health care for the poor in the United States has historically been provided in an incomplete and fragmentary manner, and yet, as is the case for all health care, it is massively expensive. Expenditures for Medicaid grew rapidly during the 1970s and 1980s (Hill 1990). One of the major causes of the general increase in medical care costs can be traced to the way in which third-party payers, including the government, have traditionally reimbursed physicians and hospitals for services rendered. For the most part, insurance companies and the government have reimbursed doctors and hospitals on a fee-for-service basis for any services provided. This reimbursement system fits well with our free market philosophy, but it makes it very difficult to control costs or even to budget for them at the beginning of the fiscal year. In such a system one has no idea until the accounting period is over just how much one must spend for medical care. As a consequence, although doctors have aggressively fought for an unregulated fee-for-service system, skyrocketing health care costs have forced both the federal and state governments to attempt to contain rates of growth in federal and state programs while still providing adequate health care to the poor.

Although some of these attempts have focused solely on rewarding efficiency among providers, most involve some form of capitation or prepayment, a system in which the provider is paid a preset amount for the care of a group of patients. In such a system, the payor (a private insurance company, an employer, or the government) is able to negotiate a set price with a health care provider for the comprehensive care of a group of patients, usually employees in the case of a private corporation or Medicaid recipients in the case of state welfare departments. Because they agree to provide all care needed by the subscribers, the health care provider organization assumes the risk of excessive medical care costs by the patient pool.

Attempts by the federal government to rationalize the health care financing system for the poor and the elderly are based on such efforts to preset the amounts paid for particular medical services. An example of such preset payment for specific medical conditions is the new Medicare Diagnosis Related Groups (DRG) hospital payment schedule (Russell 1989, Dolenc and Dougherty 1985). Because expenditures for hospital services were driving the costs of Medicare up rapidly, in 1983 the federal government adopted a plan in which a hospital is paid a preset amount for the treatment of an individual with a particular diagnosis. Any admission to a hospital under Medicare must be classified into one of approximately five hundred DRGs, each of which is assumed to be homogeneous in terms of treatment costs.

These preset amounts are based on a formula that, theoretically, reflects the average cost of treating the condition effectively. The formula is periodically updated to compensate for changing medical marketplace factors and takes account of differences between hospitals that might influence the cost of treating the average patient. These include such factors as region, case mix, local demographics, and teaching status. Provisions are also made for "outliers," or patients whose care costs far in excess of the preset amount. Despite this limited flexibility, however, the system is designed to be fairly rigid and requires that the hospital assume a substantial amount of the risk involved in caring for elderly Medicare patients.

The major shortcoming of such a system, of course, is that it may achieve significant savings but at the cost of the quality of care provided to patients (Dolenc and Dougherty 1985). Refusing to accept the sickest patients, medically premature release, insufficient testing or treatment, and generally inadequate care are always possibilities in a system that forces the provider to assume the financial risk for patients who turn out to need more services than are covered by the preset amount. A large administrative apparatus, including intensive monitoring of physician behavior, is necessary to ensure that adequate qualtiy of care is maintained. Unfortunately, what is inevitably lost as a result of the increased bureaucratization of medicine is the unencumbered doctor-patient relationship. Increasingly, doctors are businessmen who provide a fairly impersonal service to purchasers. For the poor, of course, this system may be no worse than the system that preceded it and, in fact, may improve the quality of the medical care they receive.

Although the DRG system currently applies only to Medicare, because of the clear necessity of containing the soaring costs of medical care, some form of condition-specific prepayment will probably be adopted for Medicaid and, perhaps, even by private insurers in the future. Of course, the form of prepayment in which a provider offers medical care to a group for a preset amount, thereby assuming the risk for unanticipated costs, has already been adopted by large employers who have the financial power to negotiate with providers. Most of us are familiar with prepayment plans in the form of Health Maintenance Organizations (HMOs) or Preferred Provider Organizations (PPOs), in which an individual has a preassigned primary care provider who is often a salaried employee of the organization and whose job it is to coordinate all of the care that an individual patient receives in the organization. Such plans are basically business arrangements, and they succeed or fail to the extent that they are able to operate within their annual budgets.

Many of these plans provide for profit sharing by the participating health care providers at the end of the year. Efficiency and the control of costs is imperative, therefore, if the organization is to show a profit. Since they are essentially stockholders in the corporation who share in any profit earned, the physicians who own or are employed by the organization have a personal interest in reducing the total amount spent during the year so as to increase the amount disbursed at the end of the year. Of course, physicians are not cynical, and, no doubt, the vast majority place the interests of their patients above their desire for profit. Nonetheless, as with DRGs, the structure of prepaid plans lends itself to the possibility that patients will be denied needed services in the interest of cost savings. To be sure, our current medical care system is so inefficient and services so extensively duplicated that substantial savings can undoubtedly be had without any harm to patients. Nonetheless, once market forces enter the doctor–patient relationship, the possibility of harm, especially to poor patients, must be considered. Despite the potential dangers, however, the poor may benefit by having a personal physician who works as a case manager to coordinate services.

Because of their potential cost efficiency but also because they provide comprehensive services and a primary referring physician who can act as a case manager, such prepayment schemes have been introduced into state Medicaid systems on a demonstration basis (Hill 1990, Freund et al. 1989). In 1983, the Health Care Financing Administration (HCFA) began an experimental program to encourage states to provide care to Medicaid-eligible individuals through capitated systems designed to rationalize medical care use and help control costs (Freund et al. 1989). Six states participated in the original experiment. Traditionally, Medicaid has been a standard health insurance plan, paying doctors a preset amount, albeit well below the amount paid by other insurance plans, for each patient visit. Consequently, as with indemnity insurance generally, there has been little incentive to reduce inappropriate use. Prepayment provides that incentive.

Although each state's program is a bit different, the plans typically involve a contract between the state and an HMO or some other provider organization for the care of Medicaid-eligible residents (Yudkowsky and Fleming 1990). This innovative approach has potential benefits to single mothers and their children, but it also poses certain dangers. The basic philosophy of the HMO is one of comprehensive care, including preventive services. These organizations, therefore, hold the potential for improving the overall health status of poor women and children by providing a coordinated set of services at one location. Unfortunately, as with most human organizations, reality often falls well short of the ideal, and the necessity of cost containment can undermine the quality of medical care provided. Early evaluations of the six HCFA Medicaid experimental programs indicated major deficiencies in prenatal care (Freund et al. 1989).

Our optimism concerning the potential benefits of HMO-style care for fatherless families must therefore be tempered by the realization of the difficulty inherent in providing comprehensive care to the Medicaid-eligible population. This group has extensive and complicated health care needs. The mental health care needs of single mothers and their children may be particularly difficult to address. In any insurance scheme, emotional and behavioral problems are particularly difficult to ensure against since they are often chronic and can cost a great deal to manage. Nonetheless, in light of the fragmentary and incomplete nature of the current system of providing care to single mothers and their families, this innovative approach promises at least some improvement.

For the poor, continuity of care has always been a problem. They often see a different physician each time they visit a clinic or emergency room for primary care. In addition, because of low reimbursement levels and the bureaucratic difficulties of dealing with the Medicaid system, many physicians will simply not accept Medicaid patients. State-sponsored participation in a rationalized, coordinated system of health care may be a very effective way to provide health care to poor fatherless families. No system will ever be without its problems, but we can hope that greater experience with these plans by various states will result in the development of ways of providing high-quality care at a reasonable cost to this very needy group.

Whatever becomes of this particular experiment, Medicaid will be with us for some time, and for all its shortcomings, it has clearly increased access to health care for poor women and children. Recent changes have addressed some of the traditional shortcomings of Medicaid and have increased its coverage of pregnant women and young children. As we noted before, the newer and more promising developments in providing health care to fatherless families have resulted from individual state initiatives. Let us mention some of the more promising innovations that will directly benefit poor women and their children in the future.

As we explained in chapter 2, until recently, Medicaid eligibility was determined by eligibility for AFDC. Because of the erosion in AFDC benefit levels, from an average of 75 percent of poverty level in 1975 to 48 percent of poverty level in 1986, Medicaid eligibility was uncoupled from AFDC eligibility as part of the Omnibus Budget Reconciliation Act (OBRA) of 1986. This legislation allowed states to set eligibility criteria for Medicaid substantially above those for AFDC and greatly increased the extent of preventive and curative health care available to single mothers and their children. Some states increased eligibility levels on their own; others did so in response to requirements contained in OBRA. By 1990, all states provided medical care to pregnant women and to children under six in families with incomes below 133 percent of poverty level. Several provide coverage to families with incomes as high as 185 percent of poverty level (Hill 1990).

Despite these liberalized eligibility criteria, there are still many obstacles to the use of health services by potential Medicaid recipients. These include the fact that despite the uncoupling of Medicaid from AFDC eligibility, the application procedure for the two programs is the same and is often quite laborious. Medicaid applicants must apply at the local welfare office, where they must fill out the same cumbersome forms and provide the same documentation concerning income used to determine AFDC eligibility. This, in conjunction with the forty-five-day determination period, can discourage applications or result in denials because of incomplete information. Studies consistently show that more than 60 percent of all denials are for incomplete AFDC applications (ibid.).

This cumbersome application procedure is particularly irrational in the case of pregnant women. The evidence is overwhelming that the earlier in her pregnancy that a woman seeks medical care, the higher the chances of a favorable birth outcome. This is particularly true for high-risk poor women, for whom the protracted application procedure and waiting period for Medicaid pregnancy benefits make little sense. Many of the most promising changes in Medicaid eligibility requirements have been aimed at making it easier for pregnant women to receive medical care as early as possible in their pregnancies. Some states, for example, allow pregnant women to apply for prenatal care at sites where they are likely to seek care, such as prenatal care clinics. Realizing that a forty-five-day waiting period is far too long during pregnancy, many states now allow presumptive eligibility, whereby the primary care provider can immediately certify a woman as eligible to receive prenatal care pending a more thorough review of her case (ibid.). Unfortunately, getting poor young women to participate in the Medicaid program early in their pregnancies is often difficult because they often live in inaccessible areas. Women who live in the inner city or in remote rural areas are often not tied into effective health education or communication networks. Some states have responded to this problem by adding outreach and case-finding components to their prenatal Medicaid efforts. Such efforts have their detractors, and, as yet, they are not widely employed.

Several states have dealt with the problem of the difficulty of the application procedure for Medicaid by shortening their application forms for pregnant women or children in need. Because of the uncoupling of Medicaid from AFDC, less asset and income information is required, and the forms for collecting it can be more focused to collect only relevant information. By 1990, forty-five states and the District of Columbia dropped asset restrictions for Medicaid eligibility for pregnant women and children (ibid.). Most states also continue eligibility once established through the entire pregnancy period and for a period of sixty days after the birth regardless of changes in income. These reforms are a clear improvement over the previous system. Given the indisputable benefit of early prenatal care, ensuring that a pregnant mother has adequate and continuous care throughout her pregnancy is clearly an enlightened policy. Similarly, in view of the rather high infant mortality rates among the poor, adequate postnatal care is essential. If there is a time in life when expenditures for basic nutrition and medical care have clear long-term benefits, it is during the period before and just after birth.

One of the major problems that seriously undermine these attempts to provide prenatal care to young poor mothers and that hinders preventive care for older children is the fact that many physicians will not accept Medicaid patients because of low reimbursement amounts and the bureaucratic complexity involved in dealing with the Medicaid system (ibid.). In addition, because of the dangers inherent in the birth process, obstetricians are frequently sued for malpractice, and many cite concern over the cost of malpractice insurance as a deterrent to accepting Medicaid patients, many of whom are at high risk of adverse birth outcomes because of youth or poverty (ibid.). Several states have responded by limiting malpractice liability or helping doctors pay for their malpractice insurance (ibid.).

Several states are also experimenting with the use of alternative providers, such as nurse-midwives and nurse-practitioners who are perfectly competent to provide routine prenatal care. As in medicine generally, the use of such physician extenders promises to be a very cost-effective way of providing high-quality primary care. States are also developing means of convincing physicians to participate in the Medicaid program through personal contact and education. Unfortunately, a large and almost insoluble part of the problem arises from the simple fact that physicians prefer to practice in middle-class neighborhoods, leaving the central city and rural areas underserved. These, unfortunately, are the places in which a large number of fatherless families congregate.

Other state innovations include risk assessment, in which potential problems with a pregnancy are identified early; nutritional counseling and education concerning diet during pregnancy and the postnatal period for both mother and child; and general health education. Over half of the states also include prenatal psychological counseling and counseling for real life difficulties. Given the practical difficulties that many single mothers face and the emotional trauma they often must endure, such services are crucial.

The states, therefore, are clearly at the forefront of efforts to provide health care to fatherless families. Individuals at the local level tend to be better informed about the everyday problems of the poor, and this knowledge has led to what promises to be effective programs for dealing with the problems of pregnant women. Unfortunately, despite the general progress made in extending Medicaid benefits, preventive care for children is still far from adequate. In chapter 2, we outlined the EPSDT program, which is designed to provide preventive care to Medicaid-eligible children under the age of twenty-one (Yudkowsky and Fleming 1990). The program is motivated by the clear benefit of preventive services in reducing the risk of more serious illness. As part of EPSDT, children are screened for nutritional deficiencies and for vision, dental, and hearing problems. They also receive the full range of immunizations. If adequately implemented, such a program would identify potentially serious health problems before they interfere with a child's development or schooling. As with prenatal care, intervention early in childhood saves far more than it costs in terms of preventing more expensive illnesses.

Unfortunately, though, several studies indicate that only a minority of Medicaid-eligible children receive preventive care through EPSDT (ibid.). Congress has attempted to remedy this problem as part of the 1989 OBRA by requiring states to more effectively screen for medical conditions and to treat conditions that are identified during the screening. The new law also provides more flexibility in enrolling EPSDT providers. It is hoped that these changes will increase the number of children who receive adequate preventive care and full immunization. As with prenatal care, for children, an ounce of prevention is worth much more than a pound of cure. The data consistently show that when we take a long-term view, investments in welfare and health care early in life produce clear returns.

Yet we invest much more in the treatment of the chronic diseases of the elderly than in preventive care for children. The unfortunate trade-off between expenditures for the care of poor children and expenditures for the elderly was emphasized by Samuel Preston in his 1984 presidential address to the Population Association of America, in which he chose as his theme the conflict in American society between the welfare of the elderly and the welfare of children (Preston 1984). In his address, Preston noted that programs that affect the health and welfare of elderly Americans have expanded greatly, largely at the expense of those that benefit children. In 1970, the proportion of elderly individuals aged sixty-five and older who were living below the official U.S. government poverty line was twice the average for all age groups. By 1982, however, the proportion of elderly persons living in poverty had fallen below the national average.

This pattern was exactly the opposite for children. In 1970, the proportion of children under age fourteen living in poverty was 37 percent below the national average, but by 1982, it was 56 percent greater. These figures clearly show that the elderly have benefited much more from increases in Social Security than children have from AFDC, and they also show that children and the elderly have essentially traded places in terms of relative economic well-being. Since 1972, Social Security benefits have been indexed to inflation so that they increase automatically with the price of goods and services.[1] AFDC payments, however, do not automatically increase with inflation, and since the 1970s, their real value has declined. The elderly have also benefited disproportionately from the greatly increased expenditures for noncash programs, the majority of which are for health-related programs that the elderly use far more frequently than do children. Since Preston's address, the situation has become even more extreme.

Medicaid is one program in which children and the elderly are in direct competition for the same resources. From 1979 to 1982, children's share of Medicaid payments dropped from approximately 15 percent to approximately 12 percent, despite an increase in the proportion of children among those eligible for Medicaid (Preston 1984: 437). Table 8.6 shows that the share of Medicaid spent on the elderly has continued to increase. By 1987, three-fourth of Medicaid funds were spent on the aged, blind, and disabled. Only one-fourth went to families who qualified for AFDC. In 1975, nearly 65 percent of all Medicaid recipients were eligible for AFDC, but only 35 percent of Medicaid funds were spent on them. The ratio of those eligible to the funds allocated (0.54) indicates that AFDC recipients received less than their fair share. Since 1975, the fraction of Medicaid funds spent on AFDC-eligible individuals has declined and the ratio of those qualified for AFDC to the amount spent on AFDC-qualified individuals dropped to 0.36. Clearly, this trend is largely due to the growing aged population in need of long-term care. Nonetheless, the data clearly show that funds for what we usually think of as a program for the poor only partially go toward the care of single mothers and their children; most of the money goes toward the care of the elderly. These differences between younger and older groups in health care expenditures are reflected in improvements in mortality. In recent years declines in mortality have been greater for those over sixty-five than for children and young adults (Preston 1984).

We do not want to take sides in this budgetary battle between the elderly and the young. Even with the gains they have enjoyed as a group, many elderly are poor, and all Americans deserve high-quality curative medical care. What we wish to emphasize is that the elderly as a group have benefited from the expansion of public financing for income support and health care to a far greater extent than have children, and the vast

Table 8.6. Medicaid Recipients: Trends in Participation and Expenditures by AFDC-Eligible Families

Year	% of All Medicaid Recipients AFDC Eligible	% of Total Medicaid Payment to AFDC-Eligible People	Ratio of AFDC Recipients/ AFDC Payment Amounts
1975	64.2	34.7	.54
1980	65.8	27.3	.57
1985	70.0	24.4	.35
1986	69.6	24.4	.35
1987	68.4	24.5	.36

Source: U.S. Bureau of the Census, *Statistical Abstract of the United States: 1989,* 109th ed. (Washington, D.C., 1989): tables 599, 569.

majority of the elderly who benefit from these programs are white and members of the middle class. The inevitable fact of the matter is that if the revenue pie does not grow because the American public demands tax reductions, increases in benefits for the elderly can only be financed at the expense of programs that benefit children.

Is National Health Insurance the Answer?

As innovative and promising as reforms in Medicaid have been, many medically needy women and children remain uninsured. Only a radical approach to the problem of the uninsured could provide coverage to all Americans, regardless of their ability to pay. One such proposal that is periodically offered in one form or another is a federally sponsored national health insurance scheme similar to that of most other developed nations. These proposals differ in the extent to which they combine public and private sources of financing, but they are all motivated by the desire to extend coverage to everyone regardless of income or employment status. As we noted in our introductory chapter, the United States is atypical of developed nations in that we do not have universal publicly financed health insurance. Most other developed nations provide universal health care coverage to their citizens on a non-means-tested basis.

There are several appealing features to such universal systems of health care coverage, but there are also certain unappealing features. One of the most potentially beneficial aspects of a federally sponsored and coordinated system of health care financing is that it might help solve two of the major problems plaguing our system of health care. First, it would extend coverage to the more than thirty-five million Americans who are currently uninsured. Although insurance might continue to be a fringe benefit for most employed persons, under a national health insurance program, the government would pick up the tab for the unemployed and the working poor on a nonstigmatizing basis. Second, a centralized health care financing system could help contain the rapidly rising costs of medical care by making it easier to plan and coordinate the delivery of services on a geographic basis. Such a system, for example, might help avoid the extensive duplication of services and the maldistribution of physicians that are typical of our current system.

Unfortunately, any national health insurance scheme has its drawbacks. Despite the rather substantial savings that might be attained in the long run through greater efficiency and planning, extending coverage to all Americans would be immensely expensive. In addition, any national health insurance scheme, whether fully or only partially funded by the federal government, would require a massive bureaucracy to administer.

Such a bureaucracy would intrude even further into the doctor–patient relationship and would almost inevitably infringe on individual freedom of choice. These characteristics make a nationalized system distasteful to many Americans, and a fully developed national health insurance system like those of the Western European countries may simply be impossible in this country, at least in the near future.

There is reason, however, to take seriously the possibility that some sort of national health insurance system will be adopted in the United States in the not too distant future. The explosive growth in the costs of medical care and the aging of the populations of the developed nations are forcing all governments, including our own, to attempt innovative means of rationing and rationalizing the delivery of medical care (Anderson 1989, Raffel 1984). Perhaps a system based on our current private insurance industry but in which the federal government would pay the premiums for those who would otherwise go uninsured might be compatible with our political and economic systems. Clearly, such attempts to rationalize the system will benefit some individuals and penalize others. Since a nationalized health insurance system would extend at least minimal insurance coverage to the working poor, it would improve the lot of fatherless families by ensuring care to those who are currently not covered by Medicaid.

All medical care systems represent some combination of private and public financing of health care. Odin W. Anderson arrays national health systems on a continuum, with what he calls "market-maximizing" systems, like that of the United States in which physicians, hospitals, and other health providers act as independent and uncoordinated economic actors, at one end, and market-minimizing systems, like that of the former Soviet Union in which doctors are employees of the state and hospitals public property, on the other (Anderson 1989, Field 1980). Most national health care systems fall somewhere in the middle and represent a compromise between a totally free market in medical care and complete control by the state. Even in the United States, which is perhaps the most market-maximizing system in the world, the government provides health care to the old and the poor as well as to veterans and to Native Americans through the Veterans Administration and the Indian Health Service. The question, of course, is whether or not the poor in general and single mothers and their children in particular would benefit by the movement of our entire system of medical care more toward the market-minimizing end of Anderson's continuum. Let us very briefly examine the basic features of two national health insurance schemes and ask how they might improve the delivery of preventive and curative health care to fatherless families.

The United Kingdom is perhaps the clearest example of the benefits and shortcomings of any national health insurance scheme. Anderson

(1984) places it at the extreme market-minimizing end of his public/ private continuum among liberal–democratic nations. In Britain, the vast majority of health care is financed and organized by the national government. Only a small fraction of all reimbursement occurs outside the National Health Service (Allen 1984). In addition, in Britain, the system is much more centrally coordinated and is differentiated into two levels, primary and specialty care. Nearly everyone is assigned to a general practitioner who provides primary care and serves as an entry point to the system. To see a specialist, an individual must be referred by his or her general practitioner. The general practitioner, therefore, is what in the United States we might consider a case manager. The British system is predicated on the desire to provide services to everyone on a nonstigmatizing basis.

One of the inevitable drawbacks of a system in which the ability to pay is no longer the major mechanism for rationing is that one must often wait for long periods for elective procedures. However, the system is very compatible with British attitudes concerning the role of the state in the care of its citizens, and for the most part, the British public is satisfied with it (ibid.). It is clear that the poor are far better off under this nationalized system than they would be in a more privatized system. Yet the British system is probably too foreign to the United States to serve as a model for providing care to the poor. Americans are suspicious of big government, and the restrictions on freedom of choice that the British system requires are probably incompatible with our basic cultural and political orientations.

The Canadian health care system shares most of the characteristics of our own system, with the exception of its financing mechanism (Hatcher, Hatcher, and Hatcher 1984). In Canada, unlike Britain, hospitals are privately owned and doctors are free economic actors. The one major difference between Canada and the United States is that in Canada, everyone is covered by government-sponsored health insurance. Private health insurance is restricted by law to only those services, like dental care, private rooms in hospitals, and medications, that are not covered by the official Canadian Medicare system. Physician services and hospitalizations are paid for by a combined federal provincial system of health insurance. This system provides coverage to everyone regardless of ability to pay and has the added benefit of helping to control the rise in medical care costs. Both Britain and Canada spend a substantially smaller fraction of their total gross national product on medical care than does the United States (Anderson 1984).

..lthough the Canadian medical care system as a whole is more compatible with ours than British system is, it is hard to imagine that it would be possible to do away with the private insurance industry in the United States since it is so central to our economy. Nonetheless, in combination with private health insurance, some version of public health insurance provided on a nonstigmatizing basis to those who are unemployed or uninsured might be possible. Even a fairly modest national health insurance system could help address many of the problems of access and duplication of services that are characteristic of our current system.

In coming decades, the massive medical care costs that will be incurred by aging baby boomers, in conjunction with the inevitable increases in costs that progress in medical science will bring about, may make national health insurance more of a possibility in the United States. The question we must examine then is, of all of the possible forms of national health insurance, which, if any, is most compatible with the political and economic systems of the United States. The real question that remains is how a uniquely American form of national health insurance would operate and how it would be financed. We have an answer to that intriguing question for public debate.

Conclusion: A Painful Inheritance?

Future directions in public policy concerning poverty and the particular plight of female-headed households will be determined by the resolution of political debates that are taking place during a period of economic retrenchment and renewed doubts concerning society's ability to ensure the health and economic welfare of all those who are unable to care for themselves. The coalition of blacks, labor unions, and liberal Democrats that made the Great Society programs a possibility has collapsed, and because the political basis of the welfare state has never been as secure in the United States as in Europe, social welfare programs that support fatherless families are under attack. Those concerned with ensuring the health and welfare of all Americans are searching for new policy directions that will ensure the welfare of the poor, who are increasingly made up of mother-only households, while respecting basic American values of self-sufficiency and the two-parent family.

Although resistance to taxation and to the welfare state occurs in all countries, it is particularly pronounced in the United States (Wilensky 1975, 1976). In most other industrialized countries, the state's responsibility for care of the individual from cradle to grave is taken for granted. In the United States, however, the extent of government's responsibility for the care of the poor is still a matter of debate. A general distrust of big government, in conjunction with the widely held belief in the United States that adequate work is available for all who want it, places welfare for the poor in a vulnerable political position. Reductions during the early 1980s in programs that guarantee nutrition, housing, and income to the poor have had a profound effect on the welfare of single mothers and their children (Symthe 1988; Grad 1988; Children's Defense Fund 1987; Palmer and Sawhill 1984).

Dealing with problems of poverty and homelessness will be more difficult in the years to come as the United States enters a period of slower economic growth. Although they are in many ways inadequate, public expenditures for social welfare take up a large fraction of federal and state outlays. The increasing need represented by the growing number of poor single-parent families in combination with a growing elderly population and an increasing resistance by middle-class taxpayers to the tax burden to which their care contributes have created a political climate unfavorable to the expansion of welfare programs for the poor. The outcome of the debate over the extent of the state's role in the support of fatherless families and the willingness of the middle class to pay for it have profound implications for the health and welfare of single mothers and their children in years to come.

Yet there are reasons for optimism. The shift in responsibility for the welfare of the poor from the federal government to the states has ushered in a period of innovation. Many states have expanded health care coverage to families who previously did not qualify, and many have introduced outreach and prevention programs for pregnant mothers and young children. As a result of this experimentation, programs that are more responsive to the local needs of single mothers may be developed. States that are lagging behind in their approach to health care for the poor may be enticed by the examples of the more successful states to adopt innovative programs. As we have noted, American political culture is hostile to centralized bureaucracy, and it is clear that large centralized bureaucracies, including those that deal with health, seriously interfere with the exercise of individual freedom. In the future, therefore, we can look to the states for innovation in the area of health care for fatherless families.

We have attempted to make it clear throughout this work that not all female-headed families and households are poor, nor are they dysfunctional. We do not consider female headship to be pathological in and of itself, just as we do not consider the traditional husband-wife family to be normal, in any absolute sense. Many critics of modern life lament the decline of the family, since for them it represents the foundation on which the culture and society with which they are familiar and believe in is built. Despite the desire by some to return to some more orderly past, it is clear that the rise of the fatherless family is part of the inevitable change that characterizes modern life. It is clear that we cannot embrace the technological and material progress of advanced industrialization and still expect to preserve the social relations and institutions of previous historical periods. Modernization is a package that changes all aspects of public and private life. Whatever the moral objections of traditionalists, female-headed families are here to stay (Bane 1976).

Critics of modern civilization are right, however, in their suspicion that the psychological and social implications of the decline of the two-parent family are profound. Children who grow up without a male role model and in poverty are likely to be very different people from those middle-class conservatives would like them to be. The research we have reviewed suggests that it is not family structure itself, however, so much as the poverty in which these children grow up that is the problem. Romantic appeals to the way things used to be, or objections to the increase in the number of female-headed households simply because one prefers some other arrangements, are pointless. The challenge for American society is to find ways of incorporating these new families into the economic and moral mainstream and to ensure the physical and mental health of their members. The failure to do so will guarantee a painful inheritance of shattered hopes and stunted lives.

We must once again emphasize that although the data show that many fatherless families are poor, relatively few are members of the underclass, however it is defined. Most single mothers support themselves and their children, and, indeed, for many women single motherhood is a matter of choice and represents a liberation from their traditional dependency on men. In fact, one could easily write a book showing that the female-headed household represents a functional adaptation to the changes in the family that are an apparently inevitable consequence of modernization and late industrial civilization. With sufficient income and social support, these families are a viable alternative to the two-parent traditional family.

We cannot end this book without once again returning to the issue of race. Unfortunately, although in recent years much more research on blacks and Hispanics has appeared in mainstream scholarly publications, race and ethnicity are such emotionally and politically charged topics that many writers avoid confronting the full implications of what they mean in contemporary American society. Discussions of race or Hispanic ethnicity that touch on difficult issues invariably draw criticism from those who feel that any research findings that can conceivably be construed as blaming the victim are dangerous. Unfortunately, it is almost impossible to say anything that someone will not consider denigrating. The impact of race and ethnicity in all areas of American life is simply too pervasive, even today, to ignore. As we have documented throughout, race affects all aspects of social well-being and, in combination with gender, forms one of the two major dimensions of disadvantage in the contemporary United States. Race and Hispanic ethnicity, therefore, must be taken into account in research on the health of single women and their children.

Race has played an important part in the development of the American welfare policy. Throughout the New Deal, blacks were systematically excluded from coverage by the major programs. The Social Security Act of 1936 specifically excluded domestic and agricultural workers, thereby leaving the majority of black workers unprotected.[2] The disproportionate power that the committee structure of Congress gave to southern states in earlier years ensured that programs like AFDC retained their local control provisions. For the most part, local control has meant the systematic subjugation of poor blacks to the will of local whites and the denial of coverage to many poor fatherless families. Although the majority of the poor are white, half of poor single mothers are black, and one can only wonder what our current family support system would look like if this were not the case.

The civil rights movement of the 1960s eliminated the remaining legal restrictions to the political enfranchisement of black Americans and struck down legal barriers to jobs and education. Unfortunately, as William Julius Wilson has shown, those barriers to black progress that remain are entrenched in the very structure of our occupational and economic systems. Although middle-class blacks have prospered and moved out of the ghetto, lower-class black families, many of whom are fatherless, are trapped in poverty. The barriers to full economic citizenship that blacks, and increasingly Hispanics, face in American society will be much harder to overcome than were the barriers to political enfranchisement. Restrictive covenants in real estate, segregated schools, poll taxes, and the rest of the segregationist apparatus provided clear targets against which an effective coalition of blacks and liberals could mobilize. Unfortunately, current economic barriers are much less well defined, and even many liberals who fought for the elimination of barriers to black political participation in American life are opposed to the elimination of economic barriers through affirmative action.

Many feminists and other politically sensitive observers object to female-headed families being singled out for special attention. Such attention, they fear, runs the risk of labeling fatherless families as pathological or particularly problem-ridden when, in fact, they are merely among the most visible victims of our class-stratified society, a society in which gender and race greatly influence one's opportunities for upward mobility. We basically concur with this judgment. The studies we have reviewed and our own investigations lead us to the inevitable conclusion that poverty lies at the base of many of the problems faced by single women and their families. Nonetheless, because gender affects both the likelihood of becoming a single parent and the likelihood of falling into poverty, poor single mothers and their children suffer from problems that are uniquely different from those of poor two-parent families, and, in our opinion, their problems require special solutions.

Perhaps the most intriguing aspect of the rise in the new matriarchy is the increase in the number of households headed by older women. Although the basic social welfare of the elderly as a group has been guaranteed in recent years as the result of the indexing of Social Security to inflation and the spread of privately financed retirement plans, many older women, especially many black and Hispanic older women, live in or near poverty. Social Security was never intended to be the sole source of income for the elderly, and surviving on a minimal OASDI income or SSI can be difficult. The literature we reviewed in chapter 7 clearly showed that for the elderly, the family is the most important source of social support. Among the poor and minorities, it is essential in providing basic services and help with activities of daily living. In the absence of family, poor elderly females are in a particularly unenviable situation.

The new grandmotherhood that has emerged among the poor, largely as the result of the inability of mothers to care for their children, is a disturbing phenomenon. Rather than representing the adoption of a new set of responsibilities and rights with respect to their grandchildren, many of these women find that they must raise a new generation of children in circumstances that are no better, perhaps even worse, than those in which they raised their children. This situation has serious negative implications for the physical and mental health of all concerned. Although we do not wish to suggest that all grandmothers who must raise their grandchildren are doomed to failure, this family form is usually the result of the seriously disruptive forces plaguing our society. These forces make the task of raising grandchildren a very difficult one. As yet, we know little about how these families operate or what effects this arrangement has on the health of grandmothers and their grandchildren.

The family is a close and emotionally charged unit. The emotional difficulties that any family member experiences affect all other members of the family as well. The negative consequences of poverty, therefore, reverberate throughout the family system so that no one is spared. If we have done anything in this book, we hope it is to have sensitized some individuals to the seriousness and complexity of the health problems that single mothers and their children face and to emphasize that there are no easy solutions. The forces that have given rise to the female-headed family are embedded in our way of life. We will avoid calling for dramatic new visions or new leadership, since such calls are hollow and, in any case, beg the question. Where are such new visions or such new leaders to come from?

Throughout our discussion, we have emphasized that given the current political climate, the most we can hope for is to retain the support system for single mothers that we have developed over the last three decades and, perhaps, to slowly improve it in the future. As we noted, innovative experimentation by progressive state agencies may usher in a new era in providing medical care to fatherless families. In years to come, the adoption of a more comprehensive system of health care coverage that includes all citizens may become a possibility, but for at least the immediate future ensuring the health of single women and their children requires determining which programs are essential to their welfare and providing evidence of their effectiveness. It is to be hoped that such efforts will make a difference in at least a few lives.

Notes
References
Index

Notes

Preface

1. Of course, there were some notable exceptions to this generalization. In a widely cited monograph, Heather Ross and Isabel Sawhill (1975) documented the rise in black female-headed families.

2. See Wilson and Neckerman (1986), Wilson (1987), Garfinkel and McLanahan (1986), and Bane (1988) for analyses of the causes of the rise in the proportion of households headed by women.

3. Psychological perspectives on poverty often characterized individuals in poverty as being unable to delay gratification, as having restricted linguistic and cognitive skills, and as ascribing the control of their lives to external forces. See Sarbin (1970) for a summary of the major psychological explanations of poverty.

4. See Wacquant and Wilson (1989) for a useful discussion of the process of hyperghettoization.

Chapter 1. Single Motherhood and Health across the Life Course

1. In a strict sense, the term *matrifocal* would be the more appropriate term, since it refers to residence patterns rather than to lineage.

Chapter 2. The Magnitude of the Problem: Demographic and Economic Dimensions

1. Less than 60 percent of women eligible to receive child support were awarded it by the court in 1983, and of that group, less than half received the full amount they were entitled to.

2. Bennett, Bloom, and Craig (1989) show that since the 1930s, the proportion of more recent cohorts of black women who ever marry has declined. for white women, although the number who never marry has increased, the increase has been only modest.

3. See Hetherington, Camara, and Featherman (1977) and Furstenberg, Brooks-Gunn, and Morgan (1987) for reviews of literature on the consequences of single parenthood on the adult socioeconomic achievement of adults and the cognitive development of children. See Featherman and Hauser (1976a, 1976b, 1978) for a review of the impact of gender, race and ethnicity, and number of siblings on educational and occupational attainment.

219

4. McLanahan's findings suggest that these effects are largely the result of the economic deprivation that female-headed families experience. Furstenberg, Brooks-Gunn, and Morgan (1987) also find that the long-term negative effects of single motherhood for children are largely the result of the mother's life problems rather than of single motherhood in and of itself.

Chapter 3. Family and Health Policy in the United States and Europe

1. Flora and Heidenheimer (1981) contains several chapters on the development of social welfare in Europe and America. Also see Furniss and Tilton (1977) and Weir, Orloff, and Skocpol (1988).

2. In the United States the earned income tax credit is a benefit to poor families. Unlike child payments, however, tax allowances are of little value to families with no earnings. In addition, because they are not means-tested, child payments and family allowances are not stigmatized. See Kamerman (1984) and Kamerman and Kahn (1978) for a discussion of family support policies in several developed nations.

3. See Palmer and Sawhill (1984), Colby (1989), Danziger and Weinberg (1986), and Cottingham and Ellwood (1989) for more detailed summaries of the various cash and in-kind transfer programs for the poor and how they were affected by the Reagan administration's budget cuts.

4. Eligibility for Medicaid is not lost immediately on the loss of eligibility for AFDC. Recipients who lose their AFDC eligibility are given four additional months of Medicaid, and since 1984 they can receive an additional six months of eligibility at the discretion of the states (Blank and Brock 1987)

5. The first large-scale social welfare program in the United States was designed to provide support to Civil War veterans and their widows. The Pension Act on June 27, 1890, was the first federal legislation to provide pensions on the basis of need (Axinn and Levin 1975).

6. Furniss and Tilton (1977) distinguish between two possible types of welfare state: the "social security state" that aims at a guaranteed national minimum level of welfare, and the "social welfare state" that aims at greater social equality. Absolute poverty can be eliminated by the first approach but relative poverty only by the second. Needless to say, the latter is a much more politically difficult task than the first.

7. For comparisons of social welfare programs in the United States, Canada, and several Western European nations, see Kamerman and Kahn (1978); Furniss and Tilton (1977); Myles (1984); Rodgers (1982); and Flora and Heidenheimer (1981).

8. See chapter 8 for a more detailed discussion of the legislation leading to the uncoupling of AFDC and Medicaid.

9. Kohl (1981) presents evidence for several European countries showing that although political periods dominated by pure Socialist or Socialist-dominated parties have the highest rates of social investments, periods in which coalition governments have been in charge have also shown rapid growth in social investments. Growth has even occurred during periods of conservative party domina-

tion. The growth of the welfare state cannot, then, be attributed solely to Left or Labor parties.

10. Furniss and Tilton (1977: chap. 4) present a critique of the fiscal crisis literature generally, and Kohl (1981) provides European evidence that a crisis arising from a conflict between rising public expenditures and finite revenues is not inevitable. The literature is inconclusive in any case in showing just how much of a conflict there is between public expenditure, levels of taxation, and private investment. Kuttner (1984) and Block et al. (1987) point out that there is no inherent conflict between social expenditures and productivity and that productivity can, in fact, be enhanced by investments in social welfare.

11. Wilensky (1975) shows that visible taxes, such as income and property taxes, are strongly associated with welfare backlash in both Europe and America. Less obvious taxes, such as value-added and sales taxes, especially in the highly class stratified societies of Western Europe, cause less backlash. In the United States, with its egalitarian philosophy and highly visible taxing system, is among those nations with strong antiwelfare and antitax constituencies.

Chapter 4. Measuring Health: Physical, Emotional, and Social Aspects

1. See Ware (1986) for a more detailed summary of the types of measures used to assess physical, mental, and social health in community surveys.

2. A well-developed tradition in anthropology and sociology makes it clear that culture and social class structure affect how individuals perceive and respond to illness (e.g., Velimirovic 1978; Kleinman 1980, 1986; Zborowski 1952; Zola 1964, 1966; Mechanic 1980; Fabrega 1974; Fabrega, Schwartz, and Wallace 1968; Fabrega and Silver 1973; Clark 1970; Nichter 1981). The literature makes it clear that culture places limits on the perceptual, explanatory, and behavioral options that individuals have at their disposal for understanding and responding to illness. Individuals from another culture, or even those from another ethnic group or social class, may misinterpret the meaning of an individual's behaviors.

Accompanying this extensive empirical anthropological and sociological literature, numerous illness-definition and help-seeking models have been developed to explain the process through which individuals identify and evaluate illness and seek medical care (e.g., Rosenstock 1966; Becker and Maiman 1983; Mechanic 1978; Suchman 1965a, 1965b; Fabrega 1974; Chrisman and Kleinman 1983). Sociological models identify sociocultural variables, including ethnicity, as important factors that influence the identification of and response to illness (Suchman 1965a, 1965b; Becker and Maiman 1983; Mechanic 1978), while models that are informed by an anthropological perspective (e.g., Fabrega 1974, Chrisman and Kleinman 1983) place the entire process of illness definition and help-seeking within a cultural context that comprises the symbolic system through which decisions concerning health and illness are made by individuals and groups.

3. Quay and Werry (1986) defines four major clusters of deviant child behaviors that can be used by researchers to study mental health in the community: conduct disorders (e.g., temper tantrums, disobedience, destructiveness, irritability); anxiety (e.g., withdrawal, depression, frequent crying); immaturity (e.g.,

short attention span, preoccupation, inattentiveness); and socialized aggression (e.g., bad companions, truancy from school). Some variation on these sorts of items is used in most communitywide assessments of behavioral problems in childhood and adolescence. See Achenbach and Edelbrock (1978) for a detailed discussion of the methodological issues involved in employing behavioral checklists.

4. These data are based on parental responses to the following questions:

"Now I am going to read some statements that describe the behavior problems of many children. Please tell me whether each statement has been often true, sometimes true, or not true of your child during the past three months" (U.S. Bureau of the Census–National Health Interview Survey, 1988 Child Health Supplement, 1988: 110–111).

1. Has sudden changes in mood or feelings.
2. Feels or complains that no one loves him or her.
3. Is rather high-strung, tense, or nervous.
4. Cheats or tells lies.
5. Is too fearful or anxious.
6. Argues too much.
7. Has difficulty concentrating, cannot pay attention for long.
8. Is easily confused, seems to be in a fog.
9. Bullies, or is cruel or mean to others.
10. Is disobedient at home.
11. Is disobedient at school.
12. Does not seem to feel sorry after he or she misbehaves.
13. Has trouble getting along with other children.
14. Has trouble getting along with teachers.
15. Is impulsive, or acts without thinking.
16. Feels worthless or inferior.
17. Is not liked by other children.
18. Has a lot of difficulty getting his or her mind off certain thoughts, has obsessions.
19. Is restless or overly active, cannot sit still.
20. Is stubborn, sullen, or irritable.
21. Has a very strong temper and loses it easily.
22. Is unhappy, sad, or depressed.
23. Is withdrawn, does not get involved with others.

(Only for children 11 years or younger)

24. Breaks things on purpose, deliberately destroys his or her own or others' things.
25. Clings to adults.
26. Cries too much.
27. Demands a lot of attention.
28. Is too dependent on children.

(Only for children 12 years and older)

29. Feels others are out to get him or her.
30. Hangs around with kids who get into trouble.

31. Is secretive, keeps things to (himself/herself).

32. Worries too much.

5. This table is from Angel and Guarnaccia (1989).

6. This table is from Angel and Worobey (1988a).

7. See Angel and Worobey (1988a) for a more detailed discussion of this adjustment procedure. In effect, it constrains the comparison of the mother's CES-D scores to those children with similar levels of health.

Chapter 5. Growing Up without Father: Health Consequences for Children

1. See Robins (1966).

2. Sociopathic personality was defined as a "gross, repetitive failure to conform to societal norms in many areas of life, in the absence of thought disturbance suggesting psychosis (Robins 1966: 79)." In this study, a diagnosis was made on the basis of the occurrence of a psychiatric condition (e.g., sexual promiscuity, suicide, school problems and truancy, pathological lying) during the individual's adult life.

3. See Kellam, Ensminger, and Turner (1977) for details in the methodology employed and the specific findings reported.

4. In this study the psychological development of children in two-parent and single-parent (widowed and divorced) families was compared using measures of IQ, emotional functioning, and behavioral disorders. See Hetherington and Deur (1972) for details in methodology.

5. As we suggested earlier, clinical samples can be very atypical of the general population of children. Many of the subjects who participated in this study were recruited through referrals from lawyers, doctors, ministers, and so on. Many of the children's parents had entered the clinic with a long history of psychological problems. Thus, those families who were most likely to be involved in the study needed counseling prior to the divorce, and consequently, they were more likely to have had greater emotional needs going into the study than those who did not choose to participate.

6. Most of the midtown Manhattan sample, however, consisted of adults who grew up in families in which the absence was due to the death of a father. The sample was a randomly selected study group of 1,660 residents, 20 to 59 years, residing in the midtown area of Manhattan in New York City. See L. Srole et al. (1962) and T. S. Langner and S. T. Michael (1963) for details of the study.

7. However, children in two-parent families report more depressive symptoms in situations in which the family is characterized as having greater family conflicts. These findings support the results of Robins (1966), who found that children from broken homes in which there was little parental discord were less likely to experience adult forms of sociopathology.

8. Chronic conditions consist of such things as lung disease, convulsions, rheumatic heart disease, and other heart conditions, for which the child had ever been treated.

9. Casper and Hogan (1991) used a subsample of women and children from the

NLSY to show that women who lived with a spouse or partner were more likely than those without a spouse or partner present in the household to seek prenatal care within the first trimester. Proximity to kin was not associated with the probability of receiving prenatal care, however.

Chapter 6. Single Motherhood: Consequences for Women's Health

1. From a role overload perspective, it is the inability to cope with an excessive level of demands and responsibilities that reduces one's sense of well-being. For a useful review of research covering role overload and the association between social roles and stress generally, see Pearlin (1983).

2. In reference to occupational role overload, Pearlin (1983) reports that when role overload is present at all, it is bimodal. That is, it is greater among the highest-placed white-collar workers and among the lowest-placed blue-collar workers and lower among workers of the middle rank. This role overload, however, results in stress only for those at the bottom of the occupational hierarchy who have little control over their work. Clearly, if one chooses to engage in numerous and demanding roles and gains satisfaction from them, one is really not overloaded. The negative aspects of role overload stem from the inability to deal with the multiple role demands. Thoits (1986) presents a clear theoretical model of how the accumulation of roles both enhances mental health and diminishes it for men and women.

3. See Mechanic (1989), Belle (1990), Angel and Guarnaccia (1989), and Angel and Thoits (1987) for a discussion of the linkages between culture, social class, and health status.

4. Stack assumes a strong cultural relativist position. Her work is very much a response to the culture of poverty perspective that was current when she conducted her research. From a relativist point of view, any value judgments concerning appropriate family structures and judgments about family dysfunction made by outside observers are based on white middle-class notions of what is best and are merely reflections of the preferences of the economically and politically dominant group. Stack demonstrates that the networks she identified are strong and adaptive and that they, in fact, make life possible for people who face the possibility of serious deprivation. In our opinion, such a radical relativist view makes an important point but runs the risk of glossing over much that is truly destructive about poverty in a desire not to blame the victims for their plight. As Stack notes, her subjects shared with the middle class a desire for single-family homes and a better material life (Stack 1974: 125). They simply cannot afford a middle-class lifestyle because of the discrimination and historical disadvantages they have faced. In our opinion, we have no choice but to make value judgments when material wealth is unequally distributed and when access to it depends on specific behaviors dictated by the majority. Social structures and life-styles that, as Stack notes, block one's chances to get ahead in life (to acquire an equity, in her terms) have negative aspects. We might characterize the situation as one in which the poor are denied options that middle-class individuals take for granted. Education, for exam-

ple, is a middle-class value, but it would be hard to imagine anyone objecting to the state providing it to the poor. In recent years the radical cultural relativist position has fallen on hard times as the destructiveness of the serious problems faced by single-parent families becomes increasingly difficult to normalize.

5. The Rand Health Insurance Experiment (HIE) is a national study of the patterns of health service utilization by persons residing in Dayton, Ohio; Seattle, Washington; Fitchburg and Franklin County, Massachusetts; and Charleston and Georgetown, South Carolina. The data were collected from 1974 to 1982 and involved the random assignment of 8,254 persons to one of sixteen health care plans. Subjects were enrolled in the experiment for a term of three or five years. All but one of the treatment groups received some level of health insurance coverage including free care. A separate control group was selected to receive health services from a Seattle Health Maintenance Organization (HMO). See Wells et al. (1982:22–44) for a detailed description of the research design, the sample, and the data collection procedures employed for the HIE study.

6. The CES-D is a 20-item scale designed to assess an individual's mood during the past week (Robins et al. 1984). It is one of the global affect scales that we discussed in chapter 4.

Chapter 7. Single Women in Mature Adulthood: A Health Research Agenda

1. See Blazer (1982) for a useful summary of theories concerning the etiology and treatment of depression among ther elderly.

2. See Feinson (1985), Blazer (1982), and Butler and Lewis (1977) for more detailed reviews of the literature on age and depression.

3. The Epidemiological Catchment Area Study (ECA) attempts to assess the prevalence of various specific mental illnesses, including depression, based on psychiatric criteria as stated in the American Psychiatiric Association's Diagnostic and Statistical Manual (DSM-III). Rates based on this data, then, supposedly approximate what we would find if psychiatrists evaluated the mental health of the respondents. As we explained in chapter 2, however, even when fairly strict criteria are employed, we must be cautious in interpreting findings based on survey responses.

4. See Fischer (1982) for a summary of "decline of community" theories in the social sciences and the popular mind. For the most part these theories posit that in highly urbanized modern societies, the size of the individual's interpersonal social networks has shrunk at the same time that the emotional supportiveness of the remaining relationships has been diminished. See Wirth (1938) for an early statement of this thesis. Litwak (1985) has developed a useful theoretical structure for understanding the interaction of such primary groups as the family and larger-scale formal organizations in modern life.

5. There are many reviews of theories and research on the Hispanic family. For useful reviews of studies of Hispanic health and aging, see Mindel (1985); Gelfand and Baressi (1987); Markides Martin, and Gomez (1983); Markides and Mindel

(1987); and Casas and Keefe (1978). The characterization of Hispanics as familistic is based largely on localized ethnographic studies, many of which are by now quite old, and the findings of these studies may no longer apply to contemporary Hispanic family life.

6. Taylor (1988) presents a very useful review of the literature on the family support structures of elderly blacks. As for Hispanics, what is known of the social support systems of the black elderly is based largely on small-scale ethnographic studies or inferences from aggregate statistics. Gibson and Jackson (1989) provide a review of the impact of informal support on the health and physical functioning of the black elderly.

7. See Taylor (1988) for a review of studies of the social support of the black elderly.

8. The first data set, the Survey of Program Participation (SIPP), collected by the U.S. Bureau of the Census in 1984, provides detailed information on both functional capacity and economic well-being of individuals in over 20,000 households in the United States. It includes information on earned income, assets, and transfer payments (Nelson, McMillen, and Kasprzk 1985). It is ideal, therefore, for assessing the economic welfare of single older women living in different family situations. In this analysis we employ a subsample of 2,356 unmarried women 55 years of age and older.

The second data set, the 1984 National Health Interview Survey Supplement on Aging, provides information on the functional capacity of a sample of 16,148 persons aged 55 to 99 living in the community (Fitti and Kovar 1987). In what follows we employ a subsample of 8,514 women living alone or with relatives to determine how living arrangements and functional capacity are related.

9. There are many scales that measure functional capacity (e.g., Fillenbaum 1984; Lawton 1971; Nagi 1976; Rosow and Breslau 1966; Katz et al. 1963). Perhaps the most commonly used scale of functional capacity and the one employed in the research presented in this chapter is that developed by Katz et al. (1963). It includes questions concerning one's ability to independently perform basic activities of daily living, including bathing, toileting, dressing, eating, walking, going outside, and getting into and out of chairs.

10. Chronic medical conditions and impairments were based on two questions. First, if the elderly female had ever had any of the following conditions: osteoporosis, a broken hip, hardening of the arteries or arteriosclerosis, rheumatic heart disease, coronary heart disease, angina pectoris, a myocardial infarction, any other heart attack, a stroke or a cerebrovascular accident, Alzheimer's disease, and cancer. Second, if during the past 12 months they had arthritis or rheumatism, diabetes, aneurysm, blood clot, and varicose veins.

Chapter 8. Single Motherhood, Health, and the New American Political Reality

1. Since 1972, Social Security benefits increase automatically whenever the annual increase in the Consumer Price Index increases by 3 percent or more. These

cost-of-living adjustments maintain the value of payments for the elderly (Achenbaum 1986). In contrast, the average value of food stamps and AFDC benefits for a family of four have lost 38 percent of their value since 1970 (Children's Defense Fund 1990).

2. See Hamilton and Hamilton (1986) for a summary of how black advocacy organizations, such as the National Association for the Advancement of Colored People (NAACP) and the National Urban League (NUL), attempted to influence the legislation of the New Deal and of later employment and family programs. For the most part, in the United States the focus on the history of civil rights legislation has overshadowed the history of the black struggle for economic equality.

References

Achenbach, Thomas. 1981. "Behavioral Problems and Competencies Reported by Parents of Normal and Disturbed Children Aged 4 Through 16." *Monographs of the Society for Research in Child Development* 46, no. 188.

Achenbach, Thomas J., and Craig S. Edelbrock. 1978. "Psychopathology of Childhood: Research Problems and Issues." *Journal of Consulting and Clinical Psychology* 46: 759–776.

Achenbaum, W. Andrew. 1986. *Social Security: Visions and Revisions.* New York: Cambridge University Press.

Aday, Lu Ann A., G. Y. Chiu, and Ronald Andersen. 1980. "Methodological Issues in Health Care Surveys of the Spanish Heritage Population." *American Journal of Public Health* 70: 367–374.

Adler, Leta McKinney. 1953. "The Relationship of Marital Status to Incidence of and Recovery from Mental Illness." *Social Forces* 32: 185–194.

Albert, Nina, and Aaron T. Beck. 1975. "Incidence of Depression in Early Adolescence: A Preliminary Study." *Journal of Youth and Adolescence* 4: 301–307.

Allen, David. 1984. "England." Pp. 197–257 in Marshall W. Raffel, ed., *Comparative Health Systems: Descriptive Analyses of Fourteen National Health Systems.* University Park: Pennsylvania State University Press.

Alpert, Joel, John Kosa, and Robert J. Haggerty. 1967. "A Month of Illness and Health Care among Low-income Families." *Public Health Reports* 82: 705–713.

American Psychiatric Association. 1987. *Diagnostic and Statistical Manual of Mental Disorders.* 3d ed. rev. Washington, D.C.: American Psychiatric Association.

Anderson, Elijah. 1989. "Sex Codes and Family Life among Inner-City Fathers." *Annals of the American Academy of Political and Social Science* 501: 59–78.

Anderson, Odin W. 1989. *The Health Services Continuum in Democratic States: An Inquiry into Solvable Problems.* Ann Arbor: Health Administration.

Anderson Jessie, Sheila Williams, Rob McGee, and Phil Silva. 1987. "DSM-III Disorders in Preadolescent children." *Archives of General Psychiatry* 44:69–76.

Aneshensel, Carol S., Ralph R. Frerichs, and Virginia A. Clark. 1981. "Family Roles and Sex Differences in Depression." *Journal of Health and Social Behavior* 22: 379–393.

Aneshensel, Carol S., Ralph R. Frerichs, and George J. Huba. 1984. "Depression and Physical Illness: A Multiwave, Nonrecursive Causal Model." *Journal of Health and Social Behavior* 25: 350–371.

Angel, Ronald. 1984. "The Costs of Disability for Hispanic Males." *Social Science Quarterly* 65: 426–443.

229

Angel, Ronald, and Jacqueline L. Angel. In press. "Mental and Physical Co-morbidity among the Elderly: The Role of Culture and Social Class." In Deborah Padgett, ed., *Handbook on Ethnicity, Aging, and Mental Health.* Westport, Conn.: Greenwood Press.

Angel, Ronald, and William Gronfein. 1988. "The Use of Subjective Information in Statistical Models." *American Sociological Review* 53: 464–473.

Angel, Ronald, and Peter J. Guarnaccia. 1989. "Mind, Body, and Culture: Somatization among Hispanics." *Social Science and Medicine* 28: 1229–1238.

Angel, Ronald J., and Ellen L. Idler. 1992. "Somatization and Hypochondriasis: Sociocultural Factors in Subjective Experience." Pp. 71–93 in P. J. Leaf and J. Greenley, eds., *Research in Community and Mental Health: A Research Annual.* Vol 6. Greenwich, Conn.: JAI Press.

Angel, Ronald, and Peggy Thoits. 1987. "The Impact of Culture on the Cognitive Structure of Illness." *Culture, Medicine, and Psychiatry* 11: 23–52.

Angel, Ronald, and Marta Tienda. 1982. "Determinants of Extended Household Structure: Cultural Pattern or Economic Need?" *American Journal of Sociology* 87:1360–1383.

Angel, Ronald, and Jacqueline L. Worobey. 1988*a*. "Single Motherhood and Children's Health." *Journal of Health and Social Behavior* 29: 38–52.

Angel, Ronald, and Jacqueline L. Worobey. 1988*b*. "Acculturation and Maternal Reports of Children's Health: Evidence from the Hispanic Health and Nutrition Survey." *Social Science Quarterly* 69: 707–721.

Anson, Ofra. 1988. "Living Arrangements and Women's Health." *Social Science and Medicine* 26: 201–208.

Aschenbrenner, J. 1975. *Lifelines: Black Families in Chicago.* New York: Holt, Rinehart, and Winston.

Auletta, Ken. 1982. *The Underclass.* New York: Random House.

Axinn, June, and Herman Levin. 1975. *Social Welfare: A History of the American Response to Need.* New York: Dodd, Mead.

Bachrach, Christine A. 1980. "Childlessness and Social Isolation among the Elderly." *Journal of Marriage and the Family* 42: 627–636.

Baker, Paula C., and Frank L. Mott. 1989. *NLSY Child Handbook 1989: A Guide and Resource Document for the National Longitudinal Survey of Youth 1986 Child Data.* Columbus: Center for Human Resource Research–Ohio State University.

Bane, Mary Jo. 1976. *Here to Stay: American Families in the Twentieth Century.* New York: Basic Books.

Bane, Mary Jo. 1988. "Politics and Policies of the Feminization of Poverty." Pp. 381–396 in Margaret Weir, Ann Shola Orloff, and Theda Skocpol, eds., *The Politics of Social Policy in the United States.* Princeton: Princeton University Press.

Bane, Mary Jo, and David T. Ellwood. 1986. "Slipping Into and Out of Poverty: The Dynamics of Spells." *Journal of Human Resources* 21: 1–23.

Bane, Mary Jo, and David T. Ellwood. 1989. "One Fifth of the Nation's Children: Why Are They Poor?" *Science* 245: 1047–1053.

Beck, Rubye W., and Scott H. Beck. 1989. "The Incidence of Extended Households among Middle-Aged Black and White Women: Estimates from a 15-Year Panel Study." *Journal of Family Issues* 10: 147–168.

Becker, Marshall H., and Lois A. Maiman. 1983. "Models of Health-Related Behavior." Pp. 539–568 in David Mechanic, ed. *Handbook of Health, Health Care, and the Health Professions.* New York: Free Press.

Beland, Francois. 1984. "The Family and Adults 65 Years of Age and Over: Coresidency and Availability of Help." *Canadian Review of Sociology and Anthropology* 21: 302–317.

Belle, Deborah. 1990. "Poverty and Women's Mental Health." *American Psychologist* 45: 385–389.

Bellin, Seymour S., and Robert H. Hardt. 1958. "Marital Status and Mental Disorders among the Aged." *American Sociological Review* 23: 155–162.

Bennett, Neil G., David E. Bloom, and Patricia H. Craig. 1989. "The Divergence of Black and White Marriage Patterns." *American Journal of Sociology* 95: 692–722.

Berkman, Paul L. 1969. "Spouseless Motherhood, Psychological Stress, and Physical Morbidity." *Journal of Health and Social Behavior* 10: 323–334.

Berkman, Lisa, and Leonard Syme. 1979. "Social Networks, Host Resistance, and Mortality: A Nine-Year Follow-up Study of Alameda County Residents." *American Journal of Epidemiology* 109: 186–204.

Berkman, Lisa F., Cathy S. Berkman, and Stanislav Kasl et al. 1986. "Depressive Symptoms in Relation to Physical Health and Functioning in the Elderly." *American Journal of Epidemiology* 124: 372–388.

Bird, Hector R., Madelyn S. Gould, Thomas Yager, Beatriz Staghezza, and Glorisa Canino. 1989. "Risk Factors for Maladjustment in Puerto Rican Children." *Journal of the American Academy of Child and Adolescent Psychiatry* 28: 847–850.

Bishop, Christine E. 1986. "Living Arrangement Choices of Elderly Singles: Effects of Income and Disability." *Health Care Financing Review* 7: 65–73.

Bjornsson, Sigurjon. 1974. "Epidemiological Investigation of Mental Disorders of Children in Reykjavik, Iceland." *Scandinavian Journal of Psychology* 15:244–254.

Blank, Susan, and Thomas Brock. 1987. "Health, Health Care, and Economic Self-Sufficiency." Pp. 160–186 in Jack A. Meyer and Marion Ein Lewin, eds., *Charting the Future of Health Care.* Washington, D.C.: American Enterprise Institute for Public Policy Research.

Blazer, Dan G. 1982. *Depression in Late Life.* St. Louis: C. V. Mosby.

Blazer, Dan G. 1989. "Depression in the Elderly." *New England Journal of Medicine* 320: 164–166.

Blazer, Dan, D. C. Hughes, and Linda K. George. 1987. "The Epidemiology of Depression in an Elderly Community Population." *The Gerontologist* 27: 281–287.

Blazer, Dan, and C. Williams. 1980. "Epidemiology of Dysphoria and Depression in an Elderly Population." *American Journal of Psychiatry* 137: 439–444.

Block, Fred, Richard A. Cloward, Barbara Ehrenreich, and Frances Fox Piven. 1987. *The Mean Season.* New York: Pantheon.

Block, Jeanne H., Jack Block, and Per F. Gjerde. 1986. "The Personality of Children Prior to Divorce: A Prospective Study." *Child Development* 57: 827–849.

Blum, Heather Munroe, Michael H. Boyle, and David R. Offord. 1988. "Single-Parent Families: Child Psychiatric Disorder and School Performance." *Journal of the American Academy of Child and Adolescent Psychiatry* 27: 214–219.

Bohlen, Celestine. 1989. "Number of Mothers in Jail Surges with Drug Arrests." *New York Times,* April 17, A1, B2.

Boyle, Michael H., David R. Offord, Hank G. Hofman, Gary P. Catlin, John A. Byles, David T. Cadman, John W. Crawford, Paul S. Links, Naomi I. Rae-Grant, and Peter Szatmari. 1987. Ontario Child Health Study I. *Archives of General Psychiatry* 44: 826–831.

Branch, Laurence G., and Alan M. Jette. 1982. "A Prospective Study of Long-term Care Institutionalization among the Aged." *American Journal of Public Health* 72: 1373–1379.

Broman, Sarah H. 1981. "Long-term Development of Children Born to Teenagers." Pp. 195–226 in Keith G. Scott, Tiffany Field, and Euan G. Robertson, eds., *Teenage Parents and Their Offspring.* New York: Gruen and Stratton.

Bronow, Ronald. 1990. "A National Health Program: Abyss at the End of the Tunnel—The Position of Physicians Who Care." *Journal of the American Medical Association* 263: 2488–2489.

Brooks-Gunn, J., and Frank F. Furstenberg. 1985. "Antecedents and Consequences of Parenting: The Case of Adolescent Motherhood." Pp. 233–258 in Alan Fogel and Gail F. Melson, eds., *The Origins of Nurturance: Developmental, Biological and Cultural Perspectives on Caregiving.* Hillsdale, N.J.: Erlbaum.

Brown, George W., and Tirril Harris. 1978. *The Social Origins of Depression: A Study of Psychiatric Disorder in Women.* New York: Free Press.

Bumpass, Larry. 1984. "Children and Marital Disruption: A Replication and Update." *Demography* 21: 71–82.

Bumpass, Larry, and Ronald R. Rindfuss. 1979. "Children's Experience of Marital Disruption." *American Journal of Sociology* 85: 49–65.

Bumpass, Larry, and Sara McLanahan. 1989. "Unmarried Motherhood: Recent Trends, Composition, and Black-White Differences." *Demography* 26: 279–286.

Bumpass, Larry L., Ronald R. Rindfuss, and R. B. Janosik. 1978. "Age and Marital Status at First Birth and the Pace of Subsequent Fertility." *Demography* 15: 75–86.

Burke, Vincent J., and Vee Burke. 1974. *Nixon's Good Deed: Welfare Reform.* New York: Columbia University Press.

Burr, Jeffrey A., and Jan E. Mutchler. 1992. "The Living Arrangements of Unmarried Elderly Hispanic Females." *Demography* 29: 93–112.

Burtless, Gary. 1986. "Public Spending for the Poor: Trends, Prospects, and Economic Limits." Pp. 18–49 in Sheldon H. Danziger and Daniel H. Weinberg, eds., *Fighting Poverty: What Works and What Doesn't.* Cambridge: Harvard University Press.

Burton, Linda M., and Vern L. Bengtson. 1985. "Black Grandmothers: Issues of

Timing and Continuity of Roles." Pp. 61–77 in Vern L. Bengtson and Joan Robertson, eds., *Grandparenthood*. Beverly Hills: Sage.

Butler, Robert N., and Myrna I. Lewis. 1977. *Aging and Mental Health: Positive Psychosocial Approaches*. Saint Louis: C. V. Mosby.

Cafferata, Gail Lee, Marc Berk, and Brenda Jones. 1987. "Single Parent Families and Children's Health Care." Paper presented at the 1987 Eastern Sociological Society Annual Meeting, May, Boston, Mass.

Cafferata, Gail Lee, and Judith D. Kasper. 1985. "Family Structure and Children's Use of Ambulatory Physician Services." *Medical Care* 23: 350–360.

Campbell, Colin D., and William L. Pierce. 1980. *The Earned Income Credit*. Washington, D.C.: American Enterprise Institute for Public Policy Research.

Canino, Ian A., Brian F. Earley, and Lloyd H. Rogler. 1988. *The Puerto Rican Child in New York City: Stress and Mental Health*. 2d ed. Monograph no. 4. New York: Hispanic Research Center, Fordham University.

Cantwell, D. P. 1986. "Classification." Pp. 133–147 in A. J. Solnit, D. J. Cohen, and J. E. Schowalter, eds., *Child Psychiatry*. New York: Basic Books.

Caplan, Marion Gedney, and Virginia I. Douglas. 1969. "Incidence of Parental Loss in Children with Depressed Mood." *Journal of Child Psychology and Psychiatry* 10: 225–232.

Carballo, Manuel, and Mary Jo Bane, eds. 1984. *The State and the Poor in the 1980s*. Boston: Auburn House.

Carter, Hugh, and Paul C. Glick. 1976. *Marriage and Divorce: A Social and Economic Study*. Cambridge: Harvard University Press.

Casas, J. Manuel, and Susan E. Keefe, eds. 1978. *Family and Mental Health in the Mexican American Community*. Monograph no. 7. Los Angeles: Spanish-Speaking Mental Health Research Center.

Casper, Lynne M., and Dennis P. Hogan. 1991. "Family Networks in Prenatal and Postnatal Health." *Social Biology* 37: 84–101.

Castells, Manuel. 1980. *The Economic Crisis and American Society*. Princeton: Princeton University Press.

Chamberlin, Robert W. 1975. "Behavioral Problems of Preschoolers." Pp. 95–101, in Robert J. Haggerty, Klaus J. Roghmann, and Ivan B. Pless, eds., *Child Health and the Community*. New York: John Wiley and Sons.

Chapman, Michael. 1977. "Father Absence, Stepfathers, and the Cognitive Performance of College Students." *Child Development* 48: 1155–1158.

Cherlin, Andrew J. 1981. *Marriage, Divorce, Remarriage*. Cambridge: Harvard University Press.

Cherlin, Andrew J. 1991. "Children and Divorce: Response to Myrna M. Weismann." *Science* 253: 952.

Cherlin, Andrew J., and Frank F. Furstenberg. 1986. *The New American Grandparent: A Place in the Family, a Life Apart*. New York: Basic Books.

Cherlin, Andrew J., Frank F. Furstenberg, Jr., P. Lindsay Chase-Lansdale, Kathleen E. Kiernan, Philip K. Robins, Donna Ruane Morrison, and Julien O. Teitler. 1991. "Longitudinal Studies of Effects of Divorce on Children in Great Britain and the United States." *Science* 252: 1386–1389.

Children's Defense Fund. 1987. *A Children's Defense Budget: FY1988.* Washington, D.C.: Children's Defnese Fund.

Children's Defense Fund. 1990a. *S.O.S. America! A Children's Defense Budget.* Washington, D.C.: Children's Defense Fund.

Children's Defense Fund. 1990b. *Children 1990: A Report Card, Briefing Book, and Action Primer.* Washington, D.C.: Children's Defense Fund.

Children's Defense Fund. 1991. *The State of America's Children: 1991.* Washington, D.C.: Children's Defense Fund.

Chilman, Catherine S. 1983. *Adolescent Sexuality in a Changing American Society: Social and Psychological Perspectives for the Human Services Professions.* New York: Wiley.

Chrisman, Noel J., and Arthur Kleinman. 1983. "Popular Health Care, Social Networks, and Cultural Meanings: The Orientation of Medical Anthropology." Pp. 569–590, in David Mechanic, ed., *Handbook of Health, Health Care, and the Health Professions.* New York: Free Press.

Clark, Margaret. 1970. *Health in the Mexican-American Culture.* Berkeley: University of California Press.

Cleary, Paul D., and David Mechanic. 1983. "Sex Differences in Psychological Distress among Married People." *Journal of Health and Social Behavior* 24: 111–121.

Coates, Deborah L. 1989. "Single Parenting among African-Americans." *Early Childhood Update* 5: 5.

Cohen, Patricia, and Judith Brook. 1987. "Family Factors Related to the Persistence of Psychopathology in Childhood and Adolescence." *Psychiatry* 50: 332–345.

Colby, Ira C. 1989. *Social Welfare Policy: Perspectives, Patterns, Insights.* Chicago: Dorsey.

Colle, Ann D., and Michael Grossman. 1978. "Determinants of Pediatric Care Utilization." *Journal of Human Resources* 13: 115–158.

Costello, Elizabeth J. 1989. "Developments in Child Psychiatric Epidemiology." *Journal of the American Academy of Child and Adolescent Psychiatry* 28: 836–841.

Costello, Elizabeth J. 1986. "Primary Care Pediatrics and Child Psychopathology: A Review of Diagnostic, Treatment, and Referral Practices." *Pediatrics* 78: 1044–1051.

Costello Elizabeth J., Barbara J. Burns, and Anthony J. Costello et al. 1988. "Service Utilitzation and Psychiatric Diagnosis in Pediatric Primary Care: The Role of the Gatekeeper." *Pediatrics* 82: 435–441.

Costello, Elizabeth J., Anthony J. Costello, Craig Edelbrock, Barbara J. Burns, Mina K. Dulcan, David Brent, and Susan Janiszewski. 1988. "Psychiatric Disorders in Pediatric Primary Care: Prevalence and Risk Factors." *Archives of General Psychiatry* 45: 1107–1116.

Cottingham, Phoebe H., and David T. Ellwood, eds. 1989. *Welfare Policy for the 1990s.* Cambridge: Harvard University Press.

Creed, Francis, Stephen Murphy, and Malcom V. Jayson. 1990. "Measurement of Psychiatric Disorder in Rheumatoid Arthritis." *Journal of Psychosomatic Research* 34: 79–87.

Crystal, Stephen, and Dennis Shea. 1990. "Cumulative Advantage, Cumulative Disadvantage, and Inequality among the Elderly." *Gerontologist* 30: 437–443.

Danziger, Sheldon H., and Daniel H. Weinberg, eds. 1986. *Fighting Poverty: What Works and What Doesn't.* Cambridge: Harvard University Press.

Davis, Karen. 1985. "Health Care Policies and the Aged: Observations from the United States." Pp. 727–744 in Robert H. Binstock and Ethel Shanas, eds., *Handbook of Aging and the Social Sciences.* New York: Van Nostrand Reinhold.

Davis, Karen, and Cathy Schoen. 1978. *Health and the War on Poverty: A Ten-Year Appraisal.* Washington, D.C.: Brookings Institution.

Dawson, Deborah A. 1990. "Family Structure and Children's Health and Well-Being: Data from the 1988 National Health Interview Survey on Child Health." Paper presented at the Annual Meeting of the Population Association of America, Toronto.

Dawson, Deborah A. 1991. "Family Structure and Children's Health: United States 1988." National Center for Health Statistics *Vital Health Statistics*, ser. 10, no. 178. DHHS publication no. (Public Health Service) 91-1506. Hyattsville, Md.: U.S. Department of Health and Human Services.

Derthick, Martha. 1979. *Policymaking for Social Security.* Washington, D.C.: Brookings Institution.

Dodge, Kenneth A. 1990. "Developmental Psychopathology in Children of Depressed Mothers." *Developmental Psychology* 26: 3–6.

Dohrenwend, Bruce, and Barbara Dohrenwend. 1969. *Social Status and Psychological Disorder: A Causal Inquiry.* New York: John Wiley.

Dohrenwend, Bruce P., Barbara S. Dohrenwend, Madelyn Schwartz Gould, Bruce Link, Richard Neugebauer, and Robin Wunsch-Hitzig. 1980. *Mental Illness in the United States: Epidemiological Estimates.* New York: Praeger.

Dolenc, Danielle A., and Charles J. Dougherty. 1985. "DRGs: The Counter-Revolution in Financing Health Care." *Hastings Center Report* 15: 19–29.

Dorpat, Theodore L., Joan K. Jackson, and Herbert S. Ripley. 1965. "Broken Homes and Attempted and Completed Suicide." *Archives of General Psychiatry* 12: 213–216.

Downey, Geraldine, and Phyllis Moen. 1987. "Personal Efficacy, Income and Family Transitions: A Longitudinal Study of Women Heading Households." *Journal of Health and Social Behavior* 28: 320–333.

Duncan, Greg. 1984. *Years of Poverty, Years of Plenty.* Ann Arbor: University of Michigan Press.

Duncan, Otis Dudley, David Featherman, and Beverly Duncan. 1972. *Socioeconomic Background and Achievement.* New York: Seminar.

Durkheim, Emile. 1951 [1897]. *Suicide: A Study in Sociology.* New York: Free Press.

Dutton, Diana B. 1985. "Socioeconomic Status and Children's Health." *Medical Care* 23: 142–156.

Edwards, Linda N., and Michael Grossman. 1982. "Income and Race Differences in Children's Health in the Mid-1960s." *Medical Care* 20: 915–930.

Egbuonu, Lisa, and Barbara Starfield. 1982. "Child Health and Social Status." *Pediatrics* 69: 550–557.

Egbuonu, Lisa, and Barbara Starfield. 1982. "Child Health and Social Status." *Pediatrics* 69: 550–557.

Ellwood, David T. 1988. *Poor Support: Poverty in the American Family.* New York: Basic Books.

Ellwood, David T. 1990. "Valuing the United States Income Support System for Lone Mothers." Pp. 201–220 in Elizabeth Duskin, ed., *Lone-Parent Families: The Economic Challenge No. 8.* Paris, France: Organisation for Economic Co-Operation and Development Social Policy Studies.

Esping-Andersen, Gosta. 1985. *Politics Against Markets: The Social Democratic Road to Power.* Princeton: Princeton University Press.

Essex, M., and S. Nam. 1987. "Marital Status and Loneliness among Older Women: The Differential Importance of Close Family Friends." *Journal of Marriage and the Family* 49: 93–106.

Ewert, Donnell P., J. Conley Thomas, Lorraine Y. Chun, Robert C. Enguidanos, and Stephen H. Waterman. 1991. "Measles Vaccination Coverage among Latino Children Aged 12 to 59 months in Los Angeles County: A Household Survey." *American Journal of Public Health* 81: 1057–1059.

Fabrega, Horacio, Jr. 1974. *Disease and Social Behavior: An Interdisciplinary Perspective.* Cambridge: MIT Press.

Fabrega, Horacio, Jr., and Daniel B. Silver. 1973. *Illness and Shamanistic Curing in Zinacantan.* Stanford: Stanford University Press.

Fabrega, H., Jr., J. D. Schwartz, and C. A. Wallace. 1968. "Ethnic Differences in Psychopathology, II: Specific Differences with Emphasis on a Mexican-American Group." *Journal of Psychiatric Research* 6: 221–235.

Farley, Reynolds. 1988. "After the Starting Line: Blacks and Women in an Uphill Race." *Demography* 25: 477–495.

Featherman, David L., and Robert M. Hauser. 1976a. "Changes in the Socioeconomic Stratification of the Races, 1962–1973." *American Journal of Sociology* 82: 621–649.

Featherman, David L., and Robert M. Hauser. 1976b. "Sexual Inequalities and Socioeconomic Achievement in the U.S., 1962–1973." *American Sociological Review* 41: 462–483.

Featherman, David L., and Robert M. Hauser. 1978. *Opportunity and Change.* New York: Academic Press.

Feinson, Marjorie Chary. 1985. "Aging and Mental Health: Distinguishing Myth from Reality." *Research on Aging* 7: 155–174.

Fendrich, Michael, Virginia Warner, and Myrna M. Weismann. 1990. "Family Risk Factors, Parental Depression, and Psychopathology in Offspring." *Developmental. Psychology* 26: 40–50.

Field, Mark. 1980. "The Health Care System and the Polity: A Contemporary American Dialectic." *Social Science and Medicine* 14A: 397–415.

Field, Tiffany. 1981. "Early Development of the Preterm Offspring of Teenage Mothers." Pp. 145–175 in Keith G. Scott, Tiffany Field, and Euan G. Robertson, eds., *Teenage Parents and Their Offspring.* New York: Gruen and Stratton.

Fillenbaum, Gerda G. 1984. "Development of Functional Status Scales for the

Longitudinal Retirement History Survey." *Review of Public Data Use* 12: 197–209.

Fischer, Claude S. 1982. *To Dwell among Friends: Personal Networks in Town and City.* Chicago: University of Chicago Press.

Fitti, Joseph E., and Mary Grace Kovar. 1987. "National Center for Health Statistics—The Supplement on Aging to the 1984 National Health Interview Survey." *Vital and Health Statistics* ser. 1, no. 21. DHHS publication no. (Public Health Service) 87-1321. Washington, D.C.: U.S. Government Printing Office.

Fleck, J. Roland, Cheryl C. Fuller, Sharon Z. Malin, Dixon H. Miller, and Kenneth R. Acheson. 1980. "Father Psychological Absence and Heterosexual Behavior, Personal Adjustment and Sex-Typing in Adolescent Girls." *Adolescence* 15: 847–857.

Flora, Peter, and Arnold J. Heidenheimer, eds. 1981. *The Development of Welfare States in Europe and America.* New Brunswick, N.J.: Transaction.

Fossett, James W., Janet D. Perloff, John A. Peterson, and Phillip R. Kletke. 1990. "Medicaid in the Inner City: The Case of Maternity Care in Chicago." *Milbank Memorial Fund Quarterly* 68: 111–141.

Fowler, Patrick C., and Herbert C. Richards. 1978. "Father Absence, Educational Preparedness, and Academic Achievement: A Test of the Confluence Model." *Journal of Educational Psychology* 4: 595–601.

Freeman, Richard B. 1982. "Economic Determinants of Geographic and Individual Variation in the Labor Market Position of Young Persons." Pp. 115–154 in R. B. Freeman and D. A. Wise, eds., *The Youth Labor Market Problem: Its Nature, Causes and Consequences.* Chicago: University of Chicago Press.

Freund, Deborah, Louis F. Rossiter, Peter D. Fox, Jack A. Meyer, Robert E. Hurley, Timothy S. Carey, and John E. Paul. 1989. "Evaluation of the Medicaid Competition Demonstrations." *Health Care Financing Review* 11: 81–97.

Furniss, Norman, and Timothy Tilton. 1977. *The Case for the Welfare State: From Social Security to Social Equality.* Bloomington: Indiana University Press.

Furstenberg, Frank F. 1976. *Unplanned Parenthood: The Social Consequences of Teenage Childbearing.* New York: Free Press.

Furstenberg, Frank F., J. Brooks-Gunn, and S. Philip Morgan. 1987. *Adolescent Mothers in Later Life.* New York: Cambridge University Press.

Gaines-Carter, Patrice. 1992. "Living in Shadows of a Mother's Death." *Washington Post*, Wednesday, March 4, D1–D3.

Gallagher, Dolores, and Larry W. Thompson. 1989. "Bereavement and Adjustment Disorders." Pp. 459–473 in Ewald W. Busse and Dan G. Blazer, ed., *Geriatric Psychiatry.* Washington, D.C.: American Psychiatric Press.

Gallagher, Dolores E., James N. Breckenridge, Larry W. Thompson, and James A. Peterson. 1983. "Effects of Bereavement on Indicators of Mental Health in Elderly Widows and Widowers." *Journal of Gerontology: Social Sciences* 38: 565–571.

Garfinkel, Irwin, and Sara S. McLanahan. 1986. *Single Mothers and Their Children: A New American Dilemma.* Washington, D.C.: Urban Institute.

Garmezy, Norman, and Michael Rutter, eds. 1983. *Stress, Coping and Development in Children.* New York: McGraw-Hill.

Garrison, William T., and Susan McQuiston. 1989. *Chronic Illness During Childhood and Adolescence: Psychological Aspects.* Newbury Park, Calif.: Sage.

Gelfand, Donald E., and Charles M. Baressi, eds. 1987. *Ethnic Dimensions of Aging.* New York: Springer Verlag.

General Accounting Office. 1992. *Early Intervention: Federal Investments Like WIC Can Produce Savings.* Human Resources Division, GAO/HRD-92-18. Gaithersburg, Md.: U.S. General Accounting Office.

George, Linda K. 1989. "Social and Economic Factors." Pp. 203–234 in Ewald W. Busse and Dan G. Blazer, ed., *Geriatric Psychiatry.* Washington, D.C.: American Psychiatric Press.

Gibson, Rose C., and Jamesx S. Jackson. 1989. "The Health, Physical Functioning, and Informal Supports of the Black Eldeerly." Pp. 421–454 in David P. Willis, ed., *Health Policies and Black Americans.* New Brunswick, N.J.: Transaction.

Gilbert, Jean M. 1978. "Extended Family Integration among Second-Generation Mexican Americans." Pp. 25–48 in J. Manuel Casas and Susan E. Keefe, eds., *Family and Mental Health in the Mexican American Community.* Los Angeles: Spanish-Speaking Mental Health Research Center.

Gilder, George. 1981. *Wealth and Poverty.* New York: Basic Books.

Glenn, Norval D., and Charles N. Weaver. 1979. "A Note on Family Situation and Global Happiness." *Social Forces* 57: 960–67.

Goldberg, David, and Peter Huxley. 1980. *Mental Illness in the Community: The Pathways to Psychiatric Care.* New York: Tavistock.

Goldberg, Evelyn L., George W. Comstock, and Sioban D. Harlow. 1988. "Emotional Problems and Widowhood." *Journal of Gerontology: Social Sciences* 43: S206–S208.

Goldberg, Evelyn L., Pearl Van Natta, and George W. Comstock. 1985. "Depressive Symptoms, Social Networks, and Social Support of Elderly Women." *American Journal of Epidemiology* 121: 448–456.

Goldman, Howard H., Darrel A. Regier, Carl A. Taube, Richard W. Redick, and Rosalyn Bass. 1980. "Community Mental Health Centers and the Treatment of Severe Mental Disorder." *American Journal of Psychiatry* 137: 83–86.

Gove, Walter R. 1972. "The Relationship Between Sex Roles, Marital Status, and Mental Illness." *Social Forces* 51: 34–44.

Gove, Walter R. 1973. "Sex, Marital Status, and Mortality." *American Journal of Sociology* 79: 49–67.

Gove, Walter R., and Michael R. Geerken. 1977. "The Effect of Children and Employment on the Mental Health of Married Men and Women." *Social Forces* 56: 66–76.

Gove, Walter R., and Jeanette Tudor. 1973. "Adult Sex Roles and Mental Illness." *American Journal of Sociology* 78: 812–835.

Grad, Rae. 1988. "The Fight Against Infant Mortality." *GAO Journal* Fall: 31–34.

Granger, Charles. 1982. "Maternal and Infant Deficits Related to Early Pregnancy and Parenthood." Pp. 33–45 in Nicholas J. Anastasiow, ed., *The Adolescent Parent.* Baltimore: Paul Brookes.

Gratton, Brian. 1987. "Familism among the Black and Mexican-American Elderly: Myth or Reality?" *Journal of Aging Studies* 1: 19–32.

Grebler, Leo, Joan W. Moore, and Ralph C. Guzman. 1970. *The Mexican-American People: The Nation's Second Largest Minority.* New York: Free Press.

Gronbjerg, Dirsten A. 1977. *Mass Society and the Extension of Welfare, 1960–1970.* Chicago: University of Chicago Press.

Gross, Jane. 1989. "Grandmothers Bear a Burden Sired by Drugs." *New York Times,* April 9, 1, 26.

Gross, Jane. 1991. "Help for Grandparents Caught Up in Drug War." *New York Times,* Sunday, April 14, 18.

Guarnaccia, Peter J., Ronald Angel, and Jacqueline L. Worobey. 1989. "The Factor Structure of the CES-D in the Hispanic Health and Nutrition Examination Survey: The Influences of Ethnicity, Gender and Language." *Social Sciences and Medicine* 29: 85–94.

Gubrium, Jaber F., 1976. *Time, Roles, and Self in Old Age.* New York: Human Sciences.

Guendelman, Sylvia, and Joan Schwalbe. 1986. "Medical Care Utilization by Hispanic Children." *Medical Care* 24: 925–937.

Gueron, Judith M. 1987. *Reforming Welfare with Work: Occasional Paper Number Two. Ford Foundation Project on Social Welfare and the American Future.* New York: Ford Foundation.

Guidubaldi, John, and Helene Cleminshaw. 1985. "Divorce, Family Health, and Child Adjustment." *Family Relations* 34: 35–41.

Gurin, Gerald, Joseph Veroff, and Sheila Feld. 1960. *Americans View Their Mental Health.* New York: Basic Books.

Guttentag, Marcia, S. Salasin, and Deborah Belle. 1980. *The Mental Health of Women.* New York: Academic Press.

Gutterman , Elane M., J. D. O'Brien, and J. G. Young. 1987. "Structured Diagnostic Interviews for Children and Adolescents: Current Status and Future Directions." *Journal of the American Academy of Child and Adolescent Psychiatry* 26: 621–630.

Haggerty, Robert J. 1983. "Epidemiology of Childhood Disease." Pp. 101–119 in David Mechanic, ed., *Handbook of Health, Health Care, and the Health Professions.* New York: Free Press.

Haggerty, Robert J., Klaus J. Roghmann, and Ivan B. Pless. 1975. *Child Health and the Community.* New York: John Wiley and Sons.

Hamilton, Charles V., and Dona C. Hamilton. 1986. "Social Policies, Civil Rights, and Poverty." Pp. 287–311, in Sheldon H. Danziger and Daniel H. Weinberg, eds., *Fighting Poverty: What Works and What Doesn't.* Cambridge: Harvard University Press.

Hankin, Janet, and Julianne S. Oktay. 1979. *Mental Disorder and Primary Medical Care: An Analytical Review of the Literature.* National Institute of Mental Health, Series D, no. 5. DHEW Publication no. (ADM) 78-661, Superintendent of Documents. Washington, D.C.: USGPO.

Haman, Michael T., Nancy B. Tuma, and Lyle P. Groenveld. 1987. "Income and Independence Effects on Marital Dissolution: Results from the Seattle and Denver Income-Maintenance Experiments." *American Journal of Sociology* 84: 611–633.

Hansell, Mary Jo. 1991. "Sociodemographic Factors and the Quality of Prenatal Care." *American Journal of Public Health* 33: 1135–1140.

Hanson, Shirley M. 1986. "Healthy Single Parent Families." *Family Relations* 35: 125–132.

Hatcher, Gordon Hollett, Peter Robert Hatcher, and Eleanor Clair Hatcher. 1984. "Canada." Pp. 86–132 in Marshall W. Raffel, ed., *Comparative Health Systems: Descriptive Analyses of Fourteen National Health Systems.* University Park: Pennsylvania State University Press.

Haveman, Robert, Barbara L. Wolfe, Ross E. Finnie, and Edward N. Wolff. 1988. "Disparities in Well-Being among U.S. Children over Two Decades: 1962–83." Pp. 149–170, in John L. Palmer, Timothy Smeeding, and Barbara Boyle Torrey, eds., *The Vulnerable.* Washington, D.C.: Urban Institute.

Hayes, Cheryl D., ed. 1987. *Risking the Future: Adolescent Sexuality, Pregnancy, and Childbearing.* Vol. 1. Washington, D.C.: National Academy Press.

Helz, Jean W., and Bryce Templeton. 1990. "Evidence of the Role of Psychosocial Factors in Diabetes Mellitus: A Review." *American Journal of Psychiatry* 147: 1275–1282.

Hetherington, E. Mavis. 1972. "Effects of Father Absence on Personality Development of Adolescent Daughters." *Developmental Psychology* 7:313–326.

Hetherington, E. Mavis. 1988a. "Parents, Children, and Siblings: Six Years after Divorce." Pp. 311–331 in Robert A. Hinde and Joan Stevenson-Hinde, *Relationships within Families: Mutual Influences.* New York: Oxford University Press.

Hetherington, E. Mavis. 1988b. "Family Relations Six Years after Divorce." Pp. 423–438 in E. Mavis Hetherington and Ross D. Parke, eds., *Contemporary Readings in Child Psychology.* New York: McGraw-Hill.

Hetherington, E. Mavis. 1989. "Coping with Family Transitions: Winners, Losers, and Survivors." *Child Development* 60: 1–14.

Hetherington, E. Mavis, and Joan L. Deur. 1972. "The Effects of Father Absence on Child Development." *Young Children* 26: 233–248.

Hetherington, E. Mavis, Kathleen A. Camara, and David L. Featherman. 1977. "Achievement and Intellectual Functioning of Children in One-Parent Households." Pp. 205–284 in Janet T. Spence, ed., *Achievement and Achievement Motives.* San Francisco: W. H. Freeman.

Hetherington, E. Mavis, E. M. Cox, and Robert Cox. 1979. "Play and Social Interaction in Children Following Divorce." *Journal of Social Issues* 35: 26–49.

Hetherington, E. Mavis, E. M. Cox, and Robert Cox. 1985. "Long-Term Effects of Divorce and Remarriage on the Adjustment of Children." *Journal of American Academy of Child and Adolescent Psychiatry* 24: 518–530.

Hetherington, E. Mavis, Margaret Stanley-Hagan, and Edward R. Anderson. 1989. "Marital Transitions." *American Psychologist* 44: 303–312.

Hewlett, Sylvia A. 1991. *When the Bough Breaks: The Cost of Neglecting Our Children.* New York: Basic Books.

Hill, Ian T. 1990. "Improving State Medicaid Programs for Pregnant Women and Children." *Health Care Financing Review* (Supplement): 75–87.

Hill, Martha S. 1983. "Female Household Headship and the Poverty of Children." Pp. 324–376 in Greg Duncan, *Five Thousand American Families: Patterns of Economic Progress.* vol. 10. Ann Arbor: Institute for Social Research.

Hinman, A. R., and J. P. Koplan. 1984. "Pertussis and Pertussis Vaccine: Reanalysis of Benefits, Risks, and Costs." *Journal of the American Medical Association* 251: 3109–3113.

Hofferth, Sandra L., and Kristin Moore. 1979. "Early Childbearing and Later Economic Well-Being." *American Sociological Review* 44: 784–815.

Hogan, Dennis P., Ling-sin Hao, and William L. Parish. 1990. "Race, Kin Networks, and Assistance to Mother-Headed Families." *Social Forces* 68: 797–812.

Horwitz, Sarah McCue, Hal Morgenstern, and Lisa F. Berkman. 1985. "The Impact of Social Stressors and Social Networks on Pediatric Medical Care Use." *Medical Care* 23: 946–959.

House, James S., Karl R. Landis, and Debra Umberson. 1988. "Social Relationships and Health." *Science* 241: 540–545.

Idler, Ellen, and Ronald Angel. 1990a. "Self-Rated Health and Mortality in the NHANES-I Epidemiologic Follow-up Study." *American Journal of Public Health* 80: 446–452.

Idler, Ellen, and Ronald Angel. 1990b. "Age, Pain and Self-Assessments of Health." Pp. 127–148 in Gary Albrecht and Judith Levy, eds., *Advances in Medical Sociology.* Vol. I. Greenwich: JAI.

Institute of Medicine. 1979. *Mental Health Services in General Health Care.* Washington, D.C.: National Academy of Sciences.

Jackson, James S., Patricia Newton, Adrian Ostfeld, Daniel Savage, and Edward L. Schneider, eds. 1988. *The Black American Elderly: Research on Physical and Psychosocial Health.* New York: Springer Verlag.

Jencks, Christopher. 1991. "Is the American Underclass Growing?" Pp. 28–100 in Christopher Jencks and Paul E. Peterson, eds., *The Urban Underclass.* Washington, D.C.: Brookings Institution.

Jette, Alan M., and Laurence G. Branch. 1981. "Physical Disability among the Aged." *American Journal of Public Health* 71: 1211–1216.

Jewell, K. Sue. 1988. *Survival of the Black Family: Institutional Impact of U.S. Social Policy.* New York: Praeger.

Jones, Audrey E., and Paul J. Placek. 1981. "Teenage Women in the United States: Sex, Contraception, Pregnancy, Fertility and Maternal Health." Pp. 49–72 in Theodora Ooms ed., *Teenage Pregnancy in a Family Context.* Philadelphia: Temple University Press.

Kahn, Alfred J., and Sheila B. Kammerman. 1983. *Income Transfers for Families with Children: An Eight-Country Study.* Philadelphia: Temple University Press.

Kammerman, Sheila B. 1984. "Women, Children, and Poverty: Public Policies and Female-headed Families in Industrialized Countries." *Signs: Journal of Women in Culture and Society* 10: 249–271.

Kammerman, Sheila B., and Alfred J. Kahn, eds. 1978. *Family Policy: Government and Families in Fourteen Countries.* New York: Columbia University Press.

Kamerman, Sheila B., and Alfred J. Kahn. 1988. *Mothers Alone: Strategies for a Time of Change.* Dover, Mass.: Auburn House.

Kandel, Denise B., Mark Davies, and Victoria H. Raveis. 1985. "The Stressfulness of Daily Social Roles for Women: Marital, Occupational and Household Roles." *Journal of Health and Social Behavior* 26: 64–78.

Kandel, Denise B., and Mark Davies. 1982. "Epidemiology of Depressive Mood in Adolescents." *Archives of General Psychiatry* 39: 1205–1212.

Kasarda, John D. 1985. "Urban Change and Minority Opportunities." Pp. 33–67 in Paul E. Peterson, ed., *The New Urban Reality.* Washington, D.C.: Brookings Institution.

Kasarda, John D. 1989. "Urban Industrial Transition and the Underclass." *Annals of the American Academy of Political and Social Science* 501: 26–47.

Katon, Wayne, and Mark D. Sullivan. 1990. "Depression and Chronic Medical Illness." *Journal of Clinical Psychiatry* 51(Supplement): 3–11.

Katz, Michael B. 1986. *In the Shadow of the Poorhouse: A Social History of Welfare in America.* New York: Basic Books.

Katz, Michael B. 1989. *The Undeserving Poor: From the War on Poverty to the War on Welfare.* New York: Pantheon.

Katz, Sidney, Amasa B. Ford, Roland W. Moskowitz, Beverly A. Jackson, and Marjorie W. Jaffe. 1963. "Studies of Illness in the Aged: The Index of ADL, A Standardized Measure of Biological and Psychological Functioning." *Journal of the American Medical Association* 185: 914–919.

Kellam, Sheppard G., Rebecca G. Adams, C. Hendricks Brown, and Margaret E. Ensminger. 1982. "The Long-Term Evolution of the Family Structure of Teenage and Older Mothers." *Journal of Marriage and the Family* (August): 539–554.

Kellam, Sheppard G., Jeannette D. Branch, Khazan C. Agrawal, and Margaret E. Ensminger. 1975. *Mental Hygiene and Going to School: The Woodlawn Program of Assessment, Early Intervention, and Evaluation.* Chicago: University of Chicago Press.

Kellam, Sheppard G., Margaret E. Ensminger, and R. Jay Turner. 1977. "Family Structure and the Mental Health of Children." *Archives of General Psychiatry* 34: 1012–1022.

Kelleher, Kelly J., and Ann A. Hohmann. N.d. "Access to Care: Issues for Hispanic Children." Working Paper from the Biometric and Clinical Applications Branch. Rockville, Md.: National Institute of Mental Health.

Keller, William J. "Study of Selected Outcomes of the Early and Periodic Screening, Diagnosis, and Treatment Program in Michigan." *Public Health Reports* 98: 110–119.

Kessler, Ronald C., and Marilyn Essex. 1982. "Marital Status and Depression: The Importance of Coping Resources." *Social Forces* 61: 484–507.

Kessler, Ronald C., and James A. McRae. 1982. "The Effect of Wives' Employment on the Mental Health of Married Men and Women." *American Sociological Review* 47: 216–227.

Kimmich, Madeleine H. 1985. *America's Children: Who Cares? Growing Needs and Declining Assistance in the Reagan Era.* Washington, D.C.: Urban Institute.

Kitagawa, Evelyn, and Phillip Hauser. 1973. *Differential Mortality in the United States: A Study in Socioeconomic Epidemiology.* Cambridge: Harvard University Press.

Kivnick, Helen Q. 1985. "Grandparenthood and Mental Health: Meaning, Behavior, and Satisfaction." Pp. 151–158, in Vern L. Bengtson and Joan F. Robertson, eds., *Grandparenthood.* Beverly Hills: Sage.

Kleinman, Arthur. 1977. "Depression, Somatization and the 'New Cross-Cultural Psychiatry.' " *Social Science and Medicine* 11: 3–10.

Kleinman, Arthur. 1980. *Patients and Healers in the Context of Culture.* Berkeley: University of California Press.

Kleinman, Arthur. 1986. *The Social Origins of Distress and Disease.* New Haven: Yale University Press.

Kleinman, Arthur, and Joan Kleinman. 1985. "Somatization: The Interconnections in Chinese Society among Culture, Depressive Experiences, and the Meanings of Pain." Pp. 429–490 in Arthur Kleinman and Byron Good, eds., *Culture and Depression.* Berkeley: University of California Press.

Kleinman, Arthur, Byron Good, and Peter Guarnaccia. 1986. *Critical Review of Selected Cross-Cultural Literature on Depressive and Anxiety Disorders.* Washington, D.C.: U.S. Government Printing Office.

Kobrin, Frances, E. 1976. "The Fall of Household Size and the Rise of the Primary Individual." *Demography* 13: 127–138.

Koch, Margaret Body. 1961. "Anxiety in Preschool Children from Broken Homes." *Merrill-Palmer Quarterly* 7: 225–231.

Kogan, Michael D., Mary Leary, and Thomas P. Schaetzel. 1990. "Factors Associated with Postpartum Care among Massachusetts Users of the Maternal and Infant Care Program." *Family Planning Perspectives* 22: 128–130.

Kohl, Jurgen. 1981. "Trends and Problems in Postwar Public Expenditure Development in Western Europe and North America." Pp. 307–344 in Peter Flora and Arnold J. Heidenheimer, eds., *The Development of Welfare States in Europe and America.* New Brunswick, N.J.: Transaction.

Kohn, Melvin L. 1972. "Class, Family, and Schizophrenia: A Reformulation." *Social Forces* 50: 295–304.

Krause, Neal, and Kyriakos S. Markides. 1985. "Employment and Psychological Well-Being in Mexican American Women." *Journal of Health and Social Behavior* 26: 15–26.

Krupinski, J., A. G. Baikie, Alan Stoller, John Graves, D. M. O'Day, and Patricia Polke. 1967. "A Community Mental Health Survey of Heyfield." *Medical Journal of Australia* 1: 1204–1211.

Kuttner, Robert. 1984. *The Economic Illusion: False Choice Between Prosperity and Social Justice.* Boston: Houghton Mifflin.

Langner, Thomas. 1963. "Broken Homes and Mental Disorder." *Public Health Reports* 78: 921–926.

Langner, Thomas S., Joanne C. Gersten, and Jeanne G. Eisenberg. 1974. "Approaches to Measurement and Definition in the Epidemiology of Behavior Disorders: Ethnic Background and Child Behavior." *International Journal of Health Services* 4: 483–501.

Langner, Thomas S., and S. T. Michael. 1963. *Life Stress and Mental Health.* New York: Free Press.

Lasch, Christopher. 1977. *Haven in a Heartless World: The Family Besieged.* New York: Basic Books.

Lawton, M. Powell. 1971. "The Functional Assessment of Elderly People." *Journal of the American Geriatrics Society* 19: 465–481.

Lemann, Nicholas. 1991. "Four Generations in the Taylor Projects." *New York Times Magazine,* January 13, 16–22.

Lewis, Oscar. 1966. "The Culture of Poverty." *Scientific American* 215: 19–25.

Litman, Theodor J. 1974. "The Family as a Basic Unit in Health and Medical Care: A Social Behavioral Overview." *Social Science and Medicine* 8: 495–519.

Litwak, Eugene. 1985. *Helping the Elderly: The Complementary Roles of Informal Networks and Formal Systems.* New York: Guilford.

Liu, Joseph. 1990. *Increasing the Proportion of Children Receiving EPSDT Benefits: A South Carolina Case Study.* Washington, D.C.: Children's Defense Fund.

Longino, Charles, and A. Lipman. 1982. "The Married, the Formerly Married and the Never-Married: Support System Differentials in a Planned Retirement Community." *International Journal of Aging and Human Development* 15: 285–297.

Lopata, Helen Z. 1978. "Contributions of Extended Families to the Support Systems of Metropolitan Area Widows: Limitations of the Modified Kin Network." *Journal of Marraige and the Family* 40: 355–364.

Lopata, Helene Z. 1979. *Women as Widows: Support Systems.* New York: Elsevier.

Lubben, James E., and Rosina M. Becerra. 1987. "Social Support among Black, Mexican, and Chinese Elderly." PP. 130–144 in Donald E. Gelfand and Charles M. Barresi, eds., *Ethnic Dimensions of Aging.* New York: Springer Verlag.

Malgady, Robert G., Lloyd H. Rogler, and Giuseppe Costantino. 1987. "Ethnocultural and Linguistic Bias in Mental Health Evaluation of Hispanics." *American Psychologist* 42: 228–234.

Markides, Kyriakos S., and Charles H. Mindel. 1987. *Aging and Ethnicity.* New York: Sage.

Markides, Kyriakos S., Harry W. Martin, and Ernesto Gomez. 1983. *Older Mexican Americans: A Study in an Urban Barrio.* Austin: University of Texas Press.

McAdoo, Harriet P. 1978. "Factors Related to Stability in Upwardly Mobile Black Families." *Journal of Marriage and the Family* 40: 761–776.

McAdoo, Harriet P. 1981. *Black Families.* Beverly Hills: Sage.

McCormick, Marie E. 1986. "Implications of Recent Changes in Infant Mortality." Pp. 282–306 in Linda Aiken and David Mechanic, eds., *Application of Social Science to Clinical Medicine and Health Policy.* New Brunswick: Rutgers University Press.

McLanahan, Sara S. 1983. "Family Structure and Stress: A Longitudinal Comparison of Two-Parent and Female-headed Families." *Journal of Marriage and the Family* 45: 347–357.

McLanahan, Sara. 1985a. "Family Structure and the Reproduction of Poverty." *American Journal of Sociology* 90: 873–901.

McLanahan, Sara. 1985*b*. "Single Mothers and Psychological Well-Being: A Test of the Stress and Vulnerability Hypotheses." *Research in Community and Mental Health* 5: 253–266.

McLanahan, Sara S. 1988. "Family Structure and Dependency: Early Transitions to Female Household Headship." *Demography* 25: 1–16.

McLanahan, Sara, and Irwin Garfinkel. 1989. "Single Mothers, the Underclass, and Social Policy." *Annals of the American Academy of Political and Social Science* 501: 92–104.

Mechanic, David. 1964. "The Influence of Mothers on their Children's Health Attitudes and Behavior." *Pediatrics* (March): 444–453.

Mechanic, David. 1978. *Medical Sociology.* 2d ed. New York: Free Press.

Mechanic, David. 1980. "The Experience and Reporting of Common Physical Complaints." *Journal of Health and Social Behavior* 21: 146–155.

Mechanic, David. 1989. "Socioeconomic Status and Health: An Examination of Underlying Process." Pp. 9–26 in John P. Bunker, Deanna S. Gomby, and Barbara H. Kehrer, eds., *Pathways to Health.* Menlo Park, Calif.: Henry J. Kaiser Family.

Mechanic, David, and Ronald Angel. 1987. "Some Factors Associated with the Report and Evaluation of Back Pain." *Journal of Health and Social Behavior* 28: 131–139.

Mechanic, David, and Stephen Hansell. 1989. "Divorce, Family Conflict, and Adolescents' Well-Being." *Journal of Health and Social Behavior* 30: 105–116.

Mencher, Samuel. 1967. *Poor Law to Poverty Program: Economic Security Policy in Britain and the United States.* Pittsburgh: University of Pittsburgh Press.

Menken, Jane. 1972. "The Health and Social Consequences of Teenage Childbearing." *Family Planning Perspectives* 4: 54–63.

Merton, Robert K. 1968. *Social Theory and Social Structure.* New York: Free Press.

Miller, C. Arden, Amy Fine, Sharon Adams-Taylor, and Lisbeth B. Schorr. 1986. *Monitoring Children's Health: Key Indicators.* Washington, D.C.: American Public Health Association.

Mindel, Charles H. 1980. "Extended Familism among Urban Mexican Americans, Anglos and Blacks." *Hispanic Journal of Behavioral Sciences* 2: 21–34.

Mindel, Charles H. 1985. "The Elderly in Minority Families." Pp. 369–386 in Beth Hess and Elizabeth W. Markson, eds., *Growing Old in America.* New Brunswick N.J.: Transaction.

Moore, Joan. 1989. "Is There a Hispanic Underclass?" *Social Science Quarterly* 70: 265–284.

Moore, Kristin. 1986. *Children of Teen Parents: Heterogeneity of Outcomes.* Final Report to the National Institute of Child Health and Human Development. Washington, D.C.: Child Trends, Inc.

Moore, Kristin A., and M. R. Burt. 1982. *Private Crisis, Public Cost: Policy Perspectives in Teenage Childbearing.* Washington, D.C.: Urban Institute.

Morgan, S. Philip, and Ronald Rindfuss. 1985. "Marital Disruption: Structural and Temporal Dimensions." *American Journal of Sociology* 90: 1055–1077.

Moss, Nancy, and Karen Carver. 1992. "Explaining Racial and Ethnic Differences in Birth Outcomes: The Effect of Household Structure and Resources." Paper presented at the annual meeting of the Population Association of America, Denver, Colo.

Moynihan, Daniel P. 1965. *The Negro Family: The Case for National Action*. Department of Labor, Office of Policy Planning and Research. Washington, D.C.: U.S. Government Printing Office.

Murphy, Elaine, Rae Smith, James Lindesay, and Jim Slattery. 1988. "Increased Mortality Rates in Late-Life Depression." *British Journal of Psychiatry* 152: 347–353.

Murray, Charles. 1984. *Losing Ground: American Social Policy, 1950–1980*. New York: Basic Books.

Mutran, Elizabeth. 1985. "Intergenerational Family Support among Blacks and Whites: Response to Culture or Socioeconomic Differences." *Journal of Gerontology* 3: 382–389.

Myers, J. K., Myrna M. Weissman, and Gary L. Tischler et al. 1984. "Six-Month Prevalence of Psychiatric Disorders in Three Communities: 1989–1982. *Archives of General Psychiatry* 41: 959–967.

Myles, John. 1984. *Old Age in the Welfare State: The Political Economy of Public Pensions*. Boston: Little, Brown and Company.

Nader, Philip R. 1975. "The Frequency and Nature of School Problems." Pp. 101–105 in Robert J. Haggerty, Klaus J. Roghmann, and Ivan B. Pless, eds., *Child Health and the Community*. New York: John Wiley and Sons.

Nagi, Saad Z. 1976. "An Epidemiology of Disability among Adults in the United States." *Milbank Memorial Fund Quarterly* 54: 439–467.

Nathanson, Catherine A. 1980. "Social Roles and Health Status among Women: The Significance of Employment. *Social Science and Medicine* 14: 463–471.

National Center for Health Statistics. 1985. "Plan and Operation of the Hispanic Health and Nutrition Examination Survey, 1982–1984." September 1985. *Vital and Health Statistics*, ser. 1, no. 19. DIIIIS publication no. (PHS) 85-1321. U.S. Public Health Service. Washington, D.C.: U.S. Government Printing Office.

National Center for Health Statistics. 1989. *Health, United States, 1988*. December. DHHS publication no. (PHS) 89-1232. U.S. Public Health Service. Washington, D.C.: U.S. Government Printing Office.

National Center for Health Statistics, M. G. Kovar, and G. S. Poe. 1985. "The National Health Interview Survey Design, 1973–84, and Procedures, 1975–83." August. *Vital and Health Statistics*, ser 1, no. 18. DHHS publication no. (PHS) 85-1320. Public Health Service. Washington, D.C.: U.S. Government Printing Office.

National Institute of Mental Health. 1987. *Mental Health, United States 1987*. In Ronald W. Manderscheid and S. A. Barrett, eds., DHHS publication no. (ADM) 87-1518. Washington, D.C.: U.S. Government Printing Office.

Nelson, Dawn, David McMillen, and Daniel Kasprzk. 1985. *An Overview of the Survey of Income and Program Participation, Update 1*. SIPP Working Paper Series no. 8401. Washington, D.C.: U.S. Bureau of the Census.

Newman, Joy Perkins. 1989. "Aging and Depression." *American Psychologist* 4: 150–165.

Nichter, Mark. 1981. "Idioms of Distress: Alternatives in the Expression of Psychosocial Distress: A Case Study from South India." *Culture, Medicine, and Psychiatry* 5: 379–408.

Norris, F. H., and Stanley A. Murrell. 1984. "Protective Function of Resources Related to Life Events, Global Stress, and Depression in Older Adults." *Journal of Health and Social Behavior* 25: 424–437.

Nuckolls, Katherine B., John Cassel, and Burton H. Kaplan. 1972. "Psychosocial Assets, Life Crisis and the Prognosis of Pregnancy." *American Journal of Epidemiology* 95: 431–441.

O'Connor, James. 1973. *The Fiscal Crisis of the State.* New York: St. Martins.

Offer, Daniel, Eric Ostrov, and Kenneth I. Howard. 1983. "Epidemiology of Mental Health and Mental Illness among Adolescents." Pp. 82–88 in Justin D. Call, Richard L. Cohen, Saul I. Harrison, Irving N. Berlin, and Lawrence A. Stone, eds., *Basic Handbook of Child Psychiatry.* New York: Basic Books.

Office of Technology Assessment. 1987. *Healthy Children: Investing in the Future.* OTA-H-345. Washington, D.C.: U.S. Government Printing Office.

Offord, David R., Michael H. Boyle, and Yvonne Racine. 1989. "Ontario Child Health Study: Correlates of Disorder." *Journal of the American Academy of Child and Adolescent Psychiatry* 28: 856–860.

Offord, David R., Michael H. Boyle, Peter Szatmari, Naomi I. Rae-Grant, Paul S. Links, David T. Cadman, John A. Byles, John W. Crawford, Heather Munroe Blum, Carolyn Byrne, Helen Thomas, and Christel A. Woodward. 1987. "Ontario Child Health Study II. Six-Month Prevalence of Disorder and Rates of Service Utilization." *Archives of General Psychiatry* 44: 832–836.

Orfield, Gary. 1988. "Race and the Liberal Agenda: The Loss of the Integrationist Dream, 1965–1974," Pp. 313–355 in Margaret Weir, Ann Shola Orloff, and Theda Skocpol, eds., *The Politics of Social Policy in the United States.* Princeton: Princeton University Press.

Orloff, Ann Shola. 1988. "The Political Origins of America's Belated Welfare State." Pp. 37–80 in Margaret Weir, Ann Shola Orloff, and Theda Skocpol, eds., *The Politics of Social Policy in the United States.* Princeton: Princeton University Press.

Ostrov, Eric, Daniel Offer, and Shirley Hartlage. 1984. "The Quietly Disturbed Adolescent." Pp. 73–81 in Daniel Offer, Eric Ostrov, and Kenneth I. Howard, eds., *Patterns of Adolescent Self-Image: New Directions for Mental Health Services.* San Francisco: Jossey-Bass.

Palmer, John L., and Isabel V. Sawhill, eds. 1984. *The Reagan Record: An Assessment of America's Changing Domestic Priorities.* Cambridge: Ballinger.

Palmer, John L., Timothy Smeeding, and Barbara Boyle Torrey, eds. 1988. *The Vulnerable.* Washington, D.C.: Urban Institute.

Parmelee, Arthur H. 1986. "Children's Illnesses: Their Beneficial Effects on Behavioral Development." *Child Development* 57: 1–10.

Parsons, Ellen P., and Rashid Bashshur. 1987. "The Burden of Health Care Costs for Single-Parent Versus Dual-Parent Families." Paper presented at the annual meeting of the American Sociological Association, August, Chicago, Ill.

Patterson, Charlotte J., Janis B. Kupersmidt, and Nancy A. Vaden. 1990. "Income

Level, Gender, Ethnicity, and Household Composition as Predictors of Children's School-based Competence." *Child Development* 61: 485–494.

Pear, Robert. 1990. "Many States Cut Food Allotments for Poor Families." *New York Times*, Tuesday, May 29, 1-A16, col. 3.

Pearlin, Leonard I. 1983. "Role Strains and Personal Stress." Pp. 3–32 in Howard B. Kaplan, ed., *Psychosocial Stress: Trends in Theory and Research*. New York: Academic.

Pearlin, Leonard I., and Joyce S. Johnson. 1977. "Marital Status, Life Strains and Depression." *American Sociological Review* 42: 704–715.

Pearson, Jane L., Andrea G. Hunter, Margaret E. Ensminger, and Sheppard G. Kellam. 1990. "Black Grandmothers in Multigenerational Households: Diversity in Family Structure and Parenting Involvement in the Woodlawn Community. *Child Development* 61: 434–442.

Perales, Cesar A., and Lauren S. Young, eds. 1988. *Too Little, Too Late: Dealing with the Health Needs of Women in Poverty*. New York: Harrington Park.

Peterson, James, and Nicholas Zill. 1986. "Marital Disruption, Parent-Child Relationships and Behavior Problems in Children." *Journal of Marriage and the Family* 48: 295–307.

Phifer, James F., and Stanley A. Murrell. 1986. "Etiologic Factors in the Onset of Depressive Symptoms in Older Adults." *Journal of Abnormal Psychology* 95: 282–291.

Physician Task Force on Hunger in America. 1985. *Hunger in America: The Growing Epidemic*. Middletown, Conn.: Wesleyan University Press.

Pleck, Joseph. H. 1985. *Working Wives/Working Husbands*. Beverly Hills: Sage.

Polit, Denise F. 1989. "Effects of a Comprehensive Program for Teenage Parents: Five Years after Project Redirection." *Family Planning Perspectives* 21: 164–169, 187.

Polit, Denise F., and Janet R. Kahn. 1985. "Project Redirection: Evaluation of a Comprehensive Program for Disadvantaged Teenage Mothers." *Family Planning Perspectives* 17: 150–155.

Popenoe, David. 1988. *Disturbing the Nest*. New York: Aldine De Gruyter.

Pratt, Lois. 1976. *Family Structure and Effective Health Behavior: The Energized Family*. Boston: Houghton Mifflin.

Preston, Samuel H. 1984. "Children and the Elderly: Divergent Paths for America's Dependents." *Demography* 21: 435–457.

Quadagno, Jill. 1988. "From Old-Age Assistance to Supplemental Security Income: The Political Economy of Relief in the South, 1935–1972." Pp. 235–263 in Margaret Weir, Ann Shola Orloff, and Theda Skocpol, eds., *The Politics of Social Policy in the United States*. Princeton: Princeton University Press.

Quadagno, Jill. 1990. "Race, Class, and Gender in the U.S. Welfare State: Nixon's Failed Family Assistance Plan." *American Sociological Review* 55: 11–28.

Quay, Herbert C., and John S. Werry. 1986. *Psychopathological Disorders of Childhood*. 3d ed. New York: John Wiley and Sons.

Questiaux, Nicole, and Jacques Fournier. 1978. "France." Pp. 117–182 in Sheila B. Kammerman and Alfred J. Kahn, eds., *Family Policy: Government and Families in Fourteen Countries*. New York: Columbia University Press.

Radloff, Lenore. 1975. "Sex Differences in Depression: The Effects of Occupation and Marital Status." *Sex Roles* 1: 249–265.

Raffel, Marshall W. 1984. *Comparative Health Systems: Descriptive Analyses of Fourteen National Health Systems.* University Park: Pennsylvania State University Press.

Raftery, Judith R. 1988. "Missing the Mark: Intelligence Testing in Los Angeles Public Schools, 1922–32." *History of Education Quarterly* 28: 73–93.

Rainwater, Lee, and William L. Yancey. 1967. *The Moynihan Report and the Politics of Controversy.* Cambridge: MIT Press.

Regier, Darrel A., David Goldberg, and Carl Taube. 1978. "The De Facto U.S. Mental Health Services System: A Public Health Perspective." *Archives of General Psychiatry* 35: 685–693.

Roberts, Robert E., and Stephen J. O'Keefe. 1981. "Sex Differences in Depression Reexamined." *Journal of Health and Social Behavior* 22: 394–400.

Robertson, Joan. 1977. "Grandmotherhood: A Study of Role Conceptions. *Journal of Marriage and the Family* 39: 165–74.

Robertson, Joan F., and Ronald L. Simons. 1989. "Family Factors, Self-Esteem, and Adolescent Depression." *Journal of Marriage and the Family* 51: 125–138.

Robins, Lee N. 1966. *Deviant Children Grown Up: A Sociological and Psychiatric Study of Sociopathic Personality.* Baltimore: Williams and Wilkins.

Robins, Lee N., and Michael Rutter, eds. 1990. *Straight and Devious Pathways from Childhood to Adulthood.* Cambridge: University of Cambridge Press.

Robins, Lee N., George E. Murphy, Robert A. Woodruff, and Lucy J. King. 1971. *Roots of Evaluation: The Epidemiological Basis for Planning Services.* London: Oxford University Press.

Robins, Lee, George E. Murphy, Robert A. Woodruff, and Lucy J. King. 1981. "Adult Psychiatric Status of Black Schoolboys." *Archives of General Psychiatry* 24: 338–345.

Robins, Lee N., John E. Helzer, Myrna M . Weissman, Helen Orvaschel, Ernest Gruenberg, Jack D. Burke, and Darrel A. Regier. 1984. "Lifetime Prevalence of Specific Psychiatric Disorders in Three Sites." *Archives of General Psychiatry* 41: 949–958.

Rodgers, Harrell R. 1982. *The Cost of Human Neglect.* Armonk, N.Y.: M. E. Sharpe.

Rosenbaum, Sara, and Kay Johnson. 1986. "Providing Health Care for Low-income Children: Reconciling Child Health Goals with Child Health Financing Realities." *Milbank Memorial Fund Quarterly* 64: 442–478.

Rosenbaum, Sara, Dana Hughes, Elizabeth Butler, and Deborah Howard. 1988. "Incarnations in the Dark: Medicaid, Managed Care, and Maternity Care." *Milbank Memorial Fund Quarterly* 66: 661–693.

Rosenfield, Sarah. 1989. "The Effects of Women's Employment: Personal Control and Sex Differences in Mental Health." *Journal of Health and Social Behavior* 30: 77–91.

Rosenstock, I. M. 1966. "Why People Use Health Services (Pt. 2)." *Milbank Memorial Fund Quarterly* 44: 94–127.

Rosenwaike, Ira, and Benjamin S. Bradshaw. 1989. "Mortality of the Spanish Sur-
name Population of the Southwest: 1980." *Social Science Quarterly* 70: 631–641.

Rosow, Irving, and Naomi Breslau. 1966. "A Guttman Health Scale for the Aged."
Journal of Gerontology 21: 556–559.

Ross, Catherine E., and Joan Huber. 1985. "Hardship and Depression." *Journal of
Health and Social Behavior* 26: 312–327.

Ross, Catherine E., and John Mirowsky. 1988. "Child Care and Emotional Adjustment of Wives' Employment." *Journal of Health and Social Behavior* 29:
127–138.

Ross, Catherine E., John Mirowsky, and Joan Huber. 1983. "Marriage Patterns
and Depression." *American Sociological Review* 48: 809–823.

Ross, Catherine E., John Mirwosky, and Patricia Ulbrich. 1983. "Distress and the
Traditional Female Role: A Comparison of Mexicans and Anglos." *American
Journal of Sociology* 89: 670–682.

Ross, Heather L., and Isabel V. Sawhill. 1975. *Time of Transition: The Growth of
Families Headed by Women.* Washington, D.C.: Urban Institute.

Rossi, Peter H., and James D. Wright. 1989. "The Urban Homeless: A Portrait of
Urban Dislocation." *Annals of the American Academy of Political and Social Science* 501: 132–142.

Russell, Louise B. 1989. *Medicare's New Hospital Payment System.* Washington,
D.C.: Brookings Institution.

Rutter, Michael. 1980. *Changing Youth in a Changing Society: Patterns of Adolescent Development and Disorder.* Cambridge: Harvard University Press.

Rutter, Michael. 1985. "Resilience in the Face of Adversity: Protective Factors and
Resistance to Psychiatric Disorder." *British Journal of Psychiatry* 147: 598–611.

Rutter, Michael. 1989. "Isle of White Revisited: Twenty-five Years of Child Psychiatric Epidemiology." *Journal of the American Academy of Child and Adolescent
Psychiatry* 28: 633–653.

Rutter, Michael, and A. Hussain Tuma. 1988. Pp. 437–452 in Michael Rutter, A.
Hussain Tuma, and Irma S. Lann, eds., *Assessment and Diagnosis in Child Psychopathology.* New York: Guilford.

Rutter, Michael, Antony Cox, Celia Tupling, Michael Berger, and William Yule.
1975. "Attainment and Adjustment in Two Geographical Areas: I—The Prevalence of Psychiatric Disorder." *British Journal of Psychiatry* 126: 493–509.

Sarbin, Theodore R. 1970. "The Culture of Poverty, Society Identity, and Cognitive Outcomes." Pp. 29–46 in Vernon L. Allen, ed., *Psychological Factors in
Poverty.* New York: Academic.

Schorr, Lisbeth. 1988. *Within Our Reach: Breaking the Cycle of Disadvantage.*
Garden City, N.Y.: Doubleday.

Schulberg, Herbert C., and Barbara J. Burns. 1987. "Mental Disorders in Primary
Care: Epidemiologic, Diagnostic, and Treatment Research Directions." Paper
presented in Bangalore, India. National Institute of Mental Health and Neuro-
sciences, October.

Schwarz, John E. 1988. *America's Hidden Success: A Reassessment of Public Policy from Kennedy to Reagan.* Rev. ed. New York: W. W. Norton.

Schwartz, Saul, Sheldon Danziger, and Eugene Smolensky. 1984. "The Choice of Living Arrangements Among the Aged." Pp. 229–253 in Henry Aaron and Gary Burtless, eds., *Retirement and Economic Behavior.* Washington, D.C.: Brookings Institution.

Schwartz Gould, Madelyn, Robin Wunsch-Hitzig, and Bruce Dohrenwend. 1981. "Estimating the Prevalence of Childhood Psychopathology: A Critical Review." *Journal of the American Academy of Child Psychiatry* 20: 462–476.

Seeman, Teresa E., George A. Kaplan, Lisa Knudsen, Richard Cohen, and Jack Guralnik. 1987. "Social Network Ties and Mortality among the Elderly in the Alameda County Study." *American Journal of Epidemiology* 126: 714–723.

Sena-Rivera, Jaime. 1979. "Extended Kinship in the United States: Competing Models and the Case of La Familia Chicano." *Journal of Marriage and the Family* 41: 121–129.

Shanas, Ethel. 1962. *The Health of Older People.* Cambridge: Harvard University Press.

Shapiro, Sam, Elizabeth A. Skinner, Larry G. Kessler, Michael Von Korff, Pearl S. German, Gary L. Tischler, Philip J. Leaf, Lee Benham, Linda Cottler, and Darrel Regier. 1984. "Utilization of Health and Mental Health Services: Three Epidemiological Catchment Area Sites." *Archives of General Psychiatry* 41: 971–978.

Shapiro, Sam, Elizabeth A. Skinner, Morton Kramer, Donald M. Steinwachs, and Darrrel A. Regier. 1985. "Measuring Need for Mental Health Services in a General Population." *Medical Care* 23: 1033–1043.

Shepherd, M. 1987. "Mental Illness and Primary Care." *American Journal of Public Health* 77: 12–13.

Shimkin, Dimitri B., Edith M. Shimkin, and Dennis A. Frate, eds. 1978. *The Extended Family in Black Societies.* Chicago: Aldine.

Sidel, Ruth. 1986. *Women and Children Last: The Plight of Poor Women in Affluent America.* New York: Viking.

Skocpol, Theda. 1988. "The Limits of the New Deal Systems and the Roots of Contemporary Welfare Dilemmas." Pp. 293–311 in Margaret Weir, Ann Shola Orloff, and Theda Skocpol, eds., *The Politics of Social Policy in the United States.* Princeton: Princeton University Press.

Smeeding, Timothy, Barbara Boyle Torrey, and Martin Rein. 1988. "Patterns of Income and Poverty: The Economic Status of Children and the Elderly in Eight Countries." Pp. 89–119 in John L. Palmer, Timothy Smeeding, and Barbara Boyle Torry, eds., *The Vulnerable.* Washington, D.C.: Urban Institute.

Smythe, Sheila M. 1988. "Safeguarding our Children's Health." *GAO Journal* (Fall): 26–30.

Soldo, Beth J., Maresh Sharma, and Richard T. Campbell. 1984. "Determinants of Community Living Arrangements of Older Unmarried Women." *Journal of Gerontology* 39: 492–498.

Srole, Leo, Thomas S. Langer, Stanley T. Michael, Price Kirkpatrick, Marvin K. Opler, and Thomas A. C. Rennie. 1962. *Mental Health in the Metropolis: The Midtown Manhattan Study.* New York: New York University Press.

Stack, Carol B. 1974. *All Our Kin: Strategies for Survival in a Black Community.* New York: Harper and Row.

Staples, Robert. 1986. "The Political Economy of Black Family Life." *The Black Scholar* 17: 2–11.

Starfield, Barbara. 1990. "Social Factors in Child Health." Pp. 30–36 in Morris Green and Robert J. Haggerty, eds., *Ambulatory Pediatrics.* Philadelphia: W. B. Saunders.

Starfield, Barbara, Janet Hankin, and Donald Steinwachs et al. 1985. "Utilization and Morbidity: Random or Tandem?" *Pediatrics* 75: 241–247.

Steinberg, Laurence. 1987. "Single Parents, Stepparents, and the Susceptibility of Adolescents to Antisocial Peer Pressure." *Child Development* 58: 269–275.

Stockman, David A. 1986. *The Triumph of Politics: How the Reagan Revolution Failed.* New York: Harper and Row.

Suchman, Edward A. 1965a. "Social Patterns of Illness and Medical Care." *Journal of Health and Human Behavior* 6: 2–16.

Suchman, Edward A. 1965b. "Stages of Illness and Medical Care." *Journal of Health and Human Behavior* 6: 114–128.

Sullivan, Mercer L. 1989. "Absent Fathers in the Inner City." *Annals of the American Academy of Political and Social Science* 501: 48–58.

Sutton-Smith, Brian, B. G. Rosenberg, and Frank Landy. 1968. "Father-Absence Effect in Families of Different Sibling Compositions." *Child Development* 39: 1213–1221.

Sweet, James A., and Larry L. Bumpass. 1987. *American Families and Households.* New York: Russell Sage.

Sweet, James, Larry Bumpass, and Vaughn Call. 1988. "The Design and Content of the National Survey of Families and Households." *NSFH Working Paper No. 1.* Madison: University of Wisconsin–Madison, Center for Demography and Ecology.

Taylor, Robert J. 1985. "The Extended Family as a Source of Support to Elderly Blacks." *The Gerontologist* 25: 488–495.

Taylor, Robert Joseph. 1986. "Receipt of Support from Family among Black Americans: Demographic and Familial Differences." *Journal of Marriage and the Family* 48: 67–77.

Taylor, Robert Joseph. 1988. "Aging and Supportive Relationships among Black Americans." Pp. 259–281 in James S. Jackson, Patricia Newton, Adrian Ostfield, Daniel Savage, and Edward L. Schneider, eds., *The Black American Elderly: Research on Physical and Psychosocial Health.* New York: Springer Verlag.

Taylor, Robert J., and Linda M. Chatters. 1986a. "Patterns of Informal Support to Elderly Black Adults: Family, Friends, and Church Members." *Social Work* 31: 432–438.

Taylor, Robert J., and Linda M. Chatters. 1986b. "Church-based Informal Support among Elderly Blacks." *The Gerontologist* 26: 637–642.

Tessler, Richard. 1980. "Birth Order, Family Size, and Children's Use of Physician Services." *Health Services Research* 15: 55–62.

Thoits, Peggy A. 1983. "Multiple Identities and Psychological Well-Being: A Reformulation and Test of the Social Isolation Hypothesis." *American Sociological Review* 48: 174–187.

Thoits, Peggy A. 1986. "Multiple Identities: Examining Gender and Marital Status Differences in Distress." *American Sociological Review* 51: 259–272.

Thoits, Peggy A. 1987. "Gender and Marital Status Differences in Control and Distress: Common Stress versus Unique Stress Explanations." *Journal of Health and Social Behavior* 28: 7–22.

Thomas, Alexander, and Stella Chess. 1977. *Temperament and Development*. New York: Brunner/Mazel.

Thomas, Kausar, and Wister, Andrew. 1984. "Living Arrangements of Older Women: The Ethnic Dimension." *Journal of Marriage and the Family* 46: 301–311.

Thompson, Maxine Seaborn, and Margaret E. Ensminger. 1989. "Psychological Well-Being among Mothers with School Age Children: Evolving Family Structures." *Social Forces* 67: 715–730.

Tienda, Marta. 1989. "Puerto Ricans and the Underclass Debate." *Annals of the American Academy of Political and Social Science* 501: 105–119.

Tienda, Marta, and Ronald Angel. 1982. "Female Headship and Extended Family Composition: Comparisons of Hispanics, Blacks, and Non-Hispanic Whites." *Social Forces* 61: 508–531.

Tissue, Thomas, and John L. McCoy. 1981. "Income and Living Arrangements Among Poor Aged Singles." *Social Security Bulletin* 44: 3–13.

Trad, Paul V. 1987. *Infant and Childhood Depression: Developmental Factors*. New York: John Wiley and Sons.

Umberson, Debra. 1987. "Family Status and Health Behaviors: Social Control as a Dimension of Social Integration." *Journal of Health and Social Behavior* 28: 306–319.

United Nations Children's Fund. 1989. *The State of the World's Children*. New York: Oxford University Press.

U.S. Bureau of the Census. 1986. "Child Support and Alimony: 1983 (Supplemental Report)." *Current Population Reports: Special Studies*. Series P-23, no. 148. Washington, D.C.: U.S. Government Printing Office.

U.S. Bureau of the Census. 1989a. Current Population Reports, ser. P-60, no. 166. *Money Income and Poverty Status in the United States: 1988 (Advance Data from the March 1989 Current Population Survey)*. Washington, D.C.: U.S. Government Printing Office.

U.S. Bureau of the Census. 1989b. *Statistical Abstract of the United States: 1989*. 109th ed. Washington, D.C.: U.S. Government Printing Office.

U.S. Bureau of the Census. 1989c. Current Population Reports, ser. P-20, no. 433. *Marital Status and Living Arrangements: March 1988*. Washington, D.C.: U.S. Government Printing Office.

Vanek, Joann. 1974. "Time Spent in Housework." *Scientific American* 231: 116–120.

Velimirovic, Boris, ed. 1978. *Modern Medicine and Medical Anthropology in the*

United States-Mexico Border Population. Pan American Health Organization Scientific publication no. 359. Washington, D.C.: World Health Organization.

Verbrugge, Lois M. 1983. "Multiple Roles and Physical Health of Women and Men." *Journal of Health and Social Behavior* 24: 16–30.

Veroff, Joseph, Richard A. Hulka, and Elizabeth Douvan. 1981. *Mental Health in America: Patterns of Help-Seeking from 1957–1976.* New York: Basic Books.

Voydanoff, Patricia. 1987. "Women's Work, Family, and Health." Pp. 69–96 in Karen Shallcross Koziara, Michael H. Moskow, and Lucretia Dewey Tanner, eds., *Working Women.* Washington, D.C.: Bureau of National Affairs.

Wacquant, Loïc J. D., and William Julius Wilson. 1989. "The Cost of Racial and Class Exclusion in the Inner City." *Annals of the American Academy of Political and Social Science* 501: 8–25.

Wallerstein, Judith S., and Sandra S. Blakeslee. 1989. *Second Chances: Men, Women, and Children a Decade After Divorce.* New York: Ticknor and Fields.

Wallerstein, Judith, and Joan Berlin Kelly. 1975. "The Effects of Parental Divorce: Experiences of the Preschool Child." *Journal of the American Academy of Child and Adolescent Psychiatry* 14: 600–616.

Wallerstein, Judith S., and Joan Berlin Kelly. 1980. *Surviving the Breakup: How Children and Parents Cope with Divorce.* New York: Basic Books.

Ware, John E. 1986. "The Assessment of Health Status." Pp. 204–228 in Linda H. Aiken and David Mechanic, eds., *Applications of Social Sciences to Clinical Medicine and Health Policy.* New Brunswick, N.J.: Rutgers University Press.

Warheit, George J., Charles E. Holzer, Roger A. Bell, and Sandra A. Arey. 1976. "Sex, Marital Status, and Mental Health: A Reappraisal." *Social Forces* 52: 459–470.

Webster-Stratton, Carolyn. 1989. "The Relationship of Marital Support, Conflict, and Divorce to Parent Perceptions, Behaviors, and Childhood Conduct Problems." *Journal of Marriage and the Family* 51: 417–430.

Weir, Margaret, Ann Shola Orloff, and Theda Skocpol, eds. 1988. *The Politics of Social Policy in the United States.* Princeton: Princeton University Press.

Weissman, Myrna M. 1988. "Psychopathology in the Children of Depressed Parents: Direct Interview Studies." Pp. 143–159 in D. L. Dauner, E. S. Gerston, and J. B. Barrett, eds., *Relatives At-Risk for Mental Disorder.* New York: Raven.

Weissman, Myrna M., Philip J. Leaf, and Martha Livingston Bruce. 1987. "Single-Parent Women: A Community Study." *Social Psychiatry* 22: 29–36.

Weitzman, Lenore J. 1985. *The Divorce Revolution: The Unexpected Social and Economic Consequences for Women and Children in America.* New York: Free Press.

Wells, James A., and Donald E. Strickland. 1982. "Physiogenic Bias as Invalidity in Psychiatric Symptom Scales." *Journal of Health and Social Behavior* 23: 235–252.

Wells, Kenneth B., Jacqueline M. Golding, and M. Audrey Burnam. 1988. "Psychiatric Disorder in a Sample of the General Population with and without Chronic Medical Conditions." *American Journal of Psychiatry* 145: 976–981.

Wells, Kenneth B., Willard G. Manning, Naihua Duan, Joseph P. Newhouse, and John E. Ware. 1987. "Cost-Sharing and the Use of General Medical Physicians for Outpatient Mental Health Care." *Health Services Research* 22: 1–17.

West, Guida. 1981. *The National Welfare Rights Movement: The Social Protest of Poor Women.* New York: Praeger.

Wilcox-Gok, Virginia L. 1985. "Mother's Education, Health Practices and Children's Health Needs: A Variance Components Model." *Review of Economics and Statistics* 67: 706–710.

Wilensky, Harold L. 1975. *The Welfare State and Equality: Structural and Ideological Roots of Public Expenditures.* Berkeley: University of California Press.

Wilensky, Harold L. 1976. *The "New Corporatism," Centralization, and the Welfare State.* Beverly Hills: Sage.

Wilensky, Harold L. 1981. "Leftism, Catholicism, and Democratic Corporatism: The Role of Political Parties in Recent Welfare State Development." Pp. 345–382 in Peter Flora and Arnold J. Heidenheimer, eds., *The Development of Welfare States in Europe and America.* New Brunswick, N.J.: Transaction.

Wilkinson, Greg. 1985. *Mental Health Practices in Primary Care Settings: An Annotated Bibliography 1977–85.* London: Tavistock.

Willis, Diane J., and C. Eugene Walker. 1989. "Etiology." Pp. 29–51 in Thomas H. Ollendick and Michel Hersen, eds., *Handbook of Child Psychopathology.* New York: Plenum.

Wilson, William Julius. 1987. *The Truly Disadvantaged: The Inner City, the Underclass, and Public Policy.* Chicago: University of Chicago Press.

Wilson, William Julius, and Katherine Neckerman. 1986. "Poverty and Family Structure: The Widening Gap Between Evidence and Public Policy Issues." Pp. 232–254 in Sheldon H. Danziger and Daniel H. Weinberg, eds., *Fighting Poverty: What Works and What Doesn't.* Cambridge: Harvard University Press.

Wirth, Louis. 1938. "Urbanism as a Way of Life." *American Journal of Sociology* 64: 8–20.

Wolf, Douglas A. 1984. "Kin Availability and the Living Arrangements of Older Women." *Social Science Research* 13: 72–89.

Wolf, Douglas A., and Beth J. Soldo. 1988. "Household Composition Choices of Older Unmarried Women." *Demography* 25: 387–403.

Wolfe, Barbara L. 1980. "Children's Utilization of Medical Care." *Medical Care* 18: 1196–1207.

Wolkind, Stephen, and Michael Rutter. 1985. "Separation, Loss and Family Relationships." Pp. 34–57 in Michael Rutter and Lionel Hersov, eds., *Child and Adolescent Psychiatry: Modern Approaches.* Oxford: Blackwell Scientific.

Wolters, Raymond. 1975. "The New Deal and the Negro." Pp. 170–217 in John Braeman, Robert H. Bremner, and David Brody, eds., *The New Deal: The National Level.* Vol. 1. Columbus: Ohio State University Press.

Woolhandler, Steffie, and David U. Himmelstein. 1989. "A National Health Program: Northern Light at the End of the Tunnel." *Journal of the American Medical Association* 262: 2136–2137.

Worobey, Jacqueline L., and Ronald J. Angel. 1990a. "Poverty and Health: Older

Minority Women and the Rise of the Female-Headed Household." *Journal of Health and Social Behavior* 31: 370–383.

Worobey, Jacqueline L., and Ronald J. Angel. 1990*b*. "Functional Capacity and Living Arrangements of Unmarried Elderly Persons." *Journal of Gerontology* 45: 95–101.

Worobey, Jacqueline L., Ronald J. Angel, and John Worobey. 1988. "Family Structure and Young Children's Use of Medical Care." *Topics in Early Childhood Special Education* 8: 30–40.

Yudkowsky, Beth K., and Gretchen V. Fleming. 1990. "Preventive Health Care for Medicaid Children." *Health Care Financing Review* (Supplement): 89–96.

Zborowski, Mark. 1952. "Cultural Components of Responses to Pain." *Journal of Social Issues* 8: 16–30.

Zill, Nicholas. 1988. "Behavior, Achievement, and Health Problems among Children in Stepfamilies: Findings from a National Survey of Child Health." Pp. 325–368 in E. Mavis Hetherington and J. D. Arasteh, eds., *Impact of Divorce, Single Parenting, and Stepparenting on Children*. Hillsdale, N.J.: Lawrence Erlbaum.

Zill, Nicholas, and Charlotte A. Schoenborn. 1990. "Developmental, Learning, and Emotional Problems: Health of Our Nation's Children, United States, 1988." *Advanced Data from the Vital and Health Statistics*, no. 190. Hyattsville, Md.: National Center for Health Statistics.

Zola, Irving K. 1964. "Illness Behavior of the Working Class: Implications and Recommendations." Pp. 350–361 in Arthur B. Shostak and William Gomberg, eds., *Blue-Collar World: Studies of the American Worker*. Englewood Cliffs, N.J.: Prentice-Hall.

Zola, Irving K. 1966. "Culture and Symptoms: An Analysis of Patients Presenting Complaints." *American Sociological Review* 31: 615–630.

Index

Life Course Studies

David L. Featherman
David I. Kertzer
  General Editors

Nancy W. Denney
Thomas J. Espenshade
Dennis P. Hogan
Jennie Keith
Maris A. Vinovskis
  Associate General Editors

The Healer's Tale: Transforming Medicine and Culture
Sharon R. Kaufman

Family, Political Economy, and Demographic Change:
The Transformation of Life in Casalecchio, Italy, 1861–1921
David I. Kertzer and Dennis P. Hogan

Dolor y Alegría: Woman and Social Change in Urban Mexico
Sarah LeVine,
in collaboration with
Clara Sunderland Correa

Family, Class, and Ideology in Early Industrial France: Social Policy
and the Working-Class Family, 1825–1848
Katherine A. Lynch

Event History Analysis in Life Course Research
Edited by Karl Ulrich Mayer and Nancy B. Tuma

Working Parents: Transformations in Gender Roles and
Public Policies in Sweden
Phyllis Moen

Family Dynamics in China: A Life Table Analysis
Zeng Yi

2375